MOBY ◄ REPLAY

His Life And Times

Published in 2001 by Olmstead Press, Chicago, Illinois

Editorial Sales Rights and Permission Inquiries should be addressed to:
Omstead Press, 22 Broad Street, Suite 34, Milford, CT 06460
Email: Editor@lpcgroup.com

Substantial discounts on bulk quantities of Olmstead Press books are available
to corporations, professional associations and other organizations.
If you are in the U.S.A. or Canada, contact LPC Group,
Attn: Special Sales Department, 1-800-626-4330, fax 1-800-334-3892,
or email: sales@lpcgroup.com

ISBN: 1-58754-011-8
Library of Congress Card Number: 2001086962

Photographic credits in order of appearance:
Cover Image: Jamie Reid;
Plates - 1: Courtesy of Instinct Records; 2, 3 & 4: Alexis Maryon;
5: Jim Dyson; 6: Matt Bright; 7 & 8: Mei Tao/Mute; 9: Corinne Day;
10 & 11: Angela Hayward/Mute; 12: Corinne Day/Mute

Cover Design by Philip Gambrill.
Typeset by Martin Roach.
Printed in the UK by Butler & Tanner

Published under licence from Independent Music Press,
P.O. Box 14691, London, SE1 2ZA, UK.
E-mail: info@impbooks.com

MOBY

Replay - His Life And Times

by Martin James

OLMSTEAD
P R E S S

AUTHOR'S ACKNOWLEDGEMENTS

First and foremost I have to thank Moby for all of his help on this book. From the very outset he insisted that I retain a critical distance, even suggesting at one point that I could "say nasty things" about him. OK, so this wasn't exactly necessary, but for a musician to display such a lack of ego made the writing of this book unusually unlimited. I would also like to thank him for finding time in his busy touring schedule to answer my incessant questions. It's fair to say that, without his considerable involvement, this text would have been a very different affair.

I would also like to thank Moby's management companies, DEF in the UK and MCT in the US. More specifically Barry Taylor at MCT for his great help at a very busy time for him and Su at DEF for help beyond the call of duty. Thanks are also due to Marci Weber at MCT and Eric Harle at DEF – our schedules may have made meeting up impossible, but without your input, the Moby story may have been a very different one. And also Emke who started the ball rolling before going on maternity leave.

A huge debt of gratitude must go out to Sarah Lowe, Andy Fraser and Zoë Millar at Mute Records UK, who gave me the run of their filing cabinets, photocopier and coffee machine. As well as being among the most helpful and friendliest people in the music business.

Eternal thanks and big love goes out to my best mate (and Moby's tour manager) Dick Meredith and his gorgeous wife Selina. Hey Dick, we've come a long way baby! Only seems like ten minutes ago that we were rushing around in the Oaksmobile!

For help on the Instinct details I'd like to thank Patrick Carmosino who went out of his way to make sure I had all of the information I needed, for which I am extremely grateful.

Thanks to Andrew Haslehurst for transcribing those old interviews and to Dave Stelfox for ploughing through the text, tearing his hair out, scribbling red lines everywhere and making so many very useful suggestions. Sorry about the late nights, mate.

For the excellent front cover image I'd like to big up Jamie Reid (I'll never forget going on the road with Jamie to cover Primal Scream - insane), not bad for an ex-grebo! Thanks must also go to Jim Dyson for scanning the image and digging out his old Moby stuff, Alexis Maryon for finding his superb pictures of Moby from 1993 - you're a star, Matt Bright for the 007 shots and the following talented photographers for their wonderful pictures: Mei Tao, Corinne Day and Angela Hayward. Thanks also to Instinct for the early press shot of Moby.

For their input, thoughts and ideas, no matter how small, I'd like to say cheers to Liam Howlett, Phil Hartnoll, Jon Bennet, Rob Byron, Dave Stone (and Lisa, Oscar and Emily of course), Tim Barr, Kris Needs, Sarah-Jane and Leeroy Thornhill. And also to all of the Mobility list subscribers who offered their support - specifically Mark Lincoln Seiler (owner of Moby's soul and the excellent 'Mobilicious' website at www.mobymusic.com), Bart van Eijck (for the exhaustive discography) Brad Caviness, Mimi Marrins, Anne (Crowes 3), Kimberly Best, Utah, Mike A7, Sheltering Skies. Sorry to anyone I missed.

For patience throughout this project, major props go out to my publishers Martin and Kaye at IMP. I'm sure Martin had hair when we started out down this road! Also thanks must go to Nik Moore for putting Martin in touch with me.

Finally, my everlasting love goes out to all of my family (the Thomas' and the Tanseys) and above all the three most important people in my life, Lisa, Ruby Blue and Felix Drum.

Martin James, Brighton, 2000.

To Ruby Blue, Felix Drum and Lis

INTRODUCTION

Manhattan, New York - April 9, 1999

It's the 99th day of 1999. Millennial doom-mongers are declaring this to be the day when the year-zero computer bug will start its long meltdown process, while less paranoid practitioners in the world of science suggest today to be 'make-a-millennium-baby-day'. Somewhere on the streets of Manhattan, illusionist David Blaine - Leonardo DiCaprio's best friend - has just buried himself alive in a glass coffin, six feet beneath the sidewalk. He's got nothing but a litre of water and a clear view of the world above to keep him company for the seven days of his publicity-seeking ordeal.

Richard Hall opens the door on his spacious loft conversion. It is situated on the top floor of a one-time psychiatric hospital in the trendy Little Italy district of New York. Where once junkies littered the doorways, now trendy boutiques line the sidewalks. The neighboring building is soon be home to David Bowie. Chic actress Christina Ricci lives in the block opposite. Down in the basement is the studio where The Beastie Boys recorded their *Hello Nasty* album and filmed the video for 'Three MCs And One DJ'. You could say it's an area of some standing.

Richard Hall, a.k.a. Moby's apartment is a whitewash of minimalism. The sparse furniture is by trendy American furniture design house Herman Miller. The walls contain a couple of paintings by his friend Damian Loeb, while the huge windows give a perfect view of the buildings over the road. In one open-plan room sits his bed, with little else. White beechwood stairs lead up to a sun-lounge room which in turn opens out onto a roof garden with a far more expansive view of New York. The garden is bare. Moby has considered getting some trees, but hasn't got round to it, or even fully squared the idea of putting living things in the middle of this insanely polluted environment.

In another room sits his studio; a mass of keyboards, mixing desk and effects units. The walls are adorned with many posters advertising his albums, singles and gigs while the floor is littered with records by Roxy Music and Joe Jackson, among many others.

The whole apartment has taken some three years for Moby to complete. From the empty shell in a run-down area that he first bought, the man known to his fans as the 'Little Idiot' has constructed a haven in the middle of the chaos of urban New York. A secluded space in which he conceives, writes, produces and, of course, plays his music.

Yesterday, REM's Michael Stipe was here to take photos of Moby for a fashion magazine. Today however, he's playing host to the media process. We're here to discuss his latest album *Play*, an album of quite astounding beauty. We have met many times in an interview situation, considerably more if you include saying hello backstage. In the years since our first encounter he has remained one of the most challenging interviewees I have ever come across.

His conversation is considered. He is incredibly articulate, holding seemingly well-thought-out opinions on everything from the eco-system to *The Simpsons*. He is friendly and very funny, if in a very dry way. When talking to Moby, he fixes you with an intense stare, his eyes occasionally flickering as if taking in some extra, unassociated bit of information, to be stored until needed. He rarely breaks into a smile although he remains unnervingly polite, and unusually congenial throughout. Some have said he is a humorless, poker-faced bore; the kind of person you wouldn't want to have at a party.

In reality however Moby is that rare thing in dance music, a man with opinions who is not afraid to voice them. And as for him not being a party animal - forget it. As we sit in his apartment, sun streaming in, talking through the stunning melting pot that is *Play*, it his hard to imagine that the album would soon propel him into the stellar heights of global celebrity. It's hard even to imagine that it would come to dominate the charts throughout the world. At this stage, *Play* is just another yet-to-be-released, or even fully promo'd, Moby album.

Almost two years later *Play* is one of the world's highest selling albums. It has crossed demographics with apparent disregard for such marketing limitations. It has come to soundtrack our every waking moment through aggressive licensing to film, advert and TV scores. Quite simply it is one of the biggest, and perhaps strangest success stories of Y2K.

Moby's rise to apparent global dominance can justifiably be regarded as mystifying for most music commentators. Over the course of his career, the media has regarded him as a curiosity rather than a serious musician. His extreme ethical stance on matters such as animal rights, human welfare and pollution, like his oft-proclaimed love of Christ, has all too often taken precedence over his music. Similarly, his extreme changes in musical direction have come under far more critical scrutiny than the actual songs themselves.

Indeed, from the day Moby first found European chart success with his *Twin Peaks* theme-hybrid anthem 'Go', he has garnered more column inches for what he *is* rather than what he does. All too often he has been presented as little more than a freakish side-show; always good for a quote, often good for a laugh, but rarely good for an album's worth of tunes. Until *Play* that is. For if one album ever caught the music and media industries sleeping in a pit of their own self-worth then this was it.

Written off as 'just another Moby album' by so many, the majority of those with anti-Moby opinions had probably sold or given away their promo copies long before they became aware of it through its increased presence on adverts, movie soundtracks and in the charts. Quite simply, this was an album which the people discovered for themselves, albeit through means of stealth marketing. Indeed, *Play* can be seen as one of the first albums of the 21st century to reach the public outside of the orthodox promotional machine. Another similar record of the time was

Macy Gray's *On How Life Is*, which also scored highly with the public despite little press, and even less airplay.

What makes Moby's achievement all the more interesting however is the fact that he had been universally written off by the media gatekeepers. For anyone who has followed the man's career closely, such myopic behavior seems almost unbelievable. Since his first record under the Moby moniker in 1990, he has continually intrigued and inspired his considerable fan base. And yet, despite having continuously hit the charts worldwide, when the promo of *Play* first started to appear in early 1999, Moby had somehow come be become regarded as old news in certain quarters.

So how did we get to this position where the record which would go on to become one of the most successful releases of the year could be written off with such vehemence by a music media which prides itself on an ability to see beyond the hype? A number of factors were at play, as it were. Factors which will continue to dominate Moby's career long after *Play* has disappeared into history.

The reduction to the level of "ethical freak show" as already mentioned is perhaps the most obvious. Similarly Moby's seemingly obtuse need to change direction at the drop of a hat has become viewed as a negative. This coming from a musician who rose to fame in the rave era, a time repeatedly written off as being void of any real talent by an industry still hung up on The Beatles and their copyists.

Likewise his ability to discuss matters on a highly intellectual level, in a manner which is so disarmingly honest that it seems to constantly call into question the interviewers' own honesty and integrity, has won him few friends among critics who thrive on cloak and dagger ambiguity. No wonder then that Moby has had his values scrutinized to a degree usually reserved for politicians. Calls of "hypocrite" and "liar" have become commonplace. Above all however, Moby's ongoing lack of critical respect has had more to do with the fact that everything he does, no matter how highbrow, regardless of morals, much less points a finger at society than holds a mirror up to it. This has proved far too uncomfortable for far too many.

Moby then; the eternal outsider or simply one of life's observers? A man who holds his beliefs but refuses to force them upon others; who refuses to judge others by his own standards. Someone who is prepared to change his beliefs when experience shows them to be unsound. One of the few truly eclectic artists in the oft-claimed openness of the post-tribal age. Oh, and someone who makes mistakes. Loads of them. Like any other human being with a passion for what he does.

CHAPTER ONE

"I was left on my own a lot, not in a neglectful way, but in a way in which I seem to have developed a strange need for autonomy. I am grateful that as a boy I had lots of strange and interesting places to play." Moby 2000

Growing up the poor kid in a rich town isn't an easy thing to do. You watch as your friends take everything for granted. You watch as rewards are heaped upon them. Try as you might, you can never quite keep up.

Growing up small in a town where athletes are the local heroes is equally tough. When everyone is obsessed with sporting prowess, the small, delicate child is seen as worthless. So what would you do in such a situation? Sociologists might suggest the most common option would be turning to crime. However, for Moby this was never an option. Although he does admit to having been in the thick of much in-school troublemaking, he turned to music instead.

Moby was born in Harlem, New York City on September 11th, 1965 and was given the rather grand name of Richard Melville Hall. Indeed as his parents looked on their tiny new son, they declared the name to be far too big for such a little child. So they gave him the nickname under which he would eventually achieve worldwide acclaim: Moby, after the eponymous giant whale of Herman Melville's famous novel.

This was not an entirely superficial moniker, as it drew on a family history reflected in his own middle name. The infant Moby, it would seem, was actually the latest in a line which included Melville himself, author of *Moby Dick* and the young Richard Hall's great-great-grand-uncle. "I've tried to read the book a few times" says the whale's namesake, "but I never quite got through it."

His parents, Elizabeth McBride Warner-Hall (nee-Reynolds) and James Hall, were impoverished students, barely scraping by on their meager income. It was a hard time that took its toll on the young parents. Their marriage became increasingly rocky. At the age of twenty six, Moby's father, a chemistry lecturer at Columbia University, was involved in a fatal car crash following a heavy drinking session. He drove his car into a wall. Richard Melville Hall was only two.

Moby maintains that he has no real memories of his father; he later discovered that some suspected he had actually committed suicide. With his father's death, Moby's mother was a widow at the young age of twenty three. She subsequently returned to her hometown of Darien, Connecticut. Here, Moby's maternal grandparents had a huge hand in raising him while his mother finished off her degree. She graduated in 1969 and, by way of celebration, took her young son to the hippie Mecca of Haight-Astbury in San Francisco. Upon their return to the real life of Connecticut, Moby's mother took temporary secretarial jobs to support herself and her son. Despite the fact that her parents were hugely wealthy - her father owned a company on Wall Street - Betsy, as she was affectionately known, was determined she should take responsibility for her own son.

Betsy Hall was something of a flower child herself, taking her son to stay at various communes for weekends. Moby recalls one particular commune visit vividly. Early one morning he wandered downstairs, into the kitchen to get some breakfast cereal. As he walked through the living room he was greeted by the sight of a mass of naked bodies slumped over each other. But while the commune may have inadvertently shown the youngster the more salacious sides of sexual behavior, it also opened his ears to an eclectic range of music. Drugs and drink were also commonplace among the adults in this environment. The little Moby soaked it all in, later reacting against his formative years with the beliefs he would adopt as a teenager. "Five days a week she would be a secretary, then on weekends we'd go to communes," he reveals. "It's ironic that I grew up to really hate the 60s counter-culture." [He has since told me, "I don't really hate 60's counter-culture.

I only hated it when I was little and it scared me."]

If these experiences created a cornerstone for Moby's beliefs, then his grandparents provided the wide-open spaces for his mind to roam. He would spend much of his formative years exploring their huge, rambling garden, enjoying private adventures in imaginary worlds. "I was left on my own a lot, not in a neglectful way, but in a way in which I seem to have developed a strange need for autonomy. My mother and grandmother both worked, which is why I spent a lot of time by myself. And a lot of my time was spent at my grandparents' house which was rambling and old and had big overgrown gardens, so there were lots of places to get lost and entertain myself. I am grateful that as a little boy I had lots of strange and interesting places to play."

Moby's earliest memories betray a relatively normal upbringing - despite only having one parent in a town full of average nuclear families. Of the first five years of his life, he clearly remembers being sent to a "disgusting" day-care center. He also remembers "eating too much King Vitamin cereal and throwing up, looking for a fox den in the woods, sharing peanuts with a businessman on a flight to San Francisco in 1969 (on the way to Haight-Astbury), lying in bed trying to count to 1000, drinking water from a faucet while a friend was flushing the toilet and having him tell me I was drinking pee. All of the above before I turned five, I think."

He also has memories of his mother's friends sneaking him into the movie theatre to see the X-rated Raquel Welch movie based on Gore Vidal's classic novel about transexuality *Myra Breckinridge*. However there is one memory that suggests an early love of music in Moby. At the age of three he recalls "listening to Credence Clearwater Revival in the car with my mom and being transfixed. The song was 'Proud Mary'. It was playing on the AM radio and I wouldn't get out of the car until it had finished playing."

Another recollection of "crying into a kazoo and having my mother, who was trying to be angry, laughing hysterically" may seem to have shown his nascent love of music. But what child hasn't at sometime made noises through a kazoo? Moby does however recall his mother buying him a drum at the age of five. Like most toddlers, it would seem Richard Hall simply loved to make noise. That he would develop a strong love of music was inevitable considering his mother's own passion for playing the piano and listening to records drawn from a wide variety of genres. "My mother was a piano player and she used to play me a lot of different stuff. Some of it was very weird classical stuff, not the usual thing for a young child to listen to. But this became a huge influence on me when I was growing up," he says.

In 1976, with the economy hitting a dramatic slump, Betsy, now unemployed, and her eleven-year-old son moved into the working-class district of Stratford, Connecticut. Their new home was another commune, inhabited by pot-smoking musicians. Moby and his increasingly despairing mother were forced to survive on welfare and food stamps. During this period he watched as Betsy was abused by a string of no-hope bohemian boyfriends - one, a musician who stole from her; another a man who threatened to kill her with a butcher's knife. There had been some nice 'uncles', but none who stuck around. If this wasn't enough for the young, highly-strung Moby, he also started to hear a voice whispering his name whenever he was in his room. He maintains that he wasn't frightened by this haunting. The paranormal presence, he says, seemed to like him.

After a couple of years of this life, Betsy finally agreed to move back to Darien. Sadly this came about through the death of her father, who had left her an inheritance. She bought a house with the money. A few years after she and Moby reluctantly moved out of their Stratford home, Betsy also admitted having heard the voice whispering her son's name.

Little Richard Hall's musical ability first began to surface around the age of eight when he took up the guitar. By the time he was nine, he had started taking formal guitar lessons, mastering his first song, Elton John's 'Crocodile Rock', soon after. Not that Moby considers himself to have been in any way a musical prodigy. He believes his talent has come largely from hours of hard work and perspiration. "Once I began studying music in earnest (at the age of twelve or thirteen) that was pretty much all I did. I spent most of my free time playing guitar, or playing piano, or playing bass."

It was at this time that he first started to experiment with recording his own songs. Like most youngsters with a love of music, he started to play around with his cassette recorder, taping himself singing and playing guitar. He maintains that he found this experience incredibly frustrating. Even at this point he'd have preferred a multi-track recorder. But he "was also very excited that it was in fact possible to record music that [he] had performed. So excited, and frustrated."

Moby's attention soon turned towards forming his own band. It was 1978 and he was thirteen. He had long since purchased his first record, 'Convoy' by C.W. McCall, which he then "listened to forty times straight. Put the needle down, listened to it then picked it up again. I did this over and over, I just couldn't get enough. I just sat in front of the record player, with this little three-minute song and I couldn't imagine it ever really ending."

By this time however he had developed a fascination for the music of The Doors and The Rolling Stones. He formed a band with a group of friends, specialising in cover versions. Not by The Stones, or even The Doors, instead the band was influenced by the obsession of the bass player - The Beatles. "We played a lot of Beatles covers - badly I might add, but it was euphoric nonetheless."

The band would rehearse in the basement of Moby's house. As this meant that the gear was always set up and available, he often went alone into this music room to mess around on the different instruments. As a result he taught himself how to play drums and bass. He already played guitar and was getting piano lessons from his mom.

He may have been relatively young, but Moby was already hooked on the passion, energy and process of making music. That unnamed Beatles covers band was to be the first of many groups Moby would be a part of, these groups covering a spectrum of musical styles from industrial to thrash, indie to post-punk.

Moby's school life was similarly dominated by creative pursuits. As a student of Royle Elementary School, Middlesex and Mather Junior High Schools and, finally, Darien High School, he excelled in languages, arts and, of course, music. "I was never very good at math or science. I liked science, but in a vague, esoteric way, and I could never be bothered with scientific minutiae - memorizing the periodic table of elements, etc."

According to his high school English teacher at Darien, Geraldine Marshall, the young Richard Hall was a "brilliant, eccentric child" whose "writing was very odd." Brilliant and eccentric he may have been, but the young Moby failed to excel at sports. Not that he was particularly bad, just not up to the standard to make the top grade at his schools. "I played baseball but wasn't very good at it. I loved to play American football when I was very young and I loved archery and swimming, but I wasn't very good at any of these things."

Moby may not have been a high-flyer on the sports field, but off it he found other, more rebellious ways of keeping himself interested. He had his music. He had even discovered the joys of dancing. "I went to my first ever dance when I was eleven or twelve years old," he says, "and it was the first time I'd ever danced in my life. It was the Junior High School dance and they were playing pop music, hit records in the gymnasium. It was the first time I'd ever danced and I couldn't stop, and I never, ever wanted to stop, I thought I'd discovered the best thing in the world. I've never felt that way about anything since. It was so much fun."

Among his other extra-curricular pursuits however, one could have taken Moby's life in a completely different direction. He became something of a mischief-maker. "I was a good student, for the most part. I caused my fair share of troubles, but somehow I never got caught. In fact, looking back on it I caused an awful lot of trouble and if I'd been found out, I would probably be in jail. Just juvenile delinquent stuff. Nothing too serious, but now that they try children as adults in our judicial system, it's a good thing that I grew up when I did.

"At school I was kind of small and odd, at times very quiet and other times very gregarious. I was kind of an exhibitionist. I have distinct memories of taking all of my clothes off in school and running up and down the hallways. I was kind of like a troublemaker, but with a conscience. I loved being provocative and causing trouble - breaking things, hiding things, and being a smart Alec - but I always felt awful if someone got hurt by it. In school, kids are really mean, and sometimes I would be joining in with the cool kids, picking on someone, and afterwards I would be loathing myself. I remember once, in Third Grade, a friend and I stole the librarian's purse - we took the money and hid the purse where she would find it. It was like a huge scandal in school and no one ever found out who did it - I felt so awful about it for such a long time."

However, this taste for mischief also spilled out of the school gates, into his everyday quest for fun. "Me and my friends went through this stage of breaking into people's houses, not to steal things but just for fun. Sometimes we would just move things around, we'd do subtle things like tilt a picture a bit or reset their alarm clocks, so it would gradually freak people out. But we never stole from them. We were like twelve at the time.

"I also remember back when I was ten, I found an abandoned private school, so some friends and I broke in and turned it into our home away from home. It was wonderful. We eventually settled in the old gymnasium where we would build forts and break things and paint nasty things on the walls. Just good, clean, healthy fun.

"There was also a period when we stole quite a lot. My friends and I used to steal anything we could get our hands on when we were seven or eight years old and, because we were young, no one suspected. When I was stealing from supermarkets I never felt guilty, but when it was from a person I just felt terrible. Oh, and we used to burn things – not houses though! When I was eight years old I burned down a friend of mine's backyard. It was an accident, we used to play with fire a lot, but usually the fires were contained."

If the straight-edge image that would later surround Moby seems at odds with the young Richard Hall, then consider this: the first time he took illegal drugs was at the tender age of ten. He claims he smoked marijuana, took pills and drank liquor while hanging out with some of the cool kids he wanted to be friends with.

"I started doing drugs when I was ten years old," he told *Mixmag* in 1993. "By the time I was twelve I had done the lot. We would smoke hash and take these pills my friend got from his sister going to hospital and we drank Jack Daniels. I never really enjoyed it and I have this really vivid memory of being stoned and hearing someone say, 'Imagine what he'll be like in five years.' And that sobered me up, and I didn't do anything for five years."

Of course a cynical perspective – and one no doubt assumed by many of the UK journalists who seem not to trust him – of this would be that he has just made this part of his life up so as to make his later anti-drug stance seem less narrow-minded. Just as the kid who is still a virgin boasts of his conquests, Moby's claim would put him in an indisputable position of authority. However, it is probably safe to surmise that his weekend hippie life would have brought him into contact with drugs of all kinds. That he smoked dope with his contemporaries is, in this context, hardly surprising. That he says he was only trying to impress the cool kids would also support his ever-present claims of insecurity.

It is worth noting though that, despite the encouragement of his mother and her commune friends, Moby rejected all ideas of becoming a vegetarian. He was a dedicated meat eater. An early rebellion against parental guidance perhaps, however in this light it also suggests that much of his later ideology would come from the same sense of rebellion.

If a reason for the apparent inconsistencies and hypocrisies which Moby has been accused of throughout his career exists, then it lies here in his youth. That he has been able to see the wider picture, re-evaluate his own convictions and hold true to what he believes at any one time emanated from a childhood of opposite experiences: Moby the quiet rebel. A smaller-than-average child with a penchant for mischief. A poor kid in a rich town. More poignantly, he was the impoverished grandchild of extremely wealthy grandparents. The gregarious boy who enjoyed his own company. One who would make spontaneous mischief in an almost calculated way. The excluded child who would have to lie to his school friends about his exotic holidays during school vacations rather than admit to not having enough money to leave the town. A creative child supported by a loving mother and doting grandparents who created an environment of solitary exploration during the week and communal expression at the weekends. As he says: "I did have friends, and although I did spend a lot of time on my own, I wouldn't describe myself as a loner."

In subsequent years Moby would often talk about his low self-esteem and overriding feeling of inadequacy. Through all of these oppositional forces he came to regard himself as an underachiever and harbour huge doubts about everything he did. What emerges then, is a strong picture of Moby the outsider. Little wonder that the kind of music he would be drawn to could be described as 'outsider music'. Soon after his flirtation with all things Beatles, Stones and Doors, Moby discovered the punk rock attack of The Sex Pistols and The Clash. By the age of fifteen he had formed his own skate-punk band, which he wistfully describes as "suburban punk rockers on mopeds".

The band went through a series of names, including UXB, The Banned, and Dicky Hell and the Redbeats, before finally settling on The Vatican Commandos. They played at venues like Pogo's in Bridgeport and adopted a stance of anti-everything. Soon after, in the summer of 1983, they released a seven-inch single, 'Hit Squad for God' on their own Pregnant Nun Records - a six-track romp through high-speed thrash mayhem. "The band lasted for three years. Three years of fighting with friends and driving twenty hours to play shows for ten people. It was really fun."

If the Commandos hadn't already proved his punk credentials, then Moby's next musical step certainly would. He became the singer with legendary US skate punks Flipper, albeit for only two days, after their usual vocalist Will Shatter was incarcerated in a Connecticut jail. It was pure luck really. The band had turned up to play a gig but their singer failed to materialize. They asked some of the young punks if they knew the words to their songs. Only Moby stepped forward.

"I can't imagine a world wherein punk rock had never existed," he considers. "It changed just about everything, and continues to do so. The essence of punk, for me, was/is the idea of defining the institutions in your life for yourself, and not relying on any existing definitions."

At this point Moby was starting to define himself in extreme terms. He had taken a Marxist position on things and had embraced an almost dogmatic, rigid standpoint. Not surprisingly, Moby soon tired of the limitations placed upon the punk genre. Though he loved, and identified with, its spirit, he had ambitions to express himself in more ambitious musical terrain while still retaining the punk ethos.

Little surprise then that he was drawn towards the late-70s, early-80s post-punk scene of the UK.

CHAPTER TWO

"Until house music, I associated dance music with aesthetically uninteresting music." Moby, 1991

Already a fan of electronic ambient artists like Brian Eno, thanks to the influence of his mother, it was through bands like Joy Division, A Certain Ratio and Public Image Limited (PiL) that Moby could see the disparate elements of punk rock and ambient walking common ground. He already had a love of musical extremes. Post-punk was music that knew no boundaries. It transcended genre, color and forcibly removed itself from the confines of contemporary music of the time.

By the late 70s, punk rock's anarchic nihilism had long-since turned into marketing fodder. Where the early cries of "Smash The System", "Never Trust A Hippie" and "Kill All Dinosaurs" created an ideological foundation which inspired a generation of youth to take up arms against the flaccidity of mid-70s music and politics, sadly the end of the decade saw all this creative anger turned to "product".

Of the first wave of UK punks, very few actually reacted against the standardization of the sound and style. There were the mavericks like Howard Devoto would leave The Buzzcocks to form Magazine, while Johnny Rotten, who would reclaim his real surname of Lydon, departed the increasingly grotesque Sex Pistols to form PiL. Of the remaining first-generation punk bands, only The Clash would seem to aspire to anything greater than the three-chord, three-minute rants, now so beloved of everyone and everything punk originally sought to destroy. In a matter of months, punk rock had become another part of the system.

In Magazine and PiL there was a sense of adventure never seen before. Most notably in the case of the latter, there existed a healthy irreverence towards all of the music the band had loved as youngsters. Entwined in the sonic depths of PiL were the reverberations of dub reggae, Captain Beefheart, Can and Neu, ground-breaking techno mavericks Kraftwerk and, of course, punk's original sense of euphoria. When PiL delivered their eponymous seven-inch single, wrapped in a mock-tabloid newspaper - the popular press had dogged the Sex Pistols from very early on, soon after they had caused national outrage in Britain by swearing on prime-time TV - its impact was incalculable. Quite apart from showing a way out of the punk *cul de sac*, it created real division between the old-school punks who would cling to the accepted punk norm (oxymoron as such an idea is), and those who saw punk rock as a byword for experimentation. Where punk was sonically exclusive, the post-punk sound was inclusive to an extreme, drawing on hugely disparate influences.

In many ways it is in this post-punk era (and New York's mutant disco/no wave, which would emerge soon after), where we can see the early attitudes that would be a major force in the rave movement of the late 80s. The music was driven by an underlying magpie aesthetic and black dance culture lay at the foundation. Not so surprising when you consider that at the early UK punk gigs, reggae and disco were the standard between-band soundtrack. Songs would take a linear rather than a narrative form. Also gigs gradually gave way to events, in which the visuals were as important as the music. However, it was still very much an anti-star set up.

One of the first bands to find creative resonance in the emerging post-punk era was a Manchester group by the name of Warsaw. Following their last gig as a buzzsaw punk act, they re-emerged in late 1977 as Joy Division (later, following the suicide of singer Ian Curtis, they would change their name once more, this time to New Order, a band famed for their trail-blazing use of electronics and early championing of acid house). They became more expansive, their rhythms were a contorted form of disco, guitars were fractured in a naïve take on funk's chicken grease style and melodies were drawn out, doom-laden, and some would say depressing. Suddenly the youth of Britain rejected their shorn hair and ripped clothes. Instead they grew their fringes, and adopted long raincoats and second-hand suits.

That the post-punk movement had an effect on the youth of Britain was of little surprise. This was radical music, born of a rejection of its own sub-cultural foundation. It was an oppositional music that aligned itself with all of society's outsiders. Most important of all, it came at a time of huge political unrest in Britain, coinciding with the beginning of the Conservative Party's eighteen-year reign. Soon after, the UK would see a series of riots that would show the world just how strong the social divisions of the time were. In sub-cultural terms however, the writing had been on the wall since 1976. Both original punk rock and post-punk were insurrectionist, righteous forms of music. Art, as ever, was simply mirroring life.

What is surprising is the fact that a young music obsessive living in an affluent suburb of East Coast America felt empathy with this music. What Moby heard of course was the post-punk sound stripped of both its British political connotations and its cultural pretensions. Moby first heard PiL, Joy Division, A Certain Ratio and Gang of Four in an enviable way for anyone wrapped up in the tensions of the time - purely as a form of music. Although, given Moby's Marxist perspective of the time, it could be argued that this music was inherently political, these new sounds appealed, albeit subconsciously, to his ideologies as much as his musical tastes.

At the age of eighteen, Moby formed AWOL, his own post-punk band. The line-up included Paul Johnson on bass, Andrew de Araujo on drums, while Moby himself sang, played guitar and e-bow. According to the sleeve notes for their one and only single, the self-titled twelve-inch released in 1984, Moby also provided "photography, design, annoyance and megalomania". The single itself was a dark, somber affair with an obvious nod of respect in the direction of Joy Division. "[AWOL were] post-punk, literally and figuratively," he recalls. "I tried to sound like Ian Curtis-meets-Ian McCulloch (lead singer with Liverpudlian post-punkers Echo and the Bunnymen) and ended up making some sort of interesting, if a tad po-faced, music."

Po-faced or not, Moby's fascination for this era of music would continue to raise its influential head on every subsequent Moby release. The young musician had discovered in post-punk a spirit that could make sense of often-perverse eclecticism. It is from this attitude that he has been able to switch with ease from rave to thrash punk to ambient film music as if it all makes perfect sense. For Moby these musics are interconnected.

Naturally he continued to expand his horizons. His next venture was a "fun and interesting industrial band" called Shopwell. With a penchant for the scouring soundscapes of performance artists-cum-industrial musicians Throbbing Gristle, Shopwell consisted of Moby (credited as Jim Biscuit), J Harrell and Paul Yates. Although they only played together "about five times", they did manage to put out a record. Called *Peanuts*, it consisted of only two tracks - two sides of looped noise - but clocked in at album length. The record had no song titles at all, which was the fashion for industrial noise artists of the time. This release is interesting in that it finds Moby experimenting with the concepts of minimalism and texture. Later in his career he would release a number of pieces of music which have their roots in both the brittle noise of industrial and the pastoral calm of Brian Eno's ambient sounds.

Following Shopwell, Moby enjoyed a brief spell in a new wave band called Japanese Sex Painting. It wasn't to last though. By the time Moby hit nineteen, his musical endeavors were taking precedence over his studies. He had graduated high school and been voted "the pupil most likely to leave us wondering". He went on to the University of Connecticut to study philosophy but failed to graduate. Throughout this time he was living in a derelict warehouse building in South Connecticut with a group of friends. He spent much of his time either making music or commuting to New York where he had secured a DJing residency at the legendary MARS Club, where he remained for a period of two years working under the acronym M.O.B.Y., which now stood for Master Of Beats, Y'all.

"I just sent them a tape and the next thing I was DJing there," he says with a glint in his eye. "I don't know anyone else that this has happened to." That tape was a mix-and-match collection of old punk rock, post-punk, disco and hip hop tracks. At this stage, despite his ever-growing love affair with hip hop (to which he would continually refer on future records), his interest in dance music was relatively limited. Indeed, while at the MARS he would back up rap superstars such as Big Daddy Kane and Run DMC. "Until house music, I associated dance music with aesthetically uninteresting music," he told *Alternative Press* in 1991.

It was during this time that he would meet his long-time best friend, renowned New York painter and film maker Damien Loeb. Back in those days, Damien would often film the happenings at MARS with his video camera, capturing amongst other things footage of Moby with long hair (which he still sported at the time of his first single release 'Mobility' on Instinct) playing tambourine alongside white rapper Serch from seminal crew 3rd Bass.

In 1988, Moby teamed up with the sometime brilliant psychedelic indie band Ultra Vivid Scene. It is a musical endeavor which has reached near-legendary proportions, with journalists repeating the story over and over again. UVS, as they were also known, were one of trendy UK post-punk record company 4AD's more popular bands among the critical cognoscenti. That Moby had been a member of them seemed to elevate his status in the eyes of many anti-dance journalists. The reality of this period of Moby's musical adventure was, as is often the case, less interesting than the romance. He never recorded or played live with Ultra Vivid Scene. He actually only rehearsed with them for about a month.

In 1989 at the age of twenty four, Moby finally left Connecticut and returned to his city of birth, New York. Although the reasons would seem obvious (after so many years commuting he had finally had enough), the truth provides an insight into the philosophies he had started to take on board. He simply didn't want to add to the world's pollution any more, so driving to and from Connecticut was out of the question.

"The automobile is responsible for many of the woes facing mankind today," he said in *Alternative Press* 1991. "They've helped create an insular society, they're horrible polluters, they're largely responsible for the greenhouse effect, and they kill thousands of people every year." To this apparently extreme stance Moby had also included a refusal to eat meat, wear or use animal products or anything tested on animals. He had developed an anti-alcohol and drugs stance and a deep Christian faith. This new-found religious belief, which will be discussed in depth later in this book, was to have a profound effect on every facet of Moby's life from hereon.

As Moby's life started to evolve with his new surroundings in New York, his values would be increasingly challenged. By the time house music appeared on the club scene (along with its associated drug culture), and Moby's head was turned towards the euphoric joy of repetitive beats, his ethics would not only be challenged, but also questioned, belittled and increasingly ridiculed. Moby was soon to become saddled with the title of the 'techno-monk'.

CHAPTER THREE

"The same thing that appeals to me about rave culture appealed to me about hardcore punk culture. They're both staunchly anti-establishment, community-oriented. The scene is not being fuelled by corporate interests, but rather by people interested in culture." Moby in 1991

Though he didn't realize it at the time, Moby's 1989 move to an apartment on 14th & 3rd in the East Village district of New York would coincide with the beginnings of the most powerful subculture to have emerged since punk: rave. However, for anyone with a passing interest in counter-culture, the dance and club scenes of New York would have been impossible to ignore. Since the heady days of disco in 1977, New York had been party central. Inevitably Moby, along with room-mates Damien Loeb and hip hop DJ, Adrian Bartos aka Stretch Armstrong, would be gradually drawn towards the energy.

Although Detroit and Chicago are generally regarded as the respective birthplaces of techno and house, the seeds of the scene can be traced back to New York's club scene of the late 70s and much of the 80s. For any DJ/musician, like Moby, the lure of these clubs was inescapable. Quite simply, New York has dance culture seeping through the cracks in every sidewalk.

The early history of house can actually be traced back as far as 1970. Francis Grasso, resident DJ at New York's infamously debauched club Sanctuary, a disused church in the tough Hell's Kitchen district, became the first DJ to segue records into a seamless, uninterrupted mix. It was through this technique, known as beat matching, that he was able to create a single hypnotic groove to keep clubbers locked to the dance floor.

This development was quickly taken a step further when Walter Gibbons (resident at Galaxy 21 and the first New York DJ to remix a track onto vinyl with Double Exposure's '10 Per Cent'), hired a drummer to play live in the club. The aim was to add extra rhythm and bottom end to his mixes. That drummer was Francois Kevorkian, who himself would one day be considered one of the world's best DJs.

Elsewhere in New York, the seeds of disco were also being sown by David Mancuso at the cutting-edge parties held in his own apartment, which became known around the city as The Loft. Mancuso's nights were almost unique in their anti-liquor policy. Yet they captured people's hearts to such an extent that dancers often referred to The Loft as a spiritual experience. This quasi-religious fervor was born of an open, passionate attitude and the most sophisticated soundsystem in New York. The records played by Mancuso were certainly uplifting and emotional, and these qualities would subsequently influence many spheres of dance music. Indeed, The Loft presented a spirit that would find its way into Moby's own music almost twenty years later.

Elsewhere in the city, Nicky Siano set up The Gallery. It was here that would-be DJs Frankie Knuckles and Larry Levan got their first breaks. Siano taught the pair how to beat mix and they would subsequently soon take on their own residencies - Levan went to The Continental Baths and Knuckles manned the decks at the legendary Better Days.

In early 1977, Knuckles was spirited away from New York to Chicago in order to become resident at The Warehouse. It was to become a fabled club where Knuckles would take all he had learned from his New York experiences and inspire an entirely new crowd. Until this point, with the exception of The Future - a club run by Lil' Louis - club DJs in Chicago, like much of the US, were actually jukeboxes.

Meanwhile, over the next few years, the combination of disco's energy and the futuristic noises emanating from Europe would inspire a whole new sound to develop in Detroit. Initially this would be seen through electro, however slowly the influence of artists like Kraftwerk could be heard everywhere, resulting in techno's arrival on the dance floor.

By combining the high energy of disco with Philly soul, then beat matching the tracks into extended edits, Knuckles began to develop what would later become known as the Chicago jack sound. Lil' Louis, on the other hand, was equally essential to house music's development, with his inclusion of the newer techno sounds of Detroit. It was from the fusion of Knuckles' and Louis' inspired DJ explorations that a defined Chicago house sound emerged.

Meanwhile New York continued to be at the forefront of the clubbing experience. Larry Levan opened the Paradise Garage, a concrete garage in SoHo, Manhattan redesigned as a haven for club hedonists. With its pornographic murals and anything-goes atmosphere it quickly became a favorite hang-out for players on the city's flamboyant gay scene.

"What attracted me first to dance culture," Moby told *Spin* in 2000, "as a white, straight kid from the suburbs going out to these mostly black, gay clubs, was just how foreign and interesting and wonderful it was. It really was alternative. New York was dirty and dangerous and sexual politics were weird, but at these clubs [Paradise Garage and Red Zone], Latinos, blacks, whites, men and women were celebrating."

Musically, the sound of Paradise Garage is pivotal to Moby's story. Just as Moby would subvert disco's hooklines in his work, Paradise Garage DJs Larry Levan and David DePino would concentrate of the hard-edged, euphoric sounds of the underground. Disco may have become the commercial sound-track to the dying days of the 70s through to the mid-80s, but Paradise Garage, just like Chicago's clubs, proved that the scene was developing in ways nobody could have ever predicted.

Among the sounds the club pioneered were mutant disco and no wave, New York's answer to post-punk and futurism (a precursor to the new romantics in the UK). The mutant disco/no wave sound was an interesting departure from the commercialization of the once-underground disco sound. Very much in keeping with the experimental ethos of post-punk, no wave artists such as Liquid Liquid, Was Not Was and Material drew a clear line between Sex Pistols, Brian Eno, George Clinton and Afrobeat legend Fela Anikulapo Kuti.

By the mid-80s, Levan began to incorporate electro-funk into Paradise Garage's musical menu. As a member of The Peech Boys, with vocalists Bernard Fowler (later to be found singing with industrial-funk outfit Tackhead), Levan pioneered the sound which would subsequently become synonymous with New York producers such as Arthur Baker and Francois Kevorkian, and artists from D:Train to Rockers' Revenge.

The electro-funk sonics of the Paradise Garage most certainly had its roots firmly placed in disco; a scene which itself had faced the wrath of white rock music snobbery during the infamous 'Disco Sucks' campaign. It is hard to imagine now but at the height of this anti-disco movement, DJ Steve Dahl invited the people of Chicago to bring their unwanted disco records along to a baseball game at Comiskey Park between the Chicago White Sox and the Detroit Tigers. During the intermission, some 100,000 records were piled up into a huge mound, then blown up with dynamite - a full-blown riot followed. As a result of the debris, the match was postponed and the game was forfeited by the White Sox.

But, as Simon Reynolds pointed out in his excellent history of dance music, *Energy Flash*: "The 'Disco Sucks' phenomenon recalls the Nazi book burnings, or the exhibitions of Degenerate Art. Modern day spectacles of *kulturekampf* like Comiskey were impelled by a similar disgust; the belief that disco was rootless, inauthentic, decadent, a betrayal of the virile principles of the true American *volk* Music, rock'n'roll. Hence T-shirts like 'Death Before Disco', hence organizations like D.R.E.A.D (Detroit Rockers Engaged in the Abolition of Disco) and Dahl's own Insane Coho Lips Antidisco Army."

In many ways, disco, and the later dance culture, seemed to represent the antithesis of Moby's youthful interests. His tastes were very much centered on the worthy. Bands he favored prior to his move to New York were dark, melancholic, art-school types. The dance music he enjoyed came from the street-cool hip hop scene. What the Paradise Garage represented was a sound that many (white, middle-class, straight, male) critics had rejected as being worthless and disposable. It was the music favored by blacks and gays, ironically making it more worthy of the 'outsider' tag than any of the post-punk bands Moby so loved. In reality, these artists had been disenfranchised by a media obsessed with a romantic notion of post-punk's darkness. It was a notion that Moby similarly romanticized.

"When I was at high school," he once said, "I was kind of attracted to the darker side of music. I like the suicidal aspects of bands. So people like Joy Division held a fascination for me, which went beyond the music. When I was at college I had a negative experience with acid. I just wanted to get high and ended up taking a particularly large dose. But after this I realized that I was romanticizing something I didn't really understand. I was glorifying suicide, even though I had no experience of it."

In 1991, talking to Sue Cummings of *LA Weekly*, he expanded on this subject considerably: "I had a dream once, the most meaningful dream I can remember... it was sort of about this. I was in Port Chester, the bad part of town, and was trying to pull a house from Port Chester into Greenwich, an all-white, affluent area. I was drinking Jack Daniels straight from the bottle, and I had this chain that I was pulling.

"While I was doing this, a woman with frazzled red hair, looking all disheveled, wearing a black slip, came up and said, 'Okay, let's go.' She said, 'We're supposed to have sex now.' And I got all nervous. I said, 'What are you talking about?' She said, 'You've been flirting with me for a long time.'

"I saw a psychologist for a few weeks while I had this dream. At first he thought it was about a sexual thing, and then he said 'Well, could this women have represented death to you in any way?' This was it exactly. I had been flirting with death and the dark side of things, and when it came to the time to actually do something about it, I realized I didn't want to."

In dance culture and clubs like the Paradise Garage, Moby found catharsis. A positivity which drew him away from the depressive sentiments of the post-punk era. True, his music would always have a melancholic edge, but it would never be morbidly death-obsessed, like many others who were touched by this period in music.

Throughout the growth of house and the subsequent changes in New York club culture, another development was taking place, which would ultimately shape Moby's music. From the eclectic melting pot of breakbeat culture, electro, disco and European new wave electronic music such as like Gary Numan, techno emerged from the darkened streets of Detroit. Spearheaded by the works of Juan Atkins, Derrick May and Kevin Saunderson, it formed into a cohesive sound, which seemed to open doors on the future.

With such an anti-establishment concept, it was inevitable that Moby would find a creative home among the ranks of the DJs and producers. His fledgling DJ career had developed such that he was now considered one of the New York underground's foremost attractions. He actually went by the name DJ Moby Deck for a while, before temporarily shortening the Deck to a simple D. A playlist, from the September 1989 edition of US magazine *Details*, shows Moby playing tracks like 'In Time' by The Jungle Brothers, 'The Payback' by James Brown, 'Who Is That?' by Boogie Down Productions and 'Flash Light' by Parliament. Interestingly, the list also included dancehall reggae track 'Who The Cap Fits' by Shinehead. The majority of Moby's gigs were on the roof area of MARS, although he did play the club's other rooms to startling effect. Throughout 1989, his sets were legendary among New York clubbers, as gradually house and techno music took over Moby's DJ sets.

"MARS had these great body-blowing sub-woofer speakers on the first floor that got into a more aggressive way of spinning," recalled Moby in *DJ Times* in 1991. "The atmosphere was dark and disorientating and there was something about playing loud, high-energy sounds that appealed to me."

As word spread, he gained more gigs at New York clubs like Quick!, The Beat (in Portchester), Big Haus, The Cafe, Lucky Strike, MK, Palladium, Time Cafe, La Palace De Beaute, Red Zone, Future Shock and The Limelight (the latter of which he has likened to "playing in a penitentiary"). He also regularly DJ'd in Germany at Hamburg's Opera House and Berlin's UFO and Quartier.

"He does weird, nasty shit," said Instinct Records' Jared Hoffman to *DJ Times* in 1991. "You know, he scratches, throws in sounds, plays them pitched as high as they can go, he cuts back and forth between tracks - he just doesn't merely spin records."

"I think that the music that I make would be quite different if I hadn't spent so many nights DJing to people and trying to make them all happy," Moby postulates. "I gave people what they wanted when they were nice and enthusiastic - I would even play Motown for secretaries if it made them happy - and I intentionally antagonized people if they were pricks." It has also been suggested elsewhere that Moby did pursue a hostile course in his Djing sets. At least one friend from his early days DJing at new wave club The Chase in Greenwich, Connecticut has said in a 1991 edition of *LA Weekly*, that Moby "would sometimes play weird stuff, dumb 70s records like *The Partridge Family*, to try to irk people."

Alongside these club dates, Moby also did two radio shows. *Rap It Up* was a hip hop show which was syndicated to fifty stations across the US while *Planet Radio* was a broader-based show which was broadcast on FM 802 in Osaka, Japan. While Moby may have initially made his name at the MARS Club as a hip hop DJ, his sets increasingly included house and techno. Indeed, the Japanese show was designed to represent all of the changes occurring within dance music. It was, in fact, the first techno show on the station.

"I record my segment here in New York, then send it to Osaka," he said at the time in *Discotext* magazine. "The programme is kind of in a New York nightclub format and it includes DJs like Mark

Kamins, Larry Levan and Red Alert who contribute once a month. I mainly play a mixture of hardcore techno and atmospheric electronic stuff.

As someone who has always been attracted to music as an oppositional force, it was perhaps inevitable that the DIY ethic of house and techno would grab Moby. House music erupted with an unparalleled vibrancy and immense energy, opening up new, seemingly unlimited, creative vistas for the artist.

Just as hip hop and electro producers found inspiration in post-punk electronic artists such as Gary Numan (DJ Afrikka Bambaataa has described Numan as a hero), both house and techno drew heavily on the European influence of artists such as Kraftwerk. The new dance culture also worked heavily on the tonal aspect of music, often suggesting subliminal rhythms through the creation of sub-level soundwaves, an effect first explored by the so-called *musique concrete* modern classical composers like Stockhausen and further explored by Genesis P. Orridge's post-Throbbing Gristle outfit Psychic TV. Like hip hop, it was a post-modern culture, relying heavily on the sampler. However, in the same way that punk subverted rock'n'roll by taking the standard song structure and reducing it to its basic three-chord form, house culture involved the sampling of other work which would then be contorted, filtered and twisted out of all recognition.

Finally, house culture also tapped into the visceral sense of power created by punk through the use of repetitive beats. Punk used repetitive chords, played faster than heartbeat rate to build a frantic buzz. In response, fans would pogo or slam dance, both forms of dance that placed people in an almost hypnotic state. Similarly, dance music used the continuous pulse of the four-to-the-floor kickdrums and the throbbing basslines to induce a trance-like state, which many, like The Loft's regulars years before, have claimed to be almost spiritual. With the addition of ecstasy, a drug that elevates this experience and stimulates the need to dance, the results could be compared to the shamanistic dance rituals of ancient cultures.

Many took this experience to be a doorway to a higher state of consciousness, in a New Age take on Dr Timothy Leary's lysergically charged plea to 'tune in, turn on and drop out' of the 1960s. Moby, however, found in this movement a counter-culture, which allowed for greater expression of the individual. Indeed this was the aesthetic at the core of punk rock - the individual over the mass.

It was from this central tenet that punk rock developed its own industry. No longer was there a need for the major record companies, as punk bands just set up their own labels. Similarly, fanzines challenged the established magazines. Unfortunately the punk movement still needed many of the established aspects of industry in order to exist. Studios were still needed to record those demos. Distribution companies were still required to get the record in the shops.

But house culture took this whole concept a stage further. Through the growth of affordable technology, people could build their own basic studios and create their own music. They could then get white label records pressed up and suddenly, by developing effective modes of distribution, the entire do-it-your-self punk ethos came to fruition. To many, this all-important combination of individuality and creative control was a revelation. In the UK, this concept was encouraged by the growth in the free party scene, which eschewed traditional clubs in favor of illegal site raves.

Despite the influential position New York occupied on the genesis of the clubbing phenomenon, the city didn't exactly warm to the sounds emanating from elsewhere in the world. Not even the hip house adventures of Todd Terry managed to seduce the city's audience. New Yorkers liked their dance music clean-cut and laced with disco divas. They loved the lavish garage sound. Post-disco, post-mutant disco/no wave, and riding on the crest of the momentum of Chicago house, this fresh New York sound drew on its unique history to create the perfect *joi de vivre* soundtrack.

On the more pop-dance tip, Deee Lite famously savored the developments at the Paradise Garage and created their own mélange of cut-up grooves, addictive hooklines and infectious melodies with the worldwide hit 'Groove Is In The Heart'. For a brief period in the first year of the 90s, New York seemed to be the epicentre of the new wave of club culture. In reality however it was in a state of creative decline. Only a year after 'Groove Is In The Heart', the city's dance sound came to be epitomized by the over-produced excesses of C&C Music Factory.

Garage continued to provide the club soundtrack at such venues as The Sound Factory, Better Days and Zanzibar, and DJs like Tony Humphries and Junior Vasquez chose to fly the flag for garage, to the detriment of every other musical advance in the dance scene since 1989. They were sonic adventurers among the DJ *cognoscenti* of New York, but they had to leave town and head for Europe to find appreciation.

CHAPTER FOUR

"I set up my studio in Jared's living room at his request, and I would spend my days making music and answering the phones." Moby

In Europe a different story was being told. Having tentatively embraced Chicago house beats in the late 80s warehouse scene (ironically Chicago's house scene had gone into a huge slump at the same time), the UK was literally forced out of its post-Live Aid Yuppie slumber. This happened thanks to the combined sound of a stripped-down drum machine, a bass generator and a Roland TR-303. It was the sound of acid house. An abrasive, yet funky sound which epitomized the DIY ethic. Little wonder then that a nation, which had long since reveled in the buzz of raw energy would embrace this gritty, urban genre. And for a country already experienced in the underground art of the illegal party, the acid house phenomenon simply created the perfect foundation for a network of free parties in places such as disused warehouses.

As acid house parties slowly transformed into illegal raves, where mega-soundsystems and huge light shows where the norm, so the music became ever more energetic. By 1990, hardcore had taken hold. It was a sound that pulled on the breakbeats of hip hop, explored the noisescapes of industrial, and reveled in the sense of euphoria of house music: tracks like 'Dextrous' and 'Aftermath' by Nightmares On Wax, 'Chime' by Orbital, 'The Theme' by Unique 3 and LFO's self titled, bass-booming classic single.

It was a period, which Simon Reynolds, one of the few journalists to embrace this new sound, coined as 'bleep and bass'. In hardcore (or bleep and bass) all of Moby's musical obsessions seemed to come together. This was a distinctly north of England music that drew on all of the sounds that had mapped out the post-punk years. But it also drew heavily on the ebullience of Chicago house and the rhythmic and tonal dexterity of Detroit techno. Moby couldn't help becoming excited about it, allowing these new sounds to infuse the music he was making in his East Village warehouse.

Despite his ongoing success as a DJ, Moby admitted to *Interview* magazine that he felt like "the guy in the Wizard of Oz, you know, the one behind the curtain." Despite his shy nature (in the same interview, in which he appeared sporting long hair, wearing a buttoned shirt with word-print, flipping records with a spatula, he said that it had taken him six months of working at MARS to actually introduce himself to his boss), Moby clearly had his sights set on success as a recording artist.

Soon after his move to New York, fellow DJ Moneypenny told Moby of a new dance label that was being set up. Called Instinct, the imprint was run by another DJ, Jared Hoffman who was actively looking for talent to sign. When Moby dropped by clutching a tape filled with great, original dance material, Hoffman was immediately enthusiastic. Pretty soon he moved his studio into the backroom of the label offices, due to Hoffman's intention to use Moby as the in-house producer. "I set up my studio in Jared's living room at his request, and I would spend my days making music and answering the phones," he recalls.

Despite the fact that Moby had played entirely instrumental demos to Hoffman, the label boss decided that it would be best to make the first release on the label a vocal tune. As a result he drafted in vocalist Jimmy Mack. Jared stepped forward as executive producer while Dave Brubaker was producer. The track was written around the vocals, rather than the vocals being added as an afterthought. Subsequently, rather than opt to use his own name, Moby came up with the idea of calling this one-off project The Brotherhood.

So, in September 1990, Instinct Records released their first single, 'Time's Up' by The Brotherhood. With a band moniker inspired by a New Order album and a title echoing the first single by the then-Howard Devoto-led Buzzcocks, this four-track release came in a Dave Brubaker-designed sleeve. Depicted on it were orange clock faces, with hands removed, spinning through the air against a green background. Doubtless intended to be in some way surreal, the actual effect was to make the record seem more like an old-school indie label release rather than a brave, new dance track. At this stage dance records came in plain jackets. In terms of sleeve imagery and information, 'less is more' seemed perfectly true. Therefore The Brotherhood instantly looked like it had arrived from an earlier time.

In reality, with the exception of the vocal versions of the tracks, much of the single represented Moby's fascination with the recent developments in electronic music. The street poet-style, rapped vocals sounded completely at odds with the backing track, itself slightly reminiscent of New York industrial hip hop outfit, Disposable Heroes Of Hiphoprisy. However Jimmy Mack's vocals lacked the understated anger which marked Hiphoprisy frontman Michael Franti's style. In many ways 'Time's Up' was also similar to aspects of the Acid Jazz style, popular in the UK at the time.

The leading 'Deep Mix' of the track was a simple affair to leave room for the vocal. An understated bassline coiled itself around a downtempo break, the rhythms of which were built from a subtle collage of bongos, maracas and wood block. The beats were further underpinned by an ever present 'tick tock' sound which was sampled from a Steve Miller Band record. The sound of flowing water, or rolling waves, can be heard throughout, while an "oh" sample is also woven into the grooves. In many ways, the overall sound is reminiscent of David Bowie's work with Brian Eno on albums like *Low* and *Heroes*, although there is also a nod in respect to *Empires & Dance* euro-tech-era Simple Minds.

On the 'Dope Mix', the beats are certainly sampled from an old-school hip hop track. Even more space is given to the vocal, featuring a double echo, which becomes increasingly annoying, sounding as though it is being sung in a round. Furthermore, the lyrics were almost embarrassingly uninspired - the opening verse was an uncomfortable variation of a teenage poem, before pronouncing the imminent end of time in the chorus.

Of course the quasi-religious – if ambiguous – notion behind these lyrics could have shown a hint at Moby's growing belief in God. The premise of a promised land, open to believers, being the backbone to all religion. However, with the last verse of 'Time's Up' we are left with little more than utter confusion.

The words of a great oracle they most certainly were not. The narrative was unclear, the message lost. However, laid onto the track, it was obvious that the vocalist had opted for phonetic suitability rather than lyrical meaning. This point is accentuated by the music, which although simple, crescendoed and reverberated at exactly the right moments.

The 'Dust Mix' was perhaps the best introduction to the talents of Moby that 'Time's Up' could offer. A near-instrumental mix (which would later turn up on the album *Rare: The Collected B-Sides*), the 'Dust Mix' is played at a slightly faster tempo and features a twisting 303 acid line. Ironically it has a post-club comedown vibe that would not have sounded out of place in Moby's later work on *Play*. The mood is understated, the tension restrained.

A US-only release, 'Times Up' failed to make any real mark. If the aim had been to create a commercial single with which to launch the label, the premise fell short. Essentially the track seemed at odds with the mood of the time among the dance fraternity. This was a time of new music. Instrumental electronic moods were soundtracking the cool parties in the US. In Europe, the techno vibe was growing at an amazing speed while in the UK, it was the era of rave. In this climate, The Brotherhood seemed deliberately commercial. At a time of huge creative honesty, the single seemed almost insincere in its forced eclecticism.

With the exception of the instrumental mix then, this was not exactly an auspicious start to Moby's post-Connecticut recording career. But what was to come next was a far more rewarding affair. Two months later, in November 1990 the still-long-haired Moby delivered the four track 'Mobility EP'.

This release was perhaps most notable for the original version of the Moby's soon-to-be hit 'Go!' which featured on the single's B-side. The lead track, however, found Moby drawing heavily on the influences of ambient and early house, yet with a huge, respectful reference to the sounds coming from Europe. With New York currently under the spell of garage, while UK ravers bought into the hip house of Todd Terry, Moby's take on the house/techno vibe seemed at odds with his hometown.

In fact, in many ways it seemed to have more in common with the Nu Beat sound of Belgium, where hi-NRG tracks were slowed down until they developed an eerie resonance. It was a sound that seemed to present emotions dislocated from the body. Outer-body weightlessness versus fully grounded density. Music which was stripped of its soul in order to become more functional. Moby added to this an ambience of deeply submerged dub-house spirituality. His sound, although quite unlike any other artists at the time, sat perfectly next to Warp Records' bleep and bass sounds by artists like Nightmares on Wax and LFO emanating from Sheffield in the UK.

The lead track 'Mobility' found emotive string washes built around a fluid, rolling bassline which echoed the sound of Massive Attack's 'Safe from Harm' from 1990. Beats evolved from a straight four-to-the-floor bass drum and offbeat hi-hat pattern before eventually giving way to a bongo-fuelled break.

The 'Aqua Mix' offered a far less dance floor-friendly version, with bass drum pushed to the forefront and added rhythm from a bell sample (again reminiscent of a Massive Attack track, this time the classic 'Unfinished Sympathy'). Although the string sample was still in evidence, the track built through the use of 303 and ghostly voices. The latter was offering what is perhaps a reference to Moby's paranormal experiences as a child.

Both mixes of 'Mobility' offered a view of the disparate sides of Moby's work. Here was a DJ renowned for his house sets, creating music that drew on his past as much as his present. As a result the almost mellow ambience sat in direct opposition to the hip house-flavored rhythm track. The result was unnerving in that it promoted entirely different emotions in equal measure. The strings and voices spoke of darkness, loneliness and fear, while the groove was an invite to join the warmth of the party. Where so much of the music that surrounded Moby at the time talked only of good times, in 'Mobility' we were introduced to the dark underbelly of rave culture.

The resulting atmosphere of near but far, hot but cold, energetic but relaxed, echoed a technique used by one of Moby's favorite bands, Simple Minds (considered to be one of the leading electronic bands of the early 80s until they developed into a stadium rock band around the time of Live Aid). However, far more than offer insight into Moby's musical tastes, these juxtapositions offered a glimpse into the feelings of the music's creator. 'Mobility' was clearly the work of an individual who enjoyed extremes, no matter how oppositional.

The single itself received very positive reviews in the dance press of the time. Picking up on the dichotomy of opposing atmospherics, US magazine *Rockpool* journalist DJ Ray Valesquez described the single as "the latest in ambient house soundscapes for perspiration, conversation and hallucination… a balancing act between rhythmic tension and blissful calm."

Furthermore, its strange ambience and addictive beats were quickly embraced by many of the leading DJs in the UK scene, many of whom were actively pushing the after-hours ambient house sound of The Orb and KLF. Copies of the single flew out of stores, turning it into one of the must-have records of the year.

Historically, the most interesting thing about 'Mobility' however was the inclusion of 'Go' on the flipside. At this stage the tune was a techno-inspired cut with analogue synths weaving around each other. The "alright" sample was in effect, as was the "go" chant, while the strings were pushed through a series of rave-style dynamics. Although simplistic, 'Go' found its way into the DJ sets of a number of hardcore DJs of the time - even if they did tend to push their Technics' pitch control to plus 8.

The mystery that surrounded the release added to the buzz. As a New Yorker, few DJs in the UK knew who Moby was. Indeed many assumed him to be from the UK or at least Belgium, so much did his music echo the atmospherics of the sounds being created in these territories at the time. As one UK industry magazine suggested in its talent tipsheet, "Moby's 'Mobility EP' on New York's small Instinct Records has been disappearing out of import racks and into DJ boxes of late, with one high-profile DJ mistaking it for a UK techno track."

The final track on the debut Moby release was called 'Time Signature' where he displayed his ongoing love of ambient sounds. Here he added skipping beats to repetitive echoed strings and synths, snaked by a smattering of 303. 'Time Signature' was very indicative of the music that would soon start to appear on Belgian label Apollo (offshoot of R&S) which was then given the unlikely tag of 'ambient house'.

In February 1991, Moby would return with a follow-up track under the alias of Voodoo Child. Although the idea of producers releasing tracks under a multitude of pseudonyms was common at the time, the reason behind Moby's new *nom de wax* had far more to do with the Instinct team trying to exaggerate their size. Each new Moby moniker suggested that Instinct had a large roster.

The tactic wasn't entirely illusory however. For Moby, the changing names provided him with the space to push in differing directions. Although none of these records were quite as commercially successful as his later work, Moby was still able to transcend the increasingly defined style boundaries being created by dance music purists. Despite its relatively young age, dance culture was already dividing into separate house and techno camps. Furthermore, the addition of ambient house only served to confuse matters further, as suddenly people were discovering new electronic music through laid-back vibes. Invariably, these same people had little time for either house or techno. The first signs of the style fascism which would come to dominate the dance scene (causing Moby to react with venom) were now showing.

Accordingly, 'Voodoo Child' was a more hardcore-oriented track than anything on the 'Mobility EP'. Featuring a pulsating bassline, the cut rolled like thunder through adrenalized, yet funky techno explorations. Pianos drove the melody while a distressed Moog sequence pushed hard at the rhythm. From the core of the track came the ghost of Jimi Hendrix, calling out the words "Voodoo Child" while a distorted crowd chanted "party" as if their lives depended on it. Elsewhere a voice barked the command to rave: "C'mon everybody, let's all get down." In the UK, the sample was misheard, with people thinking the words were "Let's hold it down" – a term which was popular among ravers of the time, meaning quite simply "keep it real".

It was a track that had been made with a huge soundsystem in mind. A 132 bpm slab of pulsating perfection. *Streetsound* described it as "extremely mind-blowing". *Rockpool* said "this here is high-octane house music… a definite eargasm!" while LA magazine *Urb* (who were wise to the identity of the man behind the track) said, "DJ Moby is a witchdoctor crafting a dance floor assault. Moby's style and talent shine through with his lightning transitions and beat changes from hardcore, pulsating rave to a smooth ambient groove."

Other tracks on the single included 'Permanent Green', built around a bongo-fuelled break (reminiscent of 'Flight' by UK punk-funk outfit A Certain Ratio), disco string stabs, a breathy rhythmic scat vocal and more whistles than a field full of ravers. It was a good-time track underpinned by a foreboding, bass-driven synth lick. Midway through, this sense of darkness was enhanced by a filtered analogue sound, which built through the minor scale before dropping to a four-to-the-floor kick drum. The crescendo saw all these parts brought together for a frenzied funk workout. 'Permanently Green''s almost Gothic ambience mirrored the UK's movement towards a post-hardcore sound called 'darkcore', the direct forerunner of jungle and drum'n'bass.

Also worth mentioning is the closing cut. Inspired by Detroit techno and Philip Glass, 'M Four' offered a stark, minimal exploration reminiscent of the experimental composer's most barren works. A sub-level 4/4 kick drum ground into the mix while a repeated synth-block melody was occasionally ghosted by a distant looped string motif.

After the Voodoo Child single, a period of intense activity would follow for Moby, a time that would see him pushed to the higher reaches of the UK charts achieving star status on the European rave circuit. He was about to become caught up in the phenomenon of 'Go'.

CHAPTER FIVE

"For me, techno isn't just a dance movement. It's more a continuation of electronic music. Hearing an early Derrick May record excited me because it was so reminiscent of old German electronica."   Moby, 1992

The years of 1990 to 1991 represented an incredibly fruitful period for Moby as he explored the extremes of his, still fairly basic, equipment. He created house, techno and ambient sounds which drew on the entire spectrum of the influences he'd picked up over the years. Slowly he built up a library of tracks, showing at this early stage a prolific work-rate that would become a feature of each musical development he would subsequently undergo.

As already discussed, much of Moby's inspiration came from those early post-punk and industrial bands. Indeed, until the arrival of house he had felt very little affinity with dance music. For him, the way into club culture had been through the experimental electronic artists that soundtracked his late teens. Naturally his own music found a fusion between his love of the rough-edged, abrasive techniques of Cabaret Voltaire, DAF and Throbbing Gristle, and the pastoral, minimalist calm of Brian Eno. Also present was the influence of the composer William Carlos Williams, whom Moby first heard at the age of seven.

His next venture however would hint at a love of the atmospherics of film scores. In early 1991, while watching a pilot episode of the hit TV series *Twin Peaks*, it struck him that David Lynch and Angelo Badalamenti's theme to the show would sound perfect recreated as a dance track.

Moby didn't have to go far to find exactly the right song. In fact he had already released it on his 'Mobility EP'. That track was 'Go', and with the string motif added, it was instantly lifted from being a good techno cut, to a rave classic in the making.

Sampling or appropriating TV and film themes was already

commonplace on the rave scene. However, what made this particular fusion work was the fact that Lynch and Badalamenti's score was informed by a similar sense of melancholy to that which underpinned Moby's own work. Furthermore the melody only added to the disorientating effect of his music. Here was a rolling groove with a distant girl's voice singing "alright" while another sample of a shouting crowd occasionally commanded the listener to "GO!"

The structure was based on immediacy. 'Go' demanded a positive reaction from the club crowd. The sampled command which gave the track its name hinted at the kind of totalitarian state whose aesthetics obsessed many post-punk acts. Indeed, many artists of this time referred heavily to the Futurist movement, an art school which itself was inspired by, and inspirational to, aspects of totalitarian ideology.

Here, the word "Go" was an instruction rather than an invitation. To say that the foundations of the track's positive energy had an unknowingly dark subtext is an understatement. This is obviously not to say that Moby himself held any views which could be in any way regarded as fascist, or totalitarian.

The addition of the beautiful, shimmering, yet oddly maudlin *Twin Peaks* theme - actually played by Moby himself as opposed to directly sampling the theme - brought a whole new dimension to "Go". Suddenly the track had all the classic Moby touches in place. Opposite forces like the joyful energy of the bassline and the mournful weight of the string motif; the free-falling beats and the authoritarian instruction of the song's title.

In many ways, 'Go' managed to encapsulate both the positive and negative features of club culture. Its euphoric theme captured the celebratory nature of dancing until dawn (something Moby would refer to time and again in his career) while the dark underbelly of the track hinted at a Quatermass-like subservience to a greater force - in this case, the greater force being a culmination of repetitive beats and massive use of ecstasy. Already the argument existed that ecstasy took away an individual's ability to differentiate between good and bad. Critical values, it was perceived, were the first casualty of the dance generation.

Certainly the dance-related media which was emerging everywhere, thanks to the combined forces of this powerful youth movement and affordable desktop publishing, seemed to feel awkward ever offering criticism about anything. This, apparently, being against the original supportive, pacifist vibe. Arguably, it was here that the lowest-common-denominator, dumbed-down music media culture of today was founded.

"Go" was released in the US on Instinct in March 1991 to justifiably good reviews. *DMR* magazine described it as, "Mind blowing. There's tons of spine-tingling energy in this baby. Don't miss it." Elsewhere UK Magazine *Echoes* referred to its "simply surging powergroove", while *Street Sound* celebrated its "aggressive and ground-breaking style".

If 'Mobility' had flown out of the UK shops on import, then this one barely touched the racks. It was an immediate hit on the rave scene, with copies of the vinyl commanding prices of up to £100 in some areas of the UK.

The international growth of 'Go' really started in Germany where the original version had become a huge favorite among its clubbing population. Subsequently, in February 1991, it was licensed to Low Spirit Records featuring the original from 'Mobility', a new track called 'Breath' and the 'Low Spirit Mix' of 'Go'. At this stage, however, the *Twin Peaks* theme had yet to be added.

In the same month, Instinct released a remix package of the track in the States. Featuring an 'Analog Mix' which included hardcore pulsating synths, and the 'Night Time Mix' which, not surprisingly, calmed things down to minimal techno with swathes of ambient synths. Also present was the 'Low Spirit Mix'. However, it was with the 'Woodtick Mix' (regarded by most critics as the essential version of the track), that the *Twin Peaks* motif first appeared. 'Go' subsequently reached the top five of New York's' underground tip sheet *Brand X* in February 1991.

So sought-after was the 'Woodtick Mix' on import that it was quickly bootlegged in other European territories. The sub-standard quality of this pressing was apparently outweighed by the public's need to own this music in some form or other. In order to stem the flow of bootlegs, and in response to the overwhelming interest from other record labels around the world, Jared Hoffman set about licensing 'Go' in other countries.

Of the many deals in place, perhaps the most notable was the one with Outer Rhythm. The Belgian company was the techno subsidiary of the ground-breaking hardcore label R&S. At the time no other imprint came close to R&S. Quite simply, it was changing the shape of the rave scene with its pounding releases. In picking up 'Go', not only did they put the track in a strong position throughout Europe, but it was also a seal of ultimate approval from the rave scene.

The only other approval Moby might have sort would have been from *Twin Peaks'* director David Lynch and theme composer Angelo Badalamenti. The former did come via mutual acquaintances, while the latter arrived from the horse's mouth.

"[Badalamenti] actually drove by my house to tell me how much he liked it!" recalls Moby. "We talked about working together, but nothing much came of it really."

Over the course of the next few months, 'Go' was released in a multitude of permutations with an incredible fourteen remixes. Each nuance of club culture was dealt with. The varying tastes of different territories were indulged. Divided loyalties between house and techno were covered. There seemed to be a mix for everyone involved in the dance world.

By July 1991, 'Go' finally received a full UK release on Outer Rhythm. It went straight at #1 in the Dance Chart and reached #10 in the UK charts, having already topped all of the independent and dance charts in various music magazines. Indeed, underground fashion magazine *i-D* placed the single at #1 in its 'Essential Dance Tracks' list as far back as February - five months before the song was actually released.

More recently, the track was placed at #9 in the all-time techno top ten in *Alternative Press*, having gained the unfair tag of 'the techno track that refuses to go away'. While in the UK, *Mixmag* placed the track at #35 in their '100 Greatest Dance Singles of All Time', despite going on to mistakenly say that the *Twin Peaks* theme was a sample rather than a recreation.

There is an argument that 'Go' merely picked up on the massive interest surrounding *Twin Peaks* at the time. However, this would do a disservice to the record and the scene which took it to their hearts. 'Go' touched the ravers in a very spiritual way. The combination of sounds worked perfectly with the buzz, rush and loved-up togetherness of ecstasy. Strange, when you consider Moby's abstinence from chemical stimulants.

Furthermore, if it was a dance cut of *Twin Peaks* that the ravers wanted, then there were already a number of Italian versions doing the rounds, such as 'Agent Cooper Loves Coffee' and 'Twin Freaks'. Ultimately however, why these tracks failed and Moby's worked, was that 'Go' sounded completely natural with Badalamenti's music included. It was as if the track was unknowingly created with the score in mind. And more to the point, vice-versa. The other *Twin Peaks* interpretations just sounded like tacky dance tracks with samples forced on top.

Moby's adaptation of the *Twin Peaks* theme was intended more as homage than a direct plundering. As an avid fan of the series, he was obsessed with the "Who killed Laura Palmer?" conundrum as much as the next man. "I've watched every episode around four or five times," he told me at the time. "I suppose I should have something better to do with my time. The first time I heard [the theme music] was when I watched the pilot in the States about a year and one month ago [mid-1989]. When the theme came on it just affected me. The strange thing is that it's only been recognized in Europe. In the States no one seems to know where it's come from!"

With 'Go' turning Moby into one of the best-known names in dance culture, it was inevitable that the media would catch on.

Naturally, what excited journalists most about him was not necessarily the music (although it undoubtedly drew them to Moby), but his beliefs and lifestyle.

Here, in the middle of what seemed a godless, hedonistic environment, was an openly devout Christian. While all around explored the outer reaches of decadence, here was someone who abstained from alcohol, refused to take drugs, campaigned against the abuse of animals, refused to eat meat or wear any animal product and shouted about the state of the planet. According to the press, he even refused to use a car on anything but the most essential journey.

In early interviews he was reported as offering thanks to God before he ate. In the same interviews his organic, wholefood diet would be described with some incredulity. Such a figure stood out among the increasingly identikit rave artists. His ideologies made people feel awkward. Were we allowed to take drugs and still enjoy his music? Was it OK to wear leather shoes in his presence? That Moby was, and is, eloquent enough to carry convincing arguments about his moral and religious position without making you feel guilty came almost as a shock. Yet his stance still increasingly turned him into an outsider not to be trusted, making it easier to condemn him for musical changes later in his career.

Perhaps, more than any of his strongly held beliefs, the one which obsessed the media most was Moby's faith. Unlike many artists who might have preferred to keep such personal subjects to themselves, Moby made a point, from very early on, of talking about the things that were close to him. "It would be easier for me not to talk about my faith, but I really force myself to do it. I mean, you don't find that many vegetarian Christians in the techno world!"

The question that seemingly obsessed the media however was simple; how could he call himself a Christian and still enjoy dance culture? Moby's answer was always straight to the point. He saw a spirituality in dancing akin to worship. Not that the media accepted this argument as the same questions have been leveled at him ever since. It is still unusual to pick up a magazine interview with Moby without the journalist using the sentence: "Christian, vegan, anti-smoking, teetotal, anti-drugs and anti-car, techno nutter." It is one of the only constants in Moby's career.

Moby explained this idea to Dave Palmer of *Syndicate* magazine in 1993: "I think it's very spiritual. When you're at a club, or a rave, and you're with friends, and the right song comes on that you all love. There is something transcendent happening there, and people remember that feeling. They're not always sure what that is, they just know they want more of it."

For many, the spiritual aspect of clubbing was perhaps enhanced, or exaggerated by the use of ecstasy. However, this was not a contributing factor for Moby. In fact, he ascertains that the first rave "was when the Ark of Covenant was brought into Jerusalem, and King David went out and danced like crazy. And tore off all his clothes."

However, it is fair to say that the abundant use of the drug did create an incredible, positive energy. Such euphoria would have been hard not to pick up on. Especially if, in the case of Moby, you were sensitive to such quasi-spiritual energy. It is true that people often talked of religious experiences during the raves. This was perhaps largely due to the sense of enlightenment produced by ecstasy. Although most churches believe the use of drugs blocks the road to true enlightenment, there are some religious teachers who believe in the value of MDMA (ecstasy).

In his book *Ecstasy and the Dance Culture*, the late Nicholas Saunders talked of interviews he'd conducted with a Benedictine monk, a rabbi, a Rinzai Zen monk and a Soto Zen monk. All of them spoke of the benefits of MDMA use, while the latter spoke of the drug helping you to "know how to sit, it provides you with experiential knowledge. It is like a medicine. If we look at the state of our own mind and the planet, we should be grateful for any means of help. However, like any good medicine, it can be misused.

"Ecstasy is a wonderful tool for teaching," the Zen monk continued. "For example, I had a very keen student who never succeeded in meditation until ecstasy removed the block caused by his effort when trying to meditate. That one experience helped him to make fast progress, and he has since been ordained a monk."

Of the other people interviewed, the Benedictine monk suggested that by taking ecstasy two or three times a year it helps to strengthen his faith, and subsequently makes prayer easier. Although as an aid to prayer, he also said the drug interrupted the internal dialogue, created distractions and resulted in a loss of faith. He was less positive about the use of ecstasy in raves however, saying, "the experience is sacred and is not suitable for hedonists such as teenage ravers."

The Rabbi was particularly positive in his attitudes about the use of drugs, suggesting, "traditional religions have lost the ability to provide followers with mystical experiences. Instead young people are far more likely to have such experiences while on LSD and ecstasy. If priests really want to understand young people, they should take the drugs themselves. They would learn that some drugs can produce the same quality and potential value as other mystical experiences."

Perhaps the most interesting observation in Saunders' study came from the Rinzai Monk, who felt that the use of ecstasy had helped him to become an abbot. Having admitted that he'd never actually danced under the influence of the drug, he accepted an invitation to attend a rave. Despite finding the music unbearable at first, he soon declared the rave to be "mediation – to be truly in the moment and not in your head!" He further explained that the object of mediation is to cease internal dialogue while maintaining full awareness of what is happening.

The following morning, the Rinzai monk said to Saunders that he had experienced a revelation following his raving experience. Now feeling that "his school of Zen concentrated too much on contraction such as disciplined meditation, but what was really needed by most students was the opposites, to let go and expand in the way he had just witnessed at the party."

With such religious overtones attached to the experience of dancing whilst on ecstasy, it was little surprise that many organised religions attempted to buy into the rave culture. By appearing to tap into the sense of collective communion at raves, and further working on the growing need for that feeling, many of the established organised churches attempted to seduce the youth. Ecstasy however, was most certainly not used as a holy sacrament. In fact, despite any positive aspects to ecstasy experience found by Saunders' case study, these Christian youth churches were most definitely anti-drug, drink, and anything else that might affect the conscious mind.

In the UK, perhaps the most infamous 'rave church' was Sheffield's Nine O'Clock Service, established by local vicar Chris Brain. His innovations included the introduction of lights and a soundsystem, while dancing was encouraged as a means of worship. It was an initiative which received wholesale support from the Anglican hierarchy, until it was discovered that the vicar had been sleeping with a number of his female parishioners.

Other cities in the UK followed suit, despite the problems of Chris Brain. Before long, similar services were being held in Gloucester and Bradford. Other notable attempts to attract young and impressionable ravers came in the shape of Billy Graham's Youth for Christ movement which held the Club X rave in Bath, and The Pioneer Network's Bliss night in Bournemouth.

Talking to *Muzik* magazine in 1996, Andy Hawthorne, a techno musician and member of the Christian youth group Message to Schools said: "Dance music is the music of the kids of Manchester. The fact that we love it as much as they do is almost beside the point. We think of ourselves as missionaries. Most kids in Manchester are pagans, because they don't know the basic information about the Christian faith."

As members of Christian movements fuelled by a born-again zeal, many such evangelists saw Moby as something of a figurehead. His strong faith in the face of a godless culture, alongside his rejection of ecstasy made him an ideal candidate for spokesman for Christian youth throughout the Western world. Yet Moby would continually turn down any advances from organized Christian churches. Indeed, he would even go as far as to attack the motives of many church organizations. The Christian right-wing in the US would especially come under fire, with Moby writing a damning essay about these 'greedy, intolerant bigots' in the inner sleeve of his *Everything is Wrong* album of 1995. What established churches failed to understand, no matter how much they wrapped themselves up in the accoutrements of youth, was Moby's very individualistic take on Christianity.

"I sort of became an annoying religious person around the time that I went through puberty," recalls Moby on the tour bus for his late-2000 US dates. "Then I discovered punk rock and new wave and nightclubs and Marxism. Then, upon the recommendation of a friend, I read the New Testament and I was somehow convinced of the divinity of Christ. That was in 1985. Ever since then, I've been trying to figure out how best to respond to this divinity. I had a period of trying to be a strict 'Christian', but I realized that just wasn't me. Now I basically believe that the universe is a very complicated place and that my understanding of it is bound to be pretty limited. Thus it stands to reason that my understanding of the architect of the universe is also bound to be pretty limited. But, on a subjective level, I love Christ and the teachings of Christ. Especially the emphasis placed on love and forgiveness and humility and compassion."

Moby's change from strict Christianity towards the more open-minded view he holds today was prompted by the experience of living with a youth pastor. At the time, he says he had all kinds of preconceived ideas about what Christians were like and what Christianity was. "Then I noticed my friend doing things differently than I thought he should be doing them, and that got me asking questions," he says.

Following a time spent reading the scriptures, Moby realized that the Christ he had read about was very different from the one he had always pictured. He developed a belief that pertained to Christianity only in the sense that he felt a deep love for Jesus. What he failed to accept was the pomp and ceremony surrounding the traditional church. He rejected what he saw as the hypocrisy of church hierarchy and openly deplored the organized religion's authoritarian stance. He believed in a Christ who lived more on the edge than the traditional church could ever accept.

"Christ was on that edge," he told *Syndicate* magazine in 1992. "He was killed for going over the edge. Christ was a rebellious, blasphemous figure, and while partially we're called to continue in the spirit of Christ, [that] was [essentially] a rebellious, anarchic spirit. I think its part of our job as responsible Christians. It's always a fine line of 'how close am I to the edge of heresy and blasphemy?' And I don't ever want to cross it, because I am, ultimately [Christ's] servant. 'Jesus is my Lord, I'm his vassal, his servant.'"

For Moby even creating music was, and is, an act of faith. "The first thing God did was create dramatically; dramatic, profound acts of creation. It's almost an insult for us to be so timid. We've been given the ability to create, and humans occasionally create great things, usually timidity is not a good ingredient in great creation," he said in the same article.

The music Moby was creating at this point was anything but timid. The beats were becoming rawer, the sounds more abrasive and the tempos faster. He was developing alongside a scene that demanded music from the edge.

CHAPTER SIX

"You get 2,000 people to agree on a time and a place and just go nuts for half-an-hour before the police come." Moby, 1991

Coinciding with the acclaimed reception of 'Go' was a new development in the dance arena. Belgian techno had taken hold of the rave scene with its rough-edged, high-speed breakbeats, huge running basslines, ear-splitting 303s and exaggerated hooklines. If one artist epitomized this sound it was Joey Beltram, the New Yorker, who along with fellow DJs Lenny Dee and Mundo Muzique actively pushed the rave sound in a harder, faster direction.

When Beltram released his 'Energy Flash' single in 1990, it was to have an enormous effect on the scene. The title track was a blistering shock of pulsating basslines and disorientating noises which seemed to both pull in and push away listeners at the same time. A perfect representation of the increasingly speed-based ecstasy pills that began surfacing over the following months.

Although 'Energy Flash' would remain a constant at raves for some time to come, its sound was superseded by Beltram's stunning follow up 'Mentasm' which, like its predecessor, would revolutionize the night-life soundtrack. A co-production between Beltram and Mundo Muzique and released under the alias of Second Phase, 'Mentasm' utilized a disquieting buzz sound over insistent beats. Its whining, at times nauseating, but mostly synapse-seducing tones became known as "the Hoover sound". It spread though the techno scene like a virus of epidemic proportions.

Beltram had found, in the European rave scene, the perfect antidote to the commercialized New York sound. The clubs in Europe were more open, with few door policies and apparently even fewer drug policies. In the Big Apple however, clubs still adhered to the principle of the celebrity-ego-massaging velvet rope. In order to be allowed to dance, kids first had to satisfy the doormen that they were worthy of being let in. In the UK, with the exception of the guest list, the door was open to anyone who wanted to pay his or her money. And Beltram's Hoover techno made for the perfect soundtrack to a night of unbridled madness.

Given that Moby already had a strong musical affiliation with Europe, and especially Britain, through his musical tastes, it was almost a foregone conclusion that he would be drawn to the rave arena. After all, it seemed to embrace everything he believed in.

With the aforementioned obvious exceptions however, Moby seemed to be a lonesome figure in his home country. The US lagged behind Europe in the rave stakes, still perpetuating the disco dream of bygone times, albeit through the newer musical forms of house and garage. Indeed, many well-established DJs looked down upon the new sounds coming from Europe as unmusical (itself a bizarre twist on the criticism leveled at early house and techno artists by rock musicians). The concept of rave as a form of youth rebellion also had a hard time taking root in the US. But a small pocket of people were trying to instigate some kind of movement of opposition. Even if that movement didn't involve music exactly - just the transcendent activity. These events were known as Outlaw Parties.

Moby explained to *Melody Maker* in 1991: "You get 2,000 people to agree on a time and a place and just go nuts for half-an-hour before the police come. We've had them on the subway, in garages and abandoned blocks. There's no music, everybody just shouts; it's complete anarchy, chaos and civil disobedience. Everybody's there - clubbers, drag-queens, punks, hip hoppers - and the police just don't know what to make of it. It's great."

These Outlaw Parties, which Moby helped to organize, were a way for increasingly frustrated New Yorkers to react against the growing atmosphere of self-obsession and zero-tolerance in the city. Furthermore it was a wake-up call to those who continually turned a blind eye to the rot that had set in just below the highly varnished surface. The US, said Moby at the time, was "like someone that's got cancer, somebody who puts on a lot of make-up and wears nice clothes to create a good impression, but inside they're dying. Everybody's smiling, pretending everything's fine but underneath, it's a very sick place."

Ten years later the same ethos and tactics as the Outlaw Parties would be employed by Reclaim The Streets campaigners around the world and also the global anti-capitalist activists of the late 90s.

So, unlike many of the DJs who worked in the dance underground of the day, Moby had a conscience. Furthermore, he was never afraid to express his feelings. Yet the rave circuit embraced the little New Yorker as an exceptional DJ. His sets were drawn from the hypnotic, yet uplifting end of house, while the experience of hearing six hours of "relentless techno beats in a club in Belgium had a lasting, almost spiritual effect."

As a direct result of the global success of 'Go', Moby found himself being booked to DJ at huge illegal raves in the UK. It was a boom time for him, an extremely prolific period which saw him delivering new tracks at an alarming rate. "Suddenly there was a torrent of Moby tracks," said Jared Hoffman to *DJ Times* in 1991. "It was amazing. He was banging out tracks every week. There was no stopping him."

However, success with 'Go' did have a downside with the rest of his output. For his next release, Moby was literally forced to use the name Brainstorm so as not to compete with the other track. Of course, once again by using this pseudonym he also maintained the label's original desire to appear to have a large roster, rather than a one-man set up.

"Basically I've been working by myself since 1983 when I had a little Mattel drum machine and a Task M four-track," said Moby in 1992, explaining the early solitary attempts at writing music which would go on to shape his subsequent way of working. "The only time I've tried working with someone else was in 1991 with Westbam. We were hanging out together and decided it would be fun to try and make a track. In the end we just brought the worst out in each other. I am happier working on my own. It makes little difference to me if people don't realize I'm also Voodoo Child and so on. I don't mind if they never make the connection. I do think that the time is right for techno to have a face though. The anonymous approach is quite… it doesn't excite me the way it used to."

As well as the aborted Westbam collaboration there had also been a much talk of a joint venture with DJ Moneypenny on Chapter 1's 'TNT EP'. In the end, this also failed to materialize. Instead Moby extended his list of pseudonyms.

Not to be confused with Westbam's single of the same name, 'Rock The House' by Brainstorm (and credited to Moby Hall) was released in April 1991, on Instinct in the US and Low Spirit in the UK. As a single, it showed definite signs of influence from the rave scene. The title track featured a propulsive break, clocking in at 130 bpm. Once again heavy on the bongo-style percussion, augmented by a voice repeating the song title over and again, before a scream sounds the emergency alarm. From here an analog synth riffs away like Iggy and the Stooges with keyboards instead of guitars. In many ways the track was reminiscent of the music being created by Essex boys, The Prodigy. Alternatively, 'Move The Colors', was less riff-led, featuring coiling sequencers and ghostly voices. It was more reminiscent of Orbital in fact.

UK dance music magazine *Record Mirror* described the single as being 'created in a Euro-style' while *Street Sound* suggested "you may find many dance floor situations where a record like this could save your life."

In this one single Moby managed to capture the essence of the rave at its most diverse. On the one hand, he tapped in to the post-b boy rave sound of breaks and bass attack, while on the other, he explored the post-industrial color sound of UK techno. Indeed, it was hard to imagine that Moby had never fully experienced the buzz of chasing a convoy around London's M25 Orbital ring-road, tuned into a pirate radio station looking for the location of the rave - weekly pastime central to the rave experience in the UK.

With the German version of this single, Moby was forced to change his moniker to Mindstorm. The reason was simple; R&S already had an act called Brainstorm on its roster. In fact, both their 'The Strange Attractor' and 'Cybernautical Tonalities' singles had been huge hits on the European dance underground.

Only a month later Moby unleashed two more singles. The first, a set of remixes of the 'Voodoo Child' single, the second under the alias of Barracuda. The 'Voodoo Child Remixes' also gained a release in Europe (with 'Permanent Green' from the original EP), once again through a licensing deal with R&S. There was also talk of Moby releasing material on Derrick May's legendary Transmat label at this time. Bizarrely, US magazine *WARD* declared this single to be an import-only release, newly snapped up by Instinct. The reviewer went on to call the lead track 'insidious warm, simple genius" while even giving support to the one-minute fourth track 'No Buttons To Push' which is described as a "great little Snap! rip-off that grinds fierce."

'Drug Fits the Face', the Barracuda single, came later in May 1991. Of all the pseudonymous releases, this one was perhaps the most deserving of an alter ego. It was about as far away from techno as Moby had ever gone. In fact it was a jazzy, Italian house-style number. "It's weird; in some ways I like the record a lot," said Moby at the time, "but I'm a little embarrassed by it, because it's more jazzy, with pianos and organs and it's more like traditional house."

Opening with the repeated 'Drug Fits The Face' refrain and gospel organ, the track felt like it should erupt into a Belgian hardcore epic. Instead it developed, through looped breakbeats and piano fills, into a seductive house anthem. On the other tracks, the ridiculously uplifting sound of Italian house seemed even more in evidence. 'Party Time' mixed piano with a female chorus and a lone voice repeating the song title over and over. Like the lead cut, this track also featured a very jazzy piano solo.

The only reminder that Moby had made his name primarily as a techno artist came with a throbbing 303. 'Barracuda' further pushed at the house boundaries, but with a sound which could have justifiably fit into the KLF's model of stadium house. Interestingly, the track fades out with Moby playing 'Greensleeves' - a trick he would resurrect when playing 'Go' live a couple of years later.

The Barracuda twelve-inch proved to be very important in Moby's development. Not only did it show that he was determined not to be pigeon-holed, it also displayed the musical techniques that were to feature heavily in future material: minor keys, uplifting pianos, spiritual vocals and gospel harmonies gelling to create music of quite indescribable positivity, albeit with an almost emotionally downbeat ambience. After a brace of singles experimenting with the juxtaposition of genres and moods, with 'Drug Fits The Face' finally a Moby 'sound' was found. Furthermore, if Moby was against the use of ecstasy, then the combination of track title and actual song didn't suggest it. This single was all about celebration with Moby showing an uncanny understanding of the joys experienced by the drug-addled raver.

'Drug Fits The Face' may have hinted at a Moby who was mellowing a little; however with his next venture he would go into hardcore overdrive. Working under the UHF alias, he delivered a fiercely abrasive single in November 1991. Surprisingly, this single did not appear on Instinct, but on Sonic in Europe and XL Recordings in the UK.

'UHF' offered shock-tactic synths cascading over rampant beats and buzzing alien sonics. In one track Moby perfectly captured the spirit of what was quickly becoming known as "nuttah" music (sounds which scaled high-energy limits for kids who would push their bodies to ridiculous extremes by imbibing incredible amounts of ecstasy). The ferocity of the track emulated the effects of the increasingly amphetamine-laced ecstasy tablets, while using drum rolls as aids to the ecstasy rush. The moment of genius came with the Italian house piano break over a stuttered analogue bassline, which perfectly mimicked the close but dislocated sensation of the speed-fuelled ecstasy high.

On 'Peacehead' he explored this theme further by placing buzzing synths over high-speed breaks, while distant voices mutter inaudible mantras. If Moby had never partaken of the drug, his understanding of the musical needs of his audience once again seemed to be remarkably informed.

'UHF' proved to be a massive hit at raves throughout Europe. Its edginess found immediate favor in Holland, while in the UK hardcore DJs would play it two or three times a night, such was the demand from the ravers.

As 1991 drew to a close, Instinct released what was essentially Moby's first album, *Instinct Dance.* A compilation of tracks from all of his previous singles under all of the aliases (with the notable exception of UHF), the intention of the album was to display the strength of the Instinct roster. It is true that the sheer quality of the material included made this album an unusually good compilation from an underground label at the time. There were no fillers, only some of the finest Moby output.

Furthermore the album contained three then-unreleased tracks. Firstly there was 'Besame', another Belgian hardcore-style track in the image of UHF. The second new offering was the similarly frantic 'Drop A Beat' as Brainstorm (even though the track would subsequently appear as a Moby single a few months later). And then there was 'Have You Seen My Baby?', credited to Voodoo Child, but eventually turning up on the *Moby* album the following June, described by Instinct as 'Moby's darkest, acid-tinged club masterpiece."

In only one year, Moby had become the biggest techno artist in the US, conquered the raves of Europe and broken the British pop charts. Although it should have been a time of great happiness, the incredible success disguised the fact that all was not well with his US label.

The year that was to follow found Moby trying to extricate

himself from what he viewed as an unfairly restrictive contract, while also watching albums being released under his name. If 1991 was a year of celebration, then 1992 would represent a year of pure frustration.

CHAPTER SEVEN

"It was the old story: a young desperate and naïve musician signs a not so favorable contract." Moby, 2000

During the course of 1991, Moby moved to a new apartment in Mott Street, SoHo. Essentially a run down warehouse space, with no hot water and few amenities, it was rented to him on the understanding that he wouldn't live there. He did of course. It offered a means of setting up his studio, away from the record label, where he could, in theory, concentrate more on his music.

From early 1992, however, Moby's relationship with Instinct began to deteriorate. Success with 'Go' had brought about a situation where a number of labels were looking to sign the New York rave star. Yet, Moby found himself tied to a contract that he felt, if he was to grow as an artist, would need to be improved upon. To say Moby was naïve in his business dealings is an understatement – indeed, it would seem he was desperate to sign to any label at the time. With the benefit of hindsight, he may not have signed the contract, as he explained in an article in *LA Weekly* in 1992, but at that point he was keen to start releasing records.

In the same article, Instinct's Jared Hoffman claimed that he was just as naïve as Moby when the contract was drawn up. "I resent these characterizations about our contract," he said. "There's no question that we were at the beginning of our learning curves then. It was a simplistic contract. In some cases, maybe it doesn't protect the artist as much as it could, but a lot of things that could have been taken by a record company, we didn't take. Our contract is a little naïve in that we didn't put fourteen, fifteen per cent up-front and take it away in the back pages."

Naïve or not, Instinct were not going to lay down and let their main asset just walk out on the label. "Look, this is the oldest story in the music industry: a small label works with an artist, the artist becomes successful and outgrows a small label. That transition is always stressful," said Jared.

For Moby, however, the situation with Jared went far deeper than this. The rift between artist and label had developed personal undertones. A story Moby told in the same *LA Weekly* article at the time underlined this. "I was in a record store sometime; last spring. It was when Jared and I weren't getting along. I ran into him in the record store. I was there purchasing other records, and he was there delivering some records. I wanted the records he had, and he made me pay for them."

Of course, no artists wants to pay their label for copies of their own records. If Moby's friendship with the Instinct boss was at a low, then the fighting which ensued would turn them into near-enemies. Early on in this period of turmoil the label continued to release Moby singles. 'Go' still dominated Moby's affairs with a remix package now doing the rounds. However, it was in March 1992 that the first fresh Moby material hit the streets. That new single was called 'Drop A Beat', a total reworking of the version that appeared on the *Instinct Dance* compilation.

In many ways, 'Drop A Beat' found Moby going even further down the hardcore road than 'UHF'. The track was based around an off-key stab, which span around the ultra-hardcore beats. Voices were cut up to disturbing effect, occasionally mirroring the cortex-crushing snare rolls. And, for ultimate rave effect, whistles were pitched at ear-splitting levels throughout.

'Drop A Beat' hit #8 on the *Billboard* dance chart in the US on its fifth week in the chart and quickly became a regular cut in the sets of all the main techno DJs. The other tracks included in the package were similarly popular among the in-the-know ravers, with 'Electricity' snapping at the synapses like a Frankenstein-inspired experiment. The final track was a new version of 'UHF'. This time numbered 'UHF 2', it was in fact completely different to the other tracks bearing the name.

Rockpool described 'Drop A Beat' as showing "Moby's strong musical bent, a trait so often lacking in hardcore house." 'Drop A Beat' was not however a classic Moby single. Where 'Drug Fits The Face' had seemed exciting and new, and 'UHF' simply extreme, this single fell short in both areas. In many ways, it felt like Moby was treading water.

What followed was one of the most controversial releases that had ever surfaced under the Moby name. An eponymous album, released without his consent. Indeed, so angry was the artist about the release of this album that he actively spoke out against it in any promotional work. One of the only times in the history of pop music that an artist has asked his audience to not place value on his own debut album.

"The basic problem was that I had never wanted to put an album like this out," he told me. "It was just a compilation with a few unreleased demos. Dance albums had always failed, I thought, because they didn't work over the full length of the record. Mostly they were singles collections which was exactly what I didn't want to do. At the time, the first Prodigy album impressed me because they'd managed to create a full listening experience which encompassed various styles. This was the kind of vision I had for my debut album. But Jared insisted on putting *Moby* out. Which kind of upset me a lot."

It is a point he raised in a number of interviews at the time. Talking to *Billboard* dance editor Larry Flick, he explained: "The troubling thing about [the album] is that all of the songs are at least a year old. It's not entirely reflective of where I'm coming from right now. Since the label had the legal right to put it out, the best thing for me to do right now is view it as more a retrospective, and get on with my life."

Although Moby would later describe the album, which had sold in excess of 72,000 units in the US alone by December 2000, as "an interesting artifact", at the time it was released, it did unwittingly outline one of the dilemmas facing dance artists putting out albums. The problem was – and remains to this day – that dance music, by its very nature, is a forward-looking form.

No matter what the sub-genre, the primary function of dance music is to experiment. Furthermore, this form often takes the shape of records which amount to DJ tools, singles where the actual nuances of sound are more important than any traditional song structure. These tracks are designed to be dropped into a DJ's set; tracks which push the sound forward in a subterranean manner.

As a result of this constant redefining, dance music has continually devoured itself, thus creating the illusion of being disposable. Album culture, on the other hand, aims less at propelling a scene, or sound, forward, than creating something timeless. As a result, artists are forced to look beyond the dance floor and into the needs of everyday life. Therefore, the classic dance album tends to straddle the anti-establishment ethos of the dance floor and the cultural conservatism of the traditional song.

The subtext of this dance album conundrum is the inherently political nature of the dance single. It is designed to be functional, linear and not to conform to accepted notions of songwriting. At its heart is a self-destruct mechanism. All singles are created in the knowledge that they will be replaced by a newer version. Thus, the dance single is clearly anti-industry, as the entire culture which these records soundtrack, is built on an ideology of DIY and self-supporting innovation. The album, on the other hand, represents the antithesis of everything the dance single stands for.

Although this situation has altered considerably in the 21st century, as the dance music industry has found a very strong foothold in the global market (more a result of accepting corporate ideology than pushing forward with its original maverick stance), at the time of *Moby* it was foremost in the minds of dance producers wanting to enjoy some kind of longevity.

For anyone as politically sensitive as Moby, the dilemma would have been very real. Already he had started to strip away at the equally political concept of anonymity, which most producers and many DJs adhered to, by becoming a very visual performer. However, with the album, it was clear that in order to carry forward a sense of that original dance ideology, he would have to do something special. A collection of year-old singles and demos was not it.

It is true that when *Moby* first surfaced, it did seem strangely dated; however it had a quality that *has* helped it stand the test of time. Listening to it now, with constraints of fashion and hype stripped away, it is amazing just how complete an album it is. In 1992, however, it was marred by its slightly behind-the-times ambience. Far too many of the tracks came from the hardcore arena - or, more to the point, the very short-lived Belgian hardcore sound. Already the dance underground had rejected all things hardcore, as the sound had become represented by cheesy chart fodder, often with references to children's television.

As a result of the naturally fickle scene's anti-hardcore stance, cuts like the incendiary 'Ah Ah' and 'Electricity', with their sampled and filtered guitars, may have rocked the rave scene a few months earlier, but by the time of the album release, were simply out of date. Indeed, around the time of the UHF release, Moby declared to me that, "the Belgian sound is definitely dead now. It sounded invigorating at first, but now there's too many people recreating the same sounds. It hasn't moved forward at all."

With this in mind, it is understandable that, at a time when Moby was already exploring very different avenues, he would not have wished this document to be on sale, representing his work. The critics however were impressed, no matter what problems lay behind the album. Echoing the sentiments of many of the record's reviewers, *Billboard* dubbed it "exemplary of the true creative potential of techno. Once you are served with material this powerful, it is nearly impossible to accept some of the goofy, novelty-driven tracks now hitting the streets on a regular basis."

If the relationship with Instinct had become awkward, then the release of this album pushed Moby to the very edge. He increasingly felt trapped, unable to pursue his career in the way he wanted to go. This sense of lost autonomy was intolerable for him.

Until 'Go', Jared Hoffman had looked after Moby on an *ad hoc* basis. But as the single became more and more successful, it understandably became harder for Moby and Hoffman to keep on top of everything. Soon after, Moby took on DEF management to cover Europe and two weeks later, on the eve of a US tour with UK rave act The Shamen, he also enlisted the help of MCT management in the US. Both companies have been in place ever since.

Barry Taylor of MCT recalls how both he and business partner Marci Weber first became involved with Moby. "Marci and I had just come back to the office after a meeting with 808 State about management (it didn't happen), and there was a message on the answering machine from Moby asking us if we'd be interested in talking about management. We loved 'Go' and the 'Voodoo Child' track but thought that Jared from Instinct was also his manager, so we never approached him prior to the call.

"So we met him the next day, and the day after he was set to open for the Shamen on a US tour. We told him that there was so much to be done with the tour going out and there being no [infrastructure] set up for it, we offered to just start working for him to ensure some visibility and billing on the dates as well as some publicity. Whatever we could do under the circumstances. We told him that we would do this for him and if he was happy, we could talk about formalizing the relationship when he got back from the tour. We've been working with him ever since."

In both management companies, Moby seemed to have discovered people who would go to extreme lengths to understand the artist they were looking after. Even with his numerous changes in musical direction, MCT and DEF stood up for him, brokering the best deals they possibly could. No matter what the circumstances.

CHAPTER EIGHT

"If the universe breaks two of your buses, then maybe you should listen."
Moby, 1999

With the Instinct deal deep in dispute, Moby's release schedule slowed down to a depressing minimum. In order to keep his name in the public consciousness, he was forced to take on a massive amount of touring and remixing. Not that either of these represented a chore to him.

Typically, he entered into this latest phase of his career with the same kind of energy that had marked out his output in the previous year. Moby had already created quite a stir with his live performances throughout 1991. At his New Music Seminar performance on July 17th 1991, he played in support of UK rave act N-Joi (featuring pre-Republica vocalist Saffron) who were in town to promote their recent Top Forty radio hit 'Anthem', to ecstatic reviews. Of the show, at New York's Limelight, *Rockpool* suggested that "the slight, soft-spoken New Yorker was more of an explosion than a performer. Through his short set, he fed constant movement, energy and intensity, and received the same back from the dance floor in an exchange as exciting as the sound itself."

As Moby's schedule became more complex, so too did his methods of playing live. "At first I used to set up my studio on stage in order to have some kind of spontaneity," he told me. "At this time, I had a sequencer, a drum machine, a couple of samplers and a sixteen channel mixer. But I soon found this a problem with being on the road. It became impossible for me to support myself technically on the road. Also, I realized that I wanted to perform more, I felt that performance was completely missing from live techno shows. Being tied to the studio gear impeded my performance so I started to put a lot more emphasis on DATs."

Throughout the latter half of 1991 and the whole of 1992 Moby played approximately 120 live shows. He toured the States and played gigs in Germany, Switzerland, Holland, Belgium and Britain. Among these was a tour with British, indie-turned-techno act, The Shamen. Moby traveled to almost all these dates alone, always choosing the train over road vehicles.

He became like a techno version of a travelling troubadour. His kit consisted of a DAT tape of all his rhythm tracks and a synth to play some of the lead lines. He didn't even take a sound engineer on tour with him, preferring to set up his own kit during the soundcheck and then instructing the engineers to leave the settings alone. "I constantly upgrade my studio equipment," he once said, "and the more I upgrade, the less I take on the road with me."

Indeed, in an incredibly shrewd move, Moby's only companion for these performances would invariably be a lighting engineer. The resulting show would be musically controlled, while the lighting effects would lift him above any other act on the bill. He simply *stood out* visually. Not that he needed much help in this department.

The Shamen tour proved to be a critical turning point for Moby. Although both acts drew energy from the very same gene pool, in order to create positive dance tracks, The Shamen's self-consciously British traits turned US audiences off. Furthermore, much of their ideology was based around the more hippie teachings of Dr. Timothy Leary and Terence McKenna, with the addition of hip drug references throughout. Sadly, these references were almost exclusively British, thus escaping much of this new audience.

Moby, on the other hand, approached his show with a paradoxically simplistic fervour. His intention was to create a party and provide a good time for everyone. Ironically, for someone with such strong convictions, he didn't see the stage as his soapbox. This was the arena where he gave of himself to the people who wanted to dance.

The resulting ball of fiery energy was quickly picked up on by the US press. *The New York Times* said: "He spent most of his set dancing, a frenzied twitch on every beat, while occasionally poking a note or a sequence of chords on a keyboard. Where the Shamen's songs ticked and hummed, Moby's pounded out a big beat, laced with sound bites like 'Go!' or 'I feel it!'... He dispensed music that was simultaneously ominous and exhilarating."

"My shows have become more of what I always wanted them to be," he said at the time. "One of the nice things about my shows is that they're never the same twice. Everything is so alive." Obviously, the fact that most of the music was on DAT presented a problem with this last statement. But Moby went on to explain his point: "Much of it depends on the club's atmosphere. The crowd can bring the whole thing up or down."

He developed his on-stage performance over the course of this time. He may have remained reliant on the DAT tape, but this simply left him free to add synth fills, drum pad solos or simply jump around the stage, occasionally shouting into a mic. As would be expected, his shows sparked enormous debate among the dance scene.

In January 1993, Moby took to the road on a full tour of the US. His companions for the shows were UK act The Prodigy. It was to prove disastrous, with a huge amount of friction growing between Moby and the members of The Prodigy throughout the tour.

The problem was a simple one. The Prodigy were renowned for their marijuana-smoking prowess. What is more, they were partial to the odd drink and enjoyed many of the more extreme aspects of life on the road. Add to this the fact that they had just arrived in the US following an absolutely disastrous tour of Australia and you had the makings of a band who were almost past caring what anyone else thought. And then there was the non-smoking, non-drinking Moby. Not a problem, had the touring companions traveled separately. Unfortunately, however, they were all using the same tour bus.

"There was a big lounge in the coach," recalls Prodigy's Liam Howlett. "Moby kept moaning that he was getting stoned lying in his bunk-bed because of the air-conditioning. He kept on banging on the door and going, 'hey guys, c'mon.' He was just like really pathetic. Nice guy and all that, but I couldn't get on his wavelength, although I have to say I did actually like him. But he wasn't what you'd call a party animal!"

Perhaps the first realization that the tour was doomed was the portentous discovery that the tour bus had previously belonged to The Eagles - the give-away being the fact that the sides of the vehicle where emblazoned with the legend 'Hotel California'! Not a great start for a rolling techno revue.

If the on-bus conflicts had been the only thing the unlikely companions had to deal with on tour, then it would have been fine. Unfortunately, from the moment they set off things started to go wrong. First of all, they had been booked to play a gangster's bar in LA. However, they had also been booked to play a rival venue the following night, which resulted in Moby and The Prodigy being "warned off". At every subsequent gig the promoters ripped the musicians off and as each new venue loomed, each act took to the stage not knowing if they would get paid for their shows.

And things just continued to get worse. "The bus broke down, it was freezing cold and we were, like, in the middle of nowhere; somewhere like Kansas," says Moby of an event which is burned into his subconscious mind. "We were sitting there for eight hours waiting for the next bus and that one broke down too. So we got this idea that we could rent a plane to get to the next show in Colorado."

Unfortunately the only plane they could get was a dilapidated old bathtub with wings. Leeroy Thornhill, then dancer with The Prodigy, now recording as Flightcrank, recalls the incident through gritted teeth. "It was pure hell. I'm so tall that I usually have to sit in seats on plane where there is lots of room. But in this tub, I couldn't move my legs for the whole flight. It was terrifying, I was sure we were going to die. What was worse was that we were working our arses off for nothing. And we were all getting ill."

If flying in a potential death trap wasn't bad enough, Moby remembers the gig they finally arrived at was a catastrophe. "We get there and The Prodigy play their set which goes fine. Then I start playing and at first my monitors weren't working, so I freaked out and went back-stage and kicked this floor-length mirror and it shattered everywhere. I went back out front, and the monitors were OK but the front of house wasn't working. So I was storming around, pissed off, and gradually everything that could go wrong did go wrong. I was berating the local sound guys over the PA, and they got so pissed off, they just turned off the whole system – except they couldn't even get that right because the microphone was still on! So I said to the audience, 'I want to apologize for this, and I wouldn't blame you guys if you started a riot.' Which was a kinda punk rock thing to do. I went backstage feeling awful.

"Then the owner of the club came back with four huge security guards and he starts screaming at me, then he tries to break a bottle against a table to attack me with. He was going to have me flung in jail, he was going to kill me. I owed him $10,000 and he was going to sue me. This went on for about half an hour and the guys from The Prodigy just disappeared one by one. So I was sitting there alone, just me – one of the least threatening people on the face of the Earth – surrounded by four giant bouncers and this club owner. I just sat there until he'd finished shouting, because I knew if I'd made a move to stand up, he would have attacked me. In the end, nothing actually happened. In retrospect, I look back and say, 'Hey, if the universe breaks two of your buses, then maybe you should listen.'"

It wasn't all bad for Moby however. As the so-called Rave New World tour hit the west Coast, *LA Times* celebrated Moby for rescuing the show. Obviously unable to understand the ethos behind DJ culture, the reviewer, staff writer Mike Boehm, bemoaned the lack of bands in the line-up. Of the music itself, he said: "The sparse audience of about 150 people spent most of the rave being pounded by recorded tracks, most of them nothing more than a horrid, anti-melodic, anti-pop thud. The sound had its obnoxious visual equivalent in the incessant ricochet of blinding white light off a mirrored ball."

Of The Prodigy he stated: "[They] served up festive music that kept the crowd hopping. But aerobic success wasn't accompanied by much musical value." Clearly here was a man for whom the rave movement, techno music or the party scene meant little. Strangely, however, he found something that he did like in Moby's set. Describing him as looking like "a clerk from a Charles Dickens novel," he went on to suggest that Moby "was a frenzied performer who easily carried his one-man show. As his machine-driven beats and programmed sequencer patterns intensified, Moby jerked, jumped and flailed to the music in a simultaneous display of alarm and release that mirrored the mixture of foreboding, yearning and affirmation that was at the core of his non-verbal compositions.

"There is a threatening otherness in machine-made music used to evoke the dystopian, sci-fi sounds of computers and machinery," he continued. "But Moby didn't leave a listener stranded in a grim new world without a lifeline. His set implied that the ability to feel is our most precious safeguard against forces that would crush us or turn us into automatons."

Despite his reluctance to be won over by the culture he had just witnessed at play, The *LA Times* journalist did, however, manage to put his finger on the strength of Moby as a musician in that last sentence. That he was able to inject soul into his songs at a time when techno producers were increasingly moving into colder terrain set him apart from many of the other acts of the day. Most importantly, he put on a show in the old-school, rock tradition. He tapped into the culture of the performer as a star (much in the same way as The Prodigy), and as such he gave outsiders a tool with which to translate this new musical language. Indeed, while all around Moby were increasingly pushing towards a greater attitude of élitism, he threw all of his energy into the inclusivity of dance music. In fact, despite chart success and being described as "the Iggy Pop of Techno" by Ian Gittins in the now-defunct UK music paper *Melody Maker*, he was one of the few artists who still remained true to the original rave ethos of openness.

CHAPTER NINE

"Oh my God, I can't believe after the last roasting he got that Moby is going to try again." Fan posting on alt.rave USENET

Over the next few months it became increasingly clear that a huge gap was opening up between Moby and much of the rest of the dance community. In many quarters, Moby's adherence to the traditional star system was deemed to be totally at odds with the needs of the culture. Also, his music was increasingly in opposition to the growing 'intelligent techno' and progressive house scenes which were dominating UK clubs and magazines.

Not for the first time Moby was headed for a full on collision with the dance press. "It's a ridiculous thing about Britain," he told me at the time. "Instead of responding to what people actually like, the music press champion what they think people should like. So you get these artists forced upon you, and they sell, maybe four copies of their album in the United States, and then you get the rave scene with acts like Prodigy and N-Joi and so on and they sell bucket-loads all over the world, but the press ignore them. This is a weird English phenomena which I hope doesn't spread, because it is killing English music on the global market."

At the time Moby wasn't to know just how prophetic his words were. Only eight years later and Britain's standing on the global music market is negligible. Similarly, in the same interview he lambasted the dance scene in ways that were to be vindicated a few years later.

"Basically the English dance scene is created in the image of its class system. You have hardcore rave that is essentially a working-class phenomenon, then you have progressive house which is a middle-class thing for people who don't want to be associated with the lower classes. With so-called 'intelligent techno' you have a form of music being created by white, middle-class, educated males, for white, middle-class, educated males. It's uptight music that totally denies its own cultural roots. Every last bit of fun has been drained out of this music in order to make it more palatable for the rock kids who couldn't handle rave. Dance music is being broken down into so many different sub-genres according to this class structure, in order to displace itself from its own working-class beginnings."

Furthermore Moby considered the so-called 'intelligent techno' artists to be far less experimental than they claimed to be. "There's a big difference between the spirit of something and the aesthetic," he said. "People talk about intelligent techno being progressive, just because it's clothed itself in all of the accoutrements of experimental music. I sometimes think the most experimental thing B12, Black Dog, Aphex Twin and the rest of the Warp records intelligent 'techno-fascists' could do would be to write a song with an acoustic guitar and vocals, rather than continually trying to see how esoteric or obscure they can be with more twenty minute songs of distorted 909s."

Perhaps the first very public signs of Moby's growing dissatisfaction with the way the dance scene was going came at 1992's *Mixmag* Dance Awards in the UK. Organized by the magazine's then-publishers DMC (who are behind the international DJ mixing competitions of the same name, the New York heat of which Moby had judged only a year before in 1991), the event brought many complaints from the artists being presented with awards as well as those competing or performing. For many, the entire event was plagued by technical difficulties. Rave act Altern 8 were nearly kicked off the bill when their DAT tape failed to arrive on time, only to be allowed to perform as a last minute concession. As a result, the band didn't have time to put on their trademark costumes of pollution masks and boilersuits for their show. "If we'd have won any awards tonight we'd have given them back," said the band's Mark Archer.

Moby himself was reported as saying he was "bored stiff" by his first hour in the audience. When he finally got on stage to perform, he completely destroyed the equipment that DMC had hired in for him to play. However Moby's dissatisfaction with the event went much deeper than the inadequate organization. He saw the inadequacies of the event as symptomatic of the dance scene itself.

"Dance music has splintered," he complained to *Melody Maker*. "What were all the extraneous people doing on stage? Why should one guy who makes a record feel obliged to hire a DJ, an MC, two dancers and a singer?" He then went on to further illustrate this when interviewed by myself: "It's not about the music anymore; it's what it represents. Progressive house represents the older, well-educated person who's graduated from rave. Jungle-Techno is drug music for the middle-working classes. Electronic dance music is supposed to be sexy, subversive and interesting, which in New York it still is. British people need to start relaxing."

With such an antagonistic stance, it was almost inevitable that Moby would soon fall out of favor with the dance front line. His concept of what dance music, and the greater culture, stood for was being superseded by something, in many ways, less palatable. Increasingly people became far more interested in the validity of the music. Whether a track made you feel good was no longer enough, instead it had to adhere to a concept of worthiness being set out by a self-elected élite.

Inevitably, Moby's live shows were quick to come under fire. In this increasingly uptight atmosphere, many critics took it upon themselves to condemn the rave acts that performed aided by the use of DATs. In a bizarre return to the values of pre-acid house rock bands, it suddenly became imperative that performers actually recreated their tracks live.

Of course, this was a ridiculous demand, as much of the studio-born music would be impossible to play entirely live without an army of keyboard players. How most rave artists got around this insane inverted snobbery was by employing dancers and MCs, while keyboard players would add occasional lead lines over the backing tracks - a method still used by many of today's dance acts when they play live.

In October and November 1993 however, the argument spilled over into the public arena and raged online on USENET's alt.rave. The announcement of his coast-to-coast *See the Light* US tour with Orbital and Aphex Twin – the latter of whom he developed an unusually vocal dislike for – had sparked the so-called FLAMEWAR.

In fact, even his touring companions seemed to be angry with him. They complained that Moby seemed to have been picked out for special treatment as he flew everywhere while they were stuck on the tour bus. His reasons were simple: they smoked and he was allergic to that smoke. However, his experience with The Prodigy may have had something to do with this decision as well.

Of the online FLAMEWAR, the artist himself became involved in the discussion after a series of posts – one in particular from techno artist Joe Le Sesne, who recorded under the name of 1.8.7., had criticized him personally for syncing to a DAT player and banging on "a cardboard keyboard" while dancing around. Having had the debate pointed out to him by a friend, Moby wrote: *"Regarding this whole live vs DAT debate… my shows in the past have relied on DAT for drums, samples, etc. This show will be more live, but basically, who cares? would you rather watch a totally 'live' and totally boring act that doesn't even break a sweat or an act that puts things on DAT and puts on a good show?"* He closed his posting with *"stop smoking, moby."*

With the relative newness of the internet, it is fair to say that Moby, who didn't have his own account at the time, might not have expected quite such a vitriolic response to his posting. Indeed so many people threw in their opinions that Moby's responses went from anger to outright hurt.

A sample of some of the responses were as follows – Trance 9 wrote: *"Whether or not an act sweats is completely irrelevant to me. Putting your act on DAT makes it impossible for you to react musically to the situation. Stage presence is worth nothing. I don't go to raves to watch some guy dance around on stage. If there's a live act, it better be live, and the music better be good."* Lazlo Nibble wrote: *"If a musician can't be bothered to play the show live, I can't be bothered to cough up hard-earned dough for the privilege of watching them."*

Michael Meacham, who posted Moby's original message defended his friend briefly: *"OK I think people are making too much of this. I have seen Moby play many times and I have even had him play for me at the Future rave last year. Everybody loved him. I think if I went to see U2 and the show was on DAT I would definitely be offended. But look at it this way - when a performer goes to a rave, they have no idea what they are getting in to. There are so many things that can go wrong. Also consider that he is only one person."*

On November 4th, approximately two weeks after the last posting, Moby returned with a communication of what appeared to be pure anger. Posting his message in capital letters, he explained he still felt his original position was fair, before going on to explain how a huge portion of his show was live: *FOR THE RECORD, I DON'T JUST HIT START ON A DAT MACHINE - I HAVE LIVE KEYBOARDS, A FULLY FUNCTIONING OCTAPAD, LIVE GUITAR, LIVE VOCALS, AND A LIVE PERCUSSIONIST WITH A FULL PERCUSSION SET UP."* He went on to explain how certain aspects of his show would be impossible without DAT before lambasting some of those who criticised this multi-functional approach. He signed off with *"PEACE AND RESPECT TO THOSE WITH OPEN MINDS. MOBY"*

That people would have reacted as angrily to this message as the one before must have been a foregone conclusion. In many ways it represented the kind of reaction that Moby had always thrived on. Any extreme reaction, no matter how negative, was always better than no reaction at all. However the torrent of abuse which rained down was astonishing. "Oh my God, I can't believe after the last roasting he got that Moby is going to try again," wrote one alt.rave regular.

If Moby had seemed to be enjoying the argument, then his final message told a very different story. Lane Dunlop, Moby's tour manager for a short while, posted this last remark. From the anger of his previous message, there now seemed to be an air of hurt in Moby's writing.

"dear friends, if you'll notice this post is in lower case to suitably represent my humble and contrite disposition. it's not easy being hated so much, but i guess that i asked for it. to clear the air, my keyboards, guitar, octapad, and percussion have all been live on this tour. just thought that i'd let you know...."

In retrospect, this argument was little more than a diversion from the real issues of the time. Dance music was being forced to comply with the frameworks of traditional pop culture. Arguments that backed up any of what were basically capitalistic constraints were merely proof that many people, no matter how drawn to the rave sound, were unable to take on board the ideology too.

Dance music as Moby knew and loved it was dying. In its place was a beast he had little time for. Inevitably Moby would increasingly rebel against what he considered a "myopic view". Over the coming years, he would rail against what he perceived as cultural fascism with a series of wildly eclectic releases which at times would verge on commercial suicide.

CHAPTER TEN

"I wouldn't necessarily think of myself as the Jesus Christ of techno, although I think there is definitely something prophetic about what I do."
Moby

Following the release of his eponymous album, Moby set about extricating himself from his deal with Instinct. With management working on his behalf, he was able to look to the future with some degree of confidence. However, there was still the issue that he had been signed for a set number of albums.

Despite the remaining stalemate between Moby and Jared Hoffman, in October 1992 Instinct sent out a promo of what was to be one of Moby's most enduring tracks, 'Next Is The E'. A stunning combination of driving Italo house pianos, rushing drum rolls (a trick which was later to become common on dance singles), dark, spooky synth washes and pulsating beats. Over the top of this was a montage of vocals ranging from a repeated cry, to a scat cut-up of a girl proclaiming "E to the I is the next is an E", then on to the seductive "I feel it" chorus. A gorgeous combination of the distorted disco of the Paradise Garage, the funk-drenched groove of breakbeat house and the soulful melancholy of ambient, the track itself offered the sound of Moby at his most creative, despite the original mix being almost two years old.

"The only time you'll have difficulty with this brilliantly produced, slamming twelve-inch is when it comes time to classify the record in a neatly suitable genre," wrote DJ Reese in *Rockpool* magazine, before claiming it to be "without question one of the year's greatest releases."

Elsewhere however, *URB* were only able to muster a derisory "pleasant workout from everybody's favorite New York nice guy soulman, Moby... I'm not sure how this would go over in a club (let the hardcore DJs worry about it) but it's worth a listen."

In the UK, however, *Mixmag Update* were far more impressed. Reviewing the single on import, DJ Billy Nasty exclaimed it to be "one brilliant dance groove. The second ('Victory') mix has got to be one of the best records I've heard for ages. A more progressive (hate the word) mix, a relentless, throbbing bassline, excellent percussion and deep and moody strings." Among the various mixes in the single was another track that would become something of an unusual Moby standard. Called 'Thousand' because it actually clocked in at over 1,000 bpm, the track brought with it an unusual kind of fame; it entered *The Guinness Book of Records* as the fastest track of all time. "At the time, tracks were just getting faster and faster," Moby reminisces. "I guess I was just trying to make a point."

Although 'Thousand' was written off as a novelty track, it subsequently became the last song Moby played at almost every one of his shows. Performed with DAT tape running, while a motionless Moby stood on top of his keyboard, as the track built and strobes grew faster and faster, the artist adopted the Christ-in-crucifixion posture.

Naturally, this pose was met with much derision from his critics in all quarters. Some have suggested it cheapened his faith to the level of gimmick. Others maintain that it smacked of a kind of arrogance, in that Moby sees himself as a martyr to his musical cause. He has even been accused of wanting to be the 'Jesus Christ of Techno'.

"I wouldn't necessarily think of myself as the Jesus Christ of techno," he explained a couple of years after his entry into the record books in a promotional film for Mute Records, "although I think there is definitely something prophetic about what I do. I like emotional music. I've always liked emotional music, even corny things."

Interestingly, the Mute promo was filmed in an abandoned church. During the film Moby is shown rooting around a derelict room when he reaches up to the wall and pulls down an old certificate. "Oh, this looks nice," he says before reading its transcription out loud. "Dedicated to the continuing service of our Lord Satan? What kind of place is this?" Surprisingly, for the man who was so often painted as an uptight, didactic, humorless bigot in the press, he actually found the irony of the situation funny.

What those accusations railed against Moby and his Christ's-passion pose missed, however, was that 'Thousand' offered a glimpse of the more theatrical side to Moby. Regardless of any moralistic viewpoint, the deificatory stance did make for a stunning visual and aural finale. Moby's slow-motion adoption of the pose seems almost choreographed in the fast-frame light of the strobes. Indeed, had this part of his show appeared in a dance piece by New York choreographer Twyla Tharpe, or in a multimedia performance by fellow New Yorker's The Wooster Group, it would no doubt have been hailed as a powerful work of art.

'I Feel It/Thousand' went to #17 in the *Rockpool* Record Pool Play Chart and #1 in their Techno 20. In the *Billboard* Hot Dance Club Play chart it went to #10. If Moby was unhappy about his deal with Instinct, it certainly didn't show. If, however, he was putting his best foot forward while shopping around for a new deal then he couldn't have done better. This was imaginative, experimental dance music with a pop edge at its very best.

Of course, with a title like 'Next Is The E'. The single was guaranteed to bring with it a degree of controversy. On the face of it Moby was condoning the use of ecstasy - despite having gone on record as being against drugs. He was subsequently condemned as a hypocrite, while it was also suggested that he was simply preying on the vulnerability of the kids who were being dragged into the drug culture associated with raving. The criticism was that a kid would buy the record as a part of their lifestyle just because of the 'E' reference. But the truth is that Moby was just the latest in what was fast becoming a tradition among rave producers. With 'Next Is The E' he entered the same debate which had raged around such classic tunes as Lenny De

Ice's 'We Are E'. At least Moby didn't go as far to include gunshots, a sample that was equally popular at the time.

"To me the rave is a place of positive spirituality. This track is a celebration of dancing till seven in the morning, sharing the moment with your closest friends, sweating together in a shared experience." Moby told me over the phone on the eve of the single's release that "at least I'm not celebrating the gangster lifestyle. I'm not saying to anyone to mistreat women and shoot policemen. I dunno, I just don't think that kind of thing is healthy."

In order to defuse the argument, Moby included a disclaimer on the CD single. It read: "Upon hearing 'Next Is The E', many people, make the assumption that this song is about drug use. The truth is that I disapprove of the irresponsible use of drugs. I've seen far too many lives damaged from drug use to even consider glorifying drugs in a song."

But Moby didn't actually go on say what he actually meant by the song title. Though he wasn't intentionally condoning drug use, there can be no doubt that the phrase "Next Is The E" was not chosen at random. The fact is, in the raves it did sound *amazing*. If Moby's main aim with music had always been to make people feel good, then this track worked incredibly effectively - not least because of its contentious sample.

Ironically, this was not the first time that Moby tapped into E culture for creative purposes. It was however the most obvious. Such transparency did not go down too well in the UK though. Following a European release on Rough Trade, a new mix came out on UK label Equator in June 1993 (a month before the UK release of *Moby*, this time entitled *The Story So Far*) under the less controversial name 'I Feel It'.

Accompanied by a video of Moby playing live, 'I Feel It' became Moby's second Top Forty hit in the UK, entering the charts at #38. When it came to play on the UK's most famous chart show *Top of the Pops*, Moby actually declined the offer, despite the fact that he had appeared on the programme for 'Go' and the obvious positive effect it would have had on record sales. His reasons were not due to some underground ideology as you might expect, but because he insisted on a climbing frame and women dancers with stockings over their heads for the performance. *Top of the Pops* turned down his request. Moby refused to appear and, in so doing, not only displayed the fact that he was a man of his word, but also one with more of a sense of humor than he had hitherto been given credit for.

As the debate raged over 'Next Is The E', yet another album was put out by Instinct. This time it was a collection of Moby's now-deleted back catalogue. Called *Early Underground*, it was released on March 10th 1993 and has subsequently sold in the region of 38,000 copies in the US.

Essentially a variation on the *Instinct Dance* album, there was no denying that the tracks on the record were an essential purchase for the latecomer to Moby; however it offered very little new insight into the musician. Also interesting is the fact that the packaging features a picture of Moby stretched out of all recognition. So much so that he looks like a doppelganger for a young Paul Hartnoll from Orbital! "I loath the *Early Underground* packaging," he says of the album. "One of the worst record covers ever."

In a review which pointed out Moby's contradictory nature, *URB* magazine in the US suggested that the album "exemplifies what lifts Moby above ninety nine per cent of the people working in this medium – his ability to weave a web of sound and create actual songs with meaning and emotion. In a genre of music that has quickly begun, more often than not, to live up to its worst expectations of banality and tiredness, Moby is truly an innovator."

Following the *Early Underground* came yet another LP. This time it was a collection of Moby's ambient tracks called, fittingly, *Ambient*. Released in the US in August 1993 and in the UK two months later (on Equator), *Ambient* was in many ways a more interesting proposition than the previous album, in that it offered entirely new tracks. Furthermore, Moby had often claimed that the music of his own that he preferred was the more mellow, ambient material. This then offered the first glimpse of a side to Moby that would remain constant through the years that would follow.

Despite the popularity of ambient house for the two or three years leading up to this album. *Ambient* had far more in common with the artists he'd listened to as a youth. Its melodic, pathos-laden melancholy drew heavily on the atmospheres of Joy Division and New Order. Its moods echoed the *Low* and *Heroes* collaborations between David Bowie and Brian Eno, while its structures hinted at the more relaxing output of 80s art-synth band Japan as well as the later output of the band's lead singer David Sylvian.

Indeed, on tracks such as 'My Beautiful Sky', 'Myopia' and '80', he successfully evokes the combined spirits of Bowie's 'Subterraneans' and Sylvian's *Gone to Earth* soundscapes, while both 'J Beas' and 'Piano And String' could have come from Japan's *Gentlemen Take Polaroids* – albeit in its gentler moments.

Ambient is an enjoyable album, somewhere between beautifully haunting and deeply soulful. Yet, put next to the output of the artists whose company the album was trying to keep, it is fair to say that it sounded naïve. In places it was too saccharine, in others it simply lacked depth. That Moby was totally against this release (despite describing the music as being "warm, thoughtful, and from the heart.") is understandable. Basically this collection only hinted at the kind of depth he would later achieve.

Of the album, *Village Voice* observed: "*Ambient*'s only flaw is that the tracks are more cut-up than cohesive, and in themselves sometimes don't find a purpose." Elsewhere, *Esquire*'s Mark Jacobson assessed the album as "a tad tinny, an inch-deep nirvana", despite actually admitting to liking it.

Talking to me at the time about this output, Moby explained: "I've always liked atmospheric music, even when I was a little kid and my mum used to play me classical stuff or whatever. When

Brian Eno came out with *On Land* I got really into relaxation music. I mean, the first record I bought which was in this style was *Heroes* by David Bowie."

Despite his love of relaxation music, he was however less than enamoured with the ambient house scene. Attacking much of the music's lack of any real substance and apparent shortage of ideas, he exclaimed: "I think the ambient scene is a little too lightweight, it's just like these voices saying [*whispers*] 'relax, relax' like really pretty, bucolic sounds, birds chirping and arpeggiated synths and stuff."

It was his opinion that good atmospheric music should demand something of the listener. That it simply wasn't enough for the music to drift over you. "To me a good piece of atmospheric music changes your perception of your surroundings," he said. "The listener is not simply passive." It is probable that Moby's lack of interest in much of the ambient scene was derived from his earlier spat with the intelligent techno artists. Ambient, by its very nature, attempted to appear highbrow. Often artists claimed to be modern classical composers in the tradition of Stockhausen.

Another aspect of this scene was that its output seemed to be best appreciated stoned. Indeed, it was all too often the product of marijuana. As a result, many of the so-called ambient pieces tended to be drenched in reverb and echo like so much cheap perfume. Similarly Moby held no admiration for the area of ambient which was deliberately clever. A direct descendent of intelligent techno, this strand of electronica presented itself as 'ambient music for enquiring minds'.

"Intentionally weird music often falls flat on its face because it's so contrived. Everything just fits," he exclaimed in 1994 before issuing a damning attack on the ambient scene: "Going back to ambient, look at the covers, everything so tasteful, I mean, I'm sick of ambient albums with ambient covers and ambient titles like, I dunno, *12th Degree of Nothing*. I just wish someone would make an ambient record and put a woman on the cover, in leather and baby oil, with a whip and call it *Motherfuckin' Motor Cycle Music* and then inside it's like really quiet, beautiful music - juxtaposition is a lot more interesting than sameness."

Ironically, one of the very areas in which *Ambient* actually failed was the very thing that he condemns others for; a lack of juxtaposition. As a deeply rooted theme in all of his dance output, this was one of Moby's most obvious trademarks. Yet here in his atmospheric work there were very few opposites at play. It all fits together just as you would expect. No surprises, just nice music.

CHAPTER ELEVEN

"If you consider remixing as an art form unto itself, I never paid my dues in the same way that I did as a musician. One day I wasn't a remixer, the next I was. Simple as that."   Moby, 1992

If the years of 1992 and 1993 had been quiet in terms of new material from Moby, then at least the fans could listen to his reinterpretations of other people's tracks through remix work. In fact, over the course of his career, Moby has always been an in-demand remixer.

One of the very reasons he is approached to do remix work, however, is exactly why the original artist often objects to the Moby treatment. Basically he strips the songs down to their barest fragments and writes an entirely new track. If the artists see it as vandalism of their music, paradoxically Moby's work from the debris of this beat hooliganism is all too often better than the original.

Despite already having made quite a name for himself as a remixer as early as 1991, Moby did express his surprise at this twist in the dance culture: "I think its kind of disturbing that record labels are approaching DJs and artists to do remixes because, the truth is, none of us is actually qualified to remix. We are musicians in the sense that we make music, but if you consider remixing as an art form unto itself, I never paid my dues in the same way that I did as a musician. One day I wasn't a remixer, the next I was. Simple as that."

Often, what the person who commissioned these remixes, usually without the original artists' consent, wanted was a little bit of the remixers' own music without actually having to sign them for long-term deals. In a strange twist, the choice of remixer became a creative decision. Sadly these decisions were often made by the least creative people in the music business. People who were more likely to be swayed by fashion than actual talent.

From Moby's point of view, the fact that he has known moments of media over-exposure and the hype that goes with it has meant that he has been able to earn a decent living wage from his remixing work. That he has shown the talent to make his remixes desirable songs in their own right is an added bonus.

Moby's remix methodology involves parts of the original tack being supplied on DAT. From here he takes the elements he needs to build a new track, perhaps best exemplified by his reworking of The Pet Shop Boys' 'Miserabilism' in 1995, in which he starts his version with a melancholic minor ninth chord before unfolding into shimmering electronic bleeps. Towards the end he introduces a melodic keyboard refrain which picks out parts of the original tune. Throughout the mix, vocals bob and weave in and out, part submerged by reverb.

"Remixing isn't anywhere near as satisfying as writing your own track, so I try to introduce things which will make it interesting for me. I really like the idea of transforming the original into something unexpected. Everybody would expect you to do a really hard mix of say, The Prodigy or any one of the rave acts, but if you take a pop artist and add these different stylings, it's always surprising."

Once again Moby's art form is all about juxtaposition. Something that has had a habit of upsetting some of his remix subjects. His version of the B52s' 'Good Stuff' turned the original's disjointed, awkward rhythm in to a tribal onslaught to great effect. However B52s' singer Fred Schneider was rumoured to be not at all happy that his voice had been left out.

"Moby doesn't just slap a beat onto a track," said a Warners employee at the time, "he actually turns the track into something it wasn't at all. On one of the B52s tracks he took a breath of Kate Pearson inhaling between songs and created something weird out of that. He's got a really good sense of humour. One of the remixes he turned in was 200 beats per minute." It could be that Moby's sense of humour was more at play on these remixes than anything of his own. With the remixes he found a strange sense of

A hirsute Moby's first press shot for Instinct Records, 1989

Moby, New York, 1993

Moby learning to fly, New York, 1993

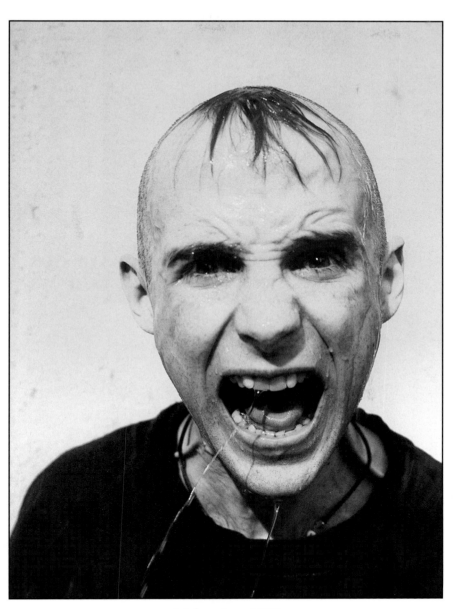

Moby, circa 1993

Live in 1997, *Animal Rights* tour

Moby Gets into 007 mode, 1997

1998, I Like To Score

Thrasher

Near his New York home, 1999

On stage touring *Play*

Live in 2000

The Little Idiot, circa *Play*

freedom. Somehow his creativity was freed from constraints of what he would term, his "own internal policemen".

Although Moby's remixes have graced the releases of artists as diverse as David Bowie, The Beastie Boys, Michael Jackson, Aerosmith and Metallica, it is perhaps more interesting to look at those mixes that were rejected.

In 1993 he was commissioned by Depeche Mode to rework 'Walking In My Shoes'. Although he turned out a number of mixes, ranging from a quiet contemplative version, through to a hardcore remix, the band rejected them as being too different. Apparently Moby's style was not what they wanted.

Another rejection came from Metallica after Moby turned in a lounge mix of 'Until It Sleeps'. "I did one remix which was sort of what they wanted, which was sort of a drum-and-bass-meets-speed-metal version. And I did another version, which was a slow quiet lounge ballad, and it's hysterical. It was with Alan Moulder who was engineering it with me and we were crying with laughter. But the guys from Metallica will never, ever release it. We sent it to them and they thought it was funny, but they said no one can ever hear this. Literally Alan and I are in the studio just weeping with laughter, 'cause it's like this gentle little piano-ey, stringy thing underneath James Hetfield, you know? Actually, I think it's the best lounge thing that I ever did."

Of the other remix oddities was Smashing Pumpkins '1979', which he recorded a disco remix of. However, he apparently loved the mix too much to actually give it to them. It remains unreleased. Also existing are remixes where Moby is credited as playing or singing on the track as well. For example, on the Jon Spencer Blues Explosion's 1998 track 'Calvin', he was credited as playing bass and percussion while ex-Depeche Mode member Alan Wilder's Recoil project released a track called 'Bloodline' which was not only co-written by Moby - he also rapped on it.

This was not the first or last time that Moby would rap. In his early shows he did a never-to-be-released and untitled track which featured him in what was described at the time as an "ill-advised rap performance". Similarly, despite a style which has more in common with a punk rock rant than an exercise in flow and cadence, he also started many of the *Play* tour gigs of 1999/2000 working Public Enemy's 'Bring The Noise' into the live version of 'The James Bond Theme'.

Another notable remix project came in 1992 when Moby was asked to work his magic for the Brian Eno track 'Fractal Zoom'. He was naturally overjoyed at the chance to work on one of his favorite artist's music. In fact it was the first time that Eno had ever allowed another producer to touch his work. According to Kevin Laffey, director of Warners A&R West Coast at the time, "Eno could see the musicality with Moby. The production was more sophisticated than most and it wasn't limited to hypnotic beats, it was multi-dimensional, passionate. And I think he liked the raw quality, and that there was a person there."

If Moby's remix work has always shown a humorous side to his approach to production, then during those difficult days of the Instinct fall-out, they offered him a welcome avenue for maintaining his public profile. They also allowed him a much-needed injection of cash.

During 1992 he was finally released from his contract with Instinct. It had been a long, drawn-out affair, but finally he signed to Elektra in the US and Mute in the UK and Europe. Although the break up with Instinct had undoubtedly effected him at the time, Moby remains philosophical about it all today. "I left on bad terms, but things got better soon after that. No hard feelings now I hope. I haven't seen Jared in maybe five years, but I certainly bear him no ill will. He's a smart man and I have a good deal of respect for him."

Moby lost no time in delivering his first single for his new record labels. On August 8th, 1993, he released 'Move'. As a single it offered a glimpse of the directions that Moby would be taking his music in. The package was more eclectic than ever before. The promos of 'Move' came in a multitude of different mixes covering the increasingly splintered dance scene. The four-track, non-remixed release, featured what was perhaps the definitive version of the lead track, and three additional essential Moby songs.

'Move' found Moby once again enjoying the euphoric power of the piano. However, rather than follow the standard Italo house pattern, he picked out strangely melancholic melodies and repeated arpeggios in the style of Philip Glass. Added to this were anthemic chord swells giving the tune an almost overblown power. The vocal hook, "You make me feel so good, so good" had a quasi-religious feel, echoing spiritualist worship.

As a single it followed an easily recognizable path from 'Next Is The E' and Barracuda's 'Drug Fits the Face' - with the obvious exception that 'Move' has no reference to drugs, beyond the fact that once again it tapped directly into the musical needs of the ecstasy user.

Accompanying the track was a video that Moby would later declare his utter dislike for. No wonder, as it offered a clumsy attempt at depicting the sexual undertones of the single (while featuring live shots of him wearing a very unflattering body stocking!). There was no doubt that Moby's music had always been charged with a strong sexual undercurrent. Some reviewers preferred to call this the "soul" in his music. However, the most powerful aspect of this sexiness was the fact that it wasn't overt. Rather than a XXX-rated exploration, Moby offered sex as indelibly linked to beauty, sadness, joy, and anger. He provided glimpses of sex through a mist of human emotions.

Yet the video for 'Move' attempted to overstate the point with shots of a girl naked but for a chiffon wrap, or occasionally flowers. Moby and the girl were depicted in a series of naked clinches while elsewhere she was shown in a series of poses hinting at masturbation. Although the actual sex acts were left to the imagination, the shots seemed unnecessarily grubby.

Furthermore, although the video was interspersed with shots of Moby standing dead still on a busy New York street while the girl stood in a doorway adopting wanting poses, the narrative wasn't clear. Was this girl someone who had seen Moby from afar and then started fantasizing about him? Or was she a hooker who was a part of his own fantasy?

Whatever the truth, it was a promo film destined to never make it onto MTV. This was a time of increased activity from the American Christian right, and sexual morals were high on the agenda. Not even the edited 'Kiddie Version' found much favor with the television stations.

With the following tracks on the EP, Moby hinted at a possible future direction. Perhaps the biggest surprise came with 'All I Need Is To Be Loved (MV)' not least because it featured a full vocal performance from Moby over a pulsating four-to-the-floor acid track. Only a year before Moby had insisted, "I'm kind of committed to not singing, at least on my records." Here, however, he delivered an impassioned plea in a voice which would not seem out of place on a Metallica record.

Lyrically 'All I Need' seemed, on a cursory listen, to reflect his religious belief. With lyrics like "All I want is to be near you, oh my god how can I love thee", the track seemed to be about the artist's sense of desolation in the face of a loss of faith. With the addition of contorted and distorted calls of "oh my god" buried deep in the mix towards the track's end, it sounded like Moby was enduring a state of living purgatory.

On a closer listen, however, it became clear that the track was concerned with far more earthly matters. With the hushed vocal intro of "Can't trust you, I wanna be with you", it revealed itself as a love song to an ex-partner. Indeed, in its entirety, 'All I Need...' encompassed the sense of urgent desperation that comes with the end, or towards the end, of a long relationship.

Other tracks on the EP included the fierce breakbeat trance attack of 'Unloved Symphony' and the contemplative ambience of 'The Rain Falls And The Sky Shudders'. The former represented one of Moby's darkest tunes to date, with its haunting strings, dislocated voices and proto-junglist breaks. However, at the point of the track's breakdown, an overwhelming journey commences as the middle eight introduces melodic arpeggiated pianos and warm strings. More than any previous track from Moby, 'Unloved Symphony' suggests some kind of personal epiphany has taken place. When considering the title, in light of 'All I Need Is To Be Loved', there is little doubt that Moby was involved in a situation of almost profound heartbreak.

The final cut, 'The Rain Falls…' offered Moby's finest ambient piece to date. By using the sounds of New York's streets in the pouring rain and adding minimal piano motifs, he managed to evoke a sense of loss reminiscent of 'The Eternal' from Joy Division's *Closer*. It remains one of Moby's most inspirationally beautiful moments.

'Move' proved to be Moby's second biggest UK hit, reaching the #21 spot in the UK pop charts. In the US it went Top Ten in the *Billboard* Dance chart. If anyone had worries that Moby might lose his ability to create classic dance floor tracks now he had signed to a major label, then this single proved such fears wrong. Indeed what the new deal provided him with was a new sense of artistic freedom.

In an ironic twist that only served to underline Moby's newly found freedom, Instinct Records actually released the aforementioned *Ambient* on exactly the same day 'Move' came out.

CHAPTER TWELVE

"There's something perversely satisfying about taking money from a car company and giving it to organizations which work to protect the environment." Moby

Moby moves crab-like across the floor on all fours. He is sprayed from head to toe in silver paint, wearing nothing but a pair of old, distressed Levi's. All around, three even more underdressed punk-angels slowly move in on him. They are painted in various colors, their wings billowing in the breeze of the wind machine. Slowly they stage a mock fight in what seems to be a cyber-heaven. It's a surreal scene, like a William Gibson-inspired update of the wicked witch of the West and her winged monkeys in *The Wizard of Oz*. Smoke spreads all around the figures, as the movement becomes more frenzied. The overhead netting starts to ripple, the silver Moby is cornered and, just as the winged angels go in for the final conflict, a voice comes over a soundsystem: "Cut." The lights come on, the smoke machine ceases coughing its sickly fumes and Moby strolls towards me to say hello. "Well, it's supposed to be like heaven," he explains of the video shoot I have just witnessed. "The idea is that I'm some kind of fallen junky, insane-type punk angel, kinda rebelling against the other angels."

It was our first face to face meeting, having previously only talked on the phone. That he was covered in silver paint somehow didn't seem in the least bit strange. In fact, had the creator of some of the most otherworldly dance music to have crossed the Atlantic been dressed in any other way, I might have been disappointed. With this meeting I finally entered the surreal universe Moby inhabits. Even if it was just a film studio in Wembley, west London.

The video was for the astounding 'Hymn' single - his fourth Top Forty hit in the UK (charting at #31). This was perhaps his most transcendental track to date, wrapping up all his key themes. Huge choral swathes envelop a host of angelic voices while beats ebb and flow through a series of build-ups and breakdowns as Moby repeats the words, "This is my dream" over and over again. 'Hymn' is a stunning collection of juxtapositions; celebratory and somber, nostalgic and futuristic, melancholic and joyous. If the previous single had hinted, no matter how tenuously, that Moby was having a crisis of faith, then this was his answer. Rarely does a track's title suit its content quite as well. This was indeed Moby's 'Hymn'.

The video however was not. In fact it wasn't even the promo he wanted. "Well, on the last single, 'Move', a ridiculous amount of money was spent on the video and I hated it, so I thought I'd have a go myself. I just think it's unnecessary to spend that kind of money. Did you see that Bjork video of her running up and down the back of a truck? Well I heard that cost about $1,000 to make and I thought it was really beautiful and entertaining. So, anyway, a friend and I filmed a video for 'Hymn'. I was really pleased with it and it only cost a fraction of a normal video, but the company felt it was too weird for MTV and *The Chart Show* [the UK's main pop video show on terrestrial TV at the time] so here we are having another go."

Indeed what was being filmed was a slightly sanitized version of a somewhat strange original, which I was later told by one of the multitude of runners, technicians etc., would probably still be too off-the-wall for MTV. In the event, however, a heavily edited version did appear for a one-minute slot on *The Chart Show*. Probably to the amusement of Moby, who had few good feelings about this new film. "There's a part of me that wants this video to fail so I can do all of my own from now on," he said.

That he had already filmed his own promo to 'Hymn' should not have come as any surprise to Moby fans. Given his long-term friendship with Paul Yates and his oft-claimed desires to further explore film-making, the step into directing seemed almost inevitable.

The original video for 'Hymn' was indeed a far more enjoyable film than the record company remake. It was neither marred by bad storyboarding nor blatant and obvious quasi-religious imagery. Called the *Yates Hall* (ie Paul Yates and Richard Hall) version, the film was in black and white, drawing from a series of observational pieces on a Super 8 camera that he and Yates had already filmed.

On the work-in-progress film (known as *New York*) Moby can be seen in various locations messing around for the camera. At one point he walks along the edge of the roof of his apartment and pretends to fall off, only to land on a ledge below. If this footage suggests anything, it is only that Moby completely lacks any of fear of heights. Of the other sections of the film, one theme starts to emerge - that of flight. For example, during one part he is seen jumping up and down. However the frames where he lands have been edited out to create a vision of levitation.

Flight and weightlessness are themes which occur over and over again in Moby's imagery. On later albums such as 1995's *Everything Is Wrong* he is depicted submerged in water, in a state of weightlessness. 1999's *Play* shows him caught in mid-flight as he jumps on a bed. In the video for 'Into The Blue', taken from *Everything Is Wrong*, he is captured floating in a fish tank.

The finished *Yates Hall* video explored this dual theme to enjoyable effect. Moby was framed by time-lapse images of traffic. The result was of him levitating in slow-motion as cars speed past. Elsewhere a series of shots depicted him floating in a swimming pool, in the last of which he was naked - apparently the main reason given for not using the video. What is certain is that the official color video paled in comparison. In fact, the most effective parts are frames from Moby and Yates's film, which were dropped in at regular intervals.

If the previous single suggested that Moby was on the verge of pushing his music into the wildest extremes possible, the accompanying track to 'Hymn' further backed this up. What Moby offered was another version of 'All I Need Is To Be Loved'.

This time it was called the 'House Of Suffering' mix and, remarkably, it featured guitars thrashing away like an old hardcore punk band. If juxtaposition was the thing that interested Moby at the time, then this entire single brought together two extremes of the dance coin. On the one hand was something uplifting, spiritual, blissful even; on the other was a track of pure rage.

As the dance scene of the time was developing a deeply rooted snobbery of what was and was not acceptable, it was almost inevitable that Moby would be condemned for this latest development. "A lot of people are really offended by it. I think people get obsessed with the form over the function, so guitars come to represent rock'n'roll, but rock'n'roll represents the 'other', and to me it's not so much the form as the function and the mentality. What I don't like about rock'n'roll is the élitist mentality of 'you have to be able to play your instrument' and you can't have synths or disco vocals. What I don't like about the dance mentality is that it's the exact opposite - or should I say, the same mentality, but with different symptoms - so instead they say you can't use guitars. It's interesting to see just how oppressive attitudes are adopted.

"When people rail against oppression, they're really going against the current form of oppression and are subsequently equally quick to enact their own forms of oppression. What I try to do is do what I enjoy and hope other people can tolerate it. If I really wanted to indulge myself I think people would just stop paying attention... so I have to work within an established context."

This last statement of course suggests that Moby was feeling increasingly limited by external constraints. It was almost as if he had fallen victim to the regulations imposed by cultural fascists. "If these constraints were taken away," he added, "then I'd probably use some speed metal, some country & western, even some experimental electronic stuff. That would be my ideal album. In fact that's probably what my next record is going to be like. I hate it when people compartmentalize things and then start saying, 'I only like this or that and don't listen to anything else.' Like, at the moment everyone is saying you have to be into intelligent techno. I mean, intelligent techno? What does that mean?"

It was obvious that Moby's dissatisfaction with dance culture was growing. Similarly, people became ever more vocal in their criticism of him. Increasingly he was painted as a humorless, hyperactive, finger-pointing dogmatist who had little time for the drug-addled, alcohol-drenched scene that surrounded him. Or he was presented as an ex-skate punk thrasher on a bible-bashing mission from God. Both images were, of course, miles from the truth; however each time Moby vented another opinion in interviews, so that particular cliché stuck even faster.

But the truth was that Moby still had a deep love of dance culture and electronic music. That he had equally deeply held beliefs should have been of little consequence on the dance floor. Indeed, it was the media who were having trouble coming to terms with the different aspects of Moby's personality co-existing, not Moby himself.

With 'Hymn' he played on these apparently opposing values by bringing together two distinctly different genres and sending them down a similar path. And, just to add to the confusion the package was completed by a 33.3333-minute ambient version of 'Hymn' called the 'Alt. Quiet Mix'.

Given the nature of Moby's promo film for 'Hymn', it was surprising that he didn't choose to add visuals to the second CD. The 'Alt. Quiet Mix' was (and still is today) Moby's most accomplished piece of ambient music. Even if he hoped it would not be tagged with the term ambient or the even stranger title of "Mobient", which Mute Records had originally marketed the CD as. Unsurprisingly, Moby hated it.

"Originally the mix was actually four different separate parts which I just put together. I'm hoping that it doesn't get called an ambient piece. What I'm hoping for is that people perceive it as a more symphonic, or classical piece - in the modern classical sense."

Despite his protestations, the 'Alt. Quiet Mix' represented the closest Moby has ever come to ambient music in its purest form. Far more in keeping with the mood pieces created by Brian Eno than the stoner symphonies of the ambient house cognoscenti, the piece is completely stripped of all sense of ego. It exists as a mood-altering presence. Though never distracting, it demands from the listener the ability to become lost in its textures while remaining completely aware of all that is happening in reality. In this sense, the music has a transcendental quality which echoes the state reached when dancing to repetitive beats – except this piece is all about repetitive textures and motifs.

Of the dance mixes that accompanied 'Hymn', perhaps the most interesting was the 'Lucky Orgasm Mix' which employed a 'White Lines'-style bassline and a vocoder, while the 'I Believe' version found Moby adding the *a capella* from rave hit 'It's Not Over' into the "better believe in God" hook. The backing tracks were minimal in the style of +8 records. Little wonder then that Richie Hawtin constantly played it in his sets. As did Pete Tong.

"Dance music still excites me a lot but more the experimental stuff that's not intentionally experimental, like, the New York deep house stuff is really weird, but it's not designed to be, like, intelligent music. It's designed to make a dance floor go crazy."

Given the intensity of the 'Hymn' package, it was somewhat shocking that Elektra didn't actually give the record a full release in the States. Even though the company sent out promo versions, when it came to the actual version that hit the record racks, they opted for a set of remixes of 'All I Need Is To Be Loved'.

Admittedly these tracks probably made more sense to the US radio playlists and indeed the American public, as electronic dance music had still not exactly taken off anywhere but the expected enclaves of LA, San Francisco, New York and Chicago. The use of punk rock vocals and the inclusion of thrash guitars on the 'House Of Suffering' mix would have mixed in far more with the

Stateside obsession with skate punk and metal funk at the time.

Most interesting, however, was a limited edition seven-inch of this single. On the flipside it featured Moby's version of the Joy Division classic 'New Dawn Fades' from the band's debut album *Unknown Pleasures.* It was a fairly faithful rendition, although it did take the original's brittle ambience deep into rock territories (complete with Slayer-like guitar solos) while Moby's almost weedy vocal performance - suffused with excessive vibrato - barely stood up to the booming melancholia in the voice of Joy Division's Ian Curtis. As an homage however, it was nothing if not heartfelt.

Moby, it seemed, was moving ever further away from dance music. His increasing use of guitars confirmed a need to explore other avenues. And then, in July 1994, just to confuse things even further, he delivered his most underground dance track since his Instinct days. What's more, he resurrected his Voodoo Child moniker for the occasion.

'Demons/Horses' was Moby showing the world he still loved dance music enough to fully understand it. These tracks were minimal DJ tools. Little surprise that they failed to make any impact on Moby's growing fan base. In fact, the general public were simply not interested in this latest venture.

Of course, it is fair to say that this was supposed to be a low-key single, however the biggest thing standing in the way of Moby at that moment was the return of 'Go'. Or a version of 'Go' on a car advert. Moby's dislike of cars had been widely reported. Indeed, even at this time he still only used cars if it was absolutely imperative, or there was no other form of transport available. Subsequently when Toyota advertised one of their new range of cars in the UK with a version of 'Go', he was furious.

On closer inspection, however, the track was not 'Go' at all. It was in fact a track called 'Laura Palmer's Theme' by FKW. When Moby tried to take legal action over the alleged lift of his music he discovered that he could not claim an infringement of copyright - he went on to say he was especially "angry [because] it's being used to sell cars."

As a direct result, and to clear up any confusion of the origination of the track, Moby reissued 'Go' with the original 'Woodtick Mix' and remixes by Jam and Spoon previously unavailable in the UK. The cover art included a no-entry-for-cars sign (in accordance with the British Highway Code) and the following declaration: "A car advert broadcast earlier this year recreated the music to Moby's song 'Go'. Many people thought it was Moby's music. This is not the case. We would like to make it clear that Moby's music was not used. Moby has not been and is not involved with this commercial and has not received any money from it. Had Moby been asked to use 'Go' he would have refused on the grounds that he would not let his songs be used to sell cars. 'Go' is available again to set the record straight. This single is available at a lower price than usual. All Moby's royalties from the single will go to the charity Transport 2000."

The outspoken attack on the car would become one of Moby's most recurrent stumbling blocks over the following years as his music was increasingly used on adverts and, eventually, on car adverts too. In 1996 he licensed the track 'God Moving Over The Face Of The Waters' (from *Everything is Wrong*) to the Rover 400 commercial. The proceeds from the track were given to environmental and animal rights organizations.

"There's something perversely satisfying about taking money from a car company and giving it to organizations which work to protect the environment," Moby said. "I figured that they were going to make the commercial with or without my music, so why not let them use the track and in the process help out some worthwhile charities."

It is in his need to present a defined and apparently unchangeable argument that Moby is most often caught out. However what is never in doubt is the fact that, at any given time, Moby fully believes in the argument he is presenting. The only problem lies in the fact that he changes his mind so much. Much like any other human being of course, except he does his opinion-changing in the public domain. It is for this reason more than any other that Moby's critics cite him as a hypocrite. That he changes his musical style as often as he alters his viewpoints has never helped matters.

As ever, with Moby's next outing he once again altered his sound. This time it was for a return to the anthemic house classics that had marked the high points of his career so far.

CHAPTER THIRTEEN

"I like dressing up in women's clothing. I'm not fetishistic about it. I don't get anything from it sexually. I just like to mess around with my identity. Instead of being a skinny little white boy." Moby, 1994

New single 'Feeling So Real' was released in October 1994 and it featured all of Moby's favorite tricks. It was every inch a classic Moby track, with a ragga intro from Kochie Banton and wailed Diva vocals literally exploding with the chorus hook. "Vocals are really important. I love the human voice. I don't know why, but I have my theories. When you're born the first sound you hear is a screaming woman, unless your mother was anaesthetized. So your most primal sounds are, first of all the heartbeat, which is like the kick drum, and then a screaming woman. So we've all been listening to techno ever since we were born."

And if the vocals weren't enough, 'Feeling So Real' combined the high camp of disco and house with the darker elements of dancehall and also featured junglist breaks, piano fills, turntable cut ups, anthemic synth melodies, a breakdown of old hardcore-style sampled guitar stabs and a live bassline which was a dead ringer for a previous bass workout by none other than Joy Division!

For the video to 'Feeling So Real', Moby chose to dress up as a woman, complete with black bobbed wig and bright red lipstick. Furthermore, in the press shots to support the single he was shown wearing a bra! With techno moving ever deeper into boys' own, macho territory – all sexuality removed – and Moby's deepening exploration of the emotional energy of gay disco, the image of Moby the transvestite brought his sexual orientation into question. "Am I heterosexual because of some biological orientation or because of conditioning?" he asked in a promotional film for his forthcoming album *Everything is Wrong*.

"For the most part, it's beaten into all men that from an early age you're only supposed to like women. I like dressing up in women's clothing. I'm not fetishistic about it. I don't get anything from it sexually. I just like to mess around with my identity. Instead of being a skinny little white boy, I can try to look like a woman, or, for the next video I would like to be a ninety-year-old man." Of course, Moby would have to wait some four years before he would finally fulfil this latter desire with one of the *Play* videos.

If Moby's intention was to follow a more eclectic path, then there could no better introduction than this. Ironically however, despite the disparate elements in the track, it still sounded like a hardcore house tune. It was either an act of pure talent that he was able to create this from so many fragments, or it might also have hinted at Moby ultimately being sonically limited. True, no matter how great 'Feeling So Real' sounded, there was still a nagging doubt that Moby was treading water. Sure, the production was much improved over those earlier tracks, but the fact remained that he was still in similar territory to tracks such as 'Next Is The E', 'Drug Fits The Face' and 'Move'.

The single also came with the gimmick of a competition for potential remixers. On one of the CD packages there were included the parts for the single to follow 'Every Time You Touch Me', so anyone could have a go at remixing the track. The winner was to receive $1,000 and their mix would be included on the next single. Mute also suggested that they would compile an album of mixes if there were enough good quality interpretations to warrant it. In this case each remixer was to be paid $500. It was the first time a competition like this had been run, although the Shamen included all the samples and effects from 'Pro-Gen' on their *Progeny* LP, saying something along the lines of "we're sick of remixing this fucker, so go out and do it yourselves."

It was an interesting twist on the remix theme for Moby. Only six months earlier he had said that he "hated listening to other people's remixes of his own work, because if they're like me, they use the best stuff for themselves anyway." Look back only a year earlier and he declared: "If record companies took the money they spent on remixing and put it into artist development, the need for remixes wouldn't be there as much."

Clearly this competition was intended as a way of putting something back into the dance community. However, there was also an aspect of it that seemed uncomfortably media-hungry. Almost as though the idea had been concocted in a development meeting by a marketing team trying to think of the best way to push Moby to the forefront of public consciousness. This is especially poignant when you consider that these singles were very much intended as a part of an overall strategy to promote the forthcoming album.

The single 'Everytime You Touch Me' was sent out as a promo at the tail end of 1994 and finally released in February 1995. The winning remix was by one Jude Sabastien. The aforementioned remix competition album failed to materialise, although a four-track promo did appear with mixes from Totalis, Quartermass, Dementia and Tabernacle.

If the video for 'Feeling So Real' had thrown into doubt Moby's sexual orientation, then what followed was even more confusing. 'Every Time You Touch Me' was supported by a promo film with imagery that verged on the homo-erotic. Moby, as ever is shirtless, while fingers stroke his chest. Although the attention comes from women, it is filmed in such a way that tapped into a certain strain of gay iconography. Heavily oiled and muscular bodies were reminiscent of Helmut Newton's photography. Furthermore the record itself evoked the spirit of The Paradise Garage like no previous Moby track.

"I like videos with romantic, sensual and sexual components to them," he explained of the footage. "Most techno videos are cold and computer-generated. I just thought it was nice to take a completely different angle on it. And I think its sort of like an ironic element in this skinny little white kid being involved in this sensual, erotic video.

"It looked like it should have been a lot of fun to make because it's me sort of oiled up, kissing models; sensual and romantic and being stroked, with me stroking them, them stroking me, feeding each other food and this kind of stuff, but it was just… it was like work."

Of the song itself, Moby suggested, "'Every Time You Touch Me' is sort of like a sensual love song mixing feminine romantic elements with quasi-spiritual. A love song to a woman that could also be a love song to God, and a kind of weird ambiguous combination of the two. A lot of times I listen to bad love songs, I think of them on a spiritual level of kind of like singing them to the person you're in love with, and singing them to God or whatever – almost turning them into a hymnal, anthemic type of thing."

In the years that would follow, Moby would further explore the range of this song by stripping it down to a simple piano and string arrangement. However, no matter how much he altered the structure, the song's sexual power would always remain. Perhaps one of the fundamental reasons why 'Every Time You Touch Me' had seemed at the time to be very much a gay love song was that this track, more than any other, underlined the void which was opening up between him and his one-time contemporaries in dance music.

As his 1993 *See The Light* tour had first shown, Moby had little time for the electronic artists of the day. In press interviews he particularly hit out at Aphex Twin and Orbital. The former because "he only seems to want to be friends with people from Cornwall [a UK county]." While his problem with Orbital (and many others) was that their live performance was, in his opinion, simply boring. Two bald men with lights on their heads was not a performance in his eyes. Of course, Orbital have proven to be one of the most enduring and popular live acts of all of the electronica brigade, with their ability to develop sounds to suit the mood of the night, along with their stunning backdrop films, creating an electrifying performance in itself.

However, Moby's problem seemed to derive from the fact that these white English electronic acts had lost all of the sexual energy that originally sparked all good dance music. "Have you heard Donna Summer's 'I Feel Love'?" he once asked me. "That was, and still is, *the* most sexual song. But it's made up of machines. There's a funny story about that song. When Brian Eno was working with David Bowie in Berlin [on the *Low* and *Heroes* sessions], he came into the studio one day and made everyone listen to the track in its entirety. When it finished he said, 'This is the future of music'. It was the first techno anthem. But these electronic acts have forgotten all about that sexual, feminine aspect."

Indeed, what had happened in the years between 1993 and 1995 was that the dance scene had became subsumed by rockist hierarchies. One of the many factors in this was the growing interest from the music press. Although many of the original writers still supported the original ethos of dance culture, this new industry demanded stars for covers of magazines. Where Moby had reacted to this by pushing himself forward as a performer, the UK artists were more reluctant to do so. This had much to do with the anti-star system attitudes that had grown through post-punk and early industrial electronica, which most UK artists had been heavily involved in.

So they were increasingly presented as bands in the traditional sense, with a seriousness that marked them out as proper musicians. The net result of this was that slowly this brand of dance music became an almost men-only area. Women, on the other hand, had largely left these dance events and gravitated to the far more visceral jungle underground. Indeed, at the same time as the *See The Light* tour was happening, the UK was being taken over by the sexually charged jungle raves.

Ironically, exactly the same thing happened to jungle as had happened to electronica before it. As the media got a hold of this vibrant new sound, the new drum'n'bass (as jungle became known) stars gradually disappeared into male-dominated musicality. The result was once again an almost women-free environment. The sexual energy again all but gone in favor of indulgent studio technique.

Where Moby's skill lay was in the fact that he was able to conjure astonishing tricks in the studio, but never forgot about the importance of that feminine side. His music was thus, like a representation of a rave, charged with the sexual power of male and female, unified in the common bond of the dance.

"I feel that things like 'intelligent techno' are indicative of people being far too sexually uptight," said Moby in 1995. "People, like Aphex Twin appear to be afraid of their own sexuality and exhibitionism, and have subsequently made a virtue of anti-sexuality and inhibition. So, because people are afraid to express certain things, they make it politically correct to not express them. What you're left with is something non-sexual and bland because the threatening elements of dance music, and indeed life, have been taken out."

CHAPTER FOURTEEN

"When I look back, I think of myself as being a didactic, narrow-minded person. Or at least this is how I always seem in interviews." Moby

Moby is not a happy man. Sitting before me in the sterile surroundings of his west London hotel room, exhausted from the never-ending round of promotional interviews, his frail demeanor and lackluster eyes present an image of inexorable resignation. Quite different from the Moby I met only a year ago on the video shoot for the 'Hymn'.

At this time he exuded an aura of positivity. Lacing his considered and articulate conversation with, at times, vitriolic humor, he seemed every inch the artist in control. Yet here, in 1995, with the imminent release of *Everything Is Wrong*, his first album for Mute Records, Moby presents the image of someone in the throes of questioning many of his most intrinsic beliefs. Defiantly anti-club culture, openly challenging towards other people and apparently involved in a personal war with Aphex Twin, a.k.a. Richard James, Moby seems weighed down with self-questioning and defensive insecurity. Just one listen to the album confirms this. To begin with, this collage of perverse style clashes drips with the kind of euphoria we'd come to expect from the "Iggy Pop Of Techno." By the album's close, 'When It's Cold I'd Like To Die', however, the listener has been taken unwittingly in a one-way trip into the depths of Moby's personal despair.

"Well, the final track perfectly sums up for me the emotions of almost quiet resignation," he says. "The song provides a nice warm environment in which to take all of your pathos and hurt. And, for my own emotional purposes, the album's structure was quite intentional because I wanted to be left feeling down at the end." This is how I read the situation with Moby when I interviewed him for the now-defunct UK dance magazine *Generator* in early 1995. This perception was largely based on Moby's less enthusiastic manner, and also the incredibly eclectic nature of his forthcoming album. In retrospect there were a number of things that I didn't take into account. He was jet-lagged. It was the end of a very long day of promotional activities of the kind that are enough to test the endurance of the most patient human being. ("More questions about being a Christian raver. More people trying to trip me up with questions I've heard over and over, and not just from journalists.") There was another factor. Moby had come to the end of a long-term relationship and his ex-partner was clearly still foremost on his mind. Indeed, so often did he refer to her that her presence was almost tangible.

It was true that Moby was questioning his most deeply held beliefs at the time. It appeared that either as a result of his experiences with Instinct, or due to the breakdown of his love life (or both), he had looked deeper into himself during the time he put together *Everything Is Wrong* than he had done for a very long time.

"When I look back, I think of myself as being a didactic, narrow-minded person. Or at least this is how I always seem in interviews. And I started to hear new arguments that would question my beliefs, which in turn made me alter my perspective. I know it's all a part of becoming old, but I think I lived in kind of an oppressive world... like my mind was almost closed, but paradoxically I thought it was extremely open.

"So, hard as it was, I sat down and questioned a few of my lifestyle choices. Why do I choose to be a vegan? Why don't I drink? Why don't I take drugs? Why don't I sleep around? I forced myself to look at my ethical understanding of the world, and I came up with a nice neat pronouncement for everybody. Which is essentially: whatever you want to do to yourself is fine. If you wanna take drugs, if you wanna kill yourself, if you wanna do whatever you want for yourself, it's fine. It's your body so it's your choice. So, as far as I'm concerned, the State shouldn't be allowed to make ethical restrictions on an individuals' actions as this action pertains to themselves.

"But any actions that individual commits that compromises or infringes the rights of anyone else, then the State is allowed to intervene. You're allowed to kill yourself, just not anyone else. You're allowed to do anything you want sexually, just as long as it is with a consenting partner. And the State should not be allowed to be involved in these decisions. For myself that's why I'm still a vegan, because if I chose to eat meat, or use animal products, that would be imposing my will violently on another creature. I don't mind getting drunk every now and then because really that's just an action that affects me. Its fun, I enjoy it, it broadens my understanding of the world. I actually quite value the different perspective that you can get when you are drunk – that is really healthy and beneficial. That's why I'm wary of fundamentalist, blanket statements about anything. Anyone that will say drugs are always bad, or drugs are always good; alcohol is always bad or alcohol is always good – I think its all relative, you know, specific to whatever context you're talking about."

Everything Is Wrong was released in March 1995. With it, Moby finally realized the album he had always wanted to put out: a multi-genred collection that ranged from thrash metal to haunting ballads, with a few dance anthems thrown in for good measure. So extensive was the sonic brew that previous singles had only hinted at how Moby would develop. To say *Everything Is Wrong* was a shock to even the most die-hard fans was an understatement.

"When I was signed to Instinct (because they were a dance label) I was only encouraged to put out dance records," he explained of the creative catharsis that the album represented. "I would come up with these guitar tracks and these, like ballads written on acoustic guitar in a folky, or classical, way, and they would just reject them. It was really restrictive to me. So when I had the chance to be more open I just took it. I had to."

Everything Is Wrong opened with a disappointing version of 'Hymn'. Unlike the single versions, this album mix lacked the rushing crescendos, in fact it acted more as an intro. What followed was the upbeat positivity of 'Feeling So Real' and the emotional angst of 'All I Need Is To Be Loved' (in its heavy guitar form). 'Let's Go Free', the first entirely new track, featured a hip hop groove and added an industrial-style noise which led into 'Everytime You Touch Me'. Collected together in this context, the previously released tracks provided an emotional rollercoaster - albeit one which rode a positive course. It was an ambience further backed up by the 303 and Italo-house piano driven 'Bring Back My Happiness'.

However in light of Moby's post-relationship state of mind, the first half of *Everything Is Wrong* took on entirely different connotations. 'Hymn' became an anthem to concentrated prayer. It was almost transformed into a search for relief from his sense of loss through faith. 'Feeling So Real' and 'Everytime You Touch Me' were love songs for the girl he had lost while 'All I Need...' was the sound of hurt and isolation. 'Bring Back My Happiness' was perhaps the most poignant of these "lost" love tracks in that it presented an air of upbeat positivity which was juxtaposed against a female vocal lamenting, "It's hard to let you go..."

'What Love' also seemed to deal with loss, but in this case the loss of youth. It was as though his recent life-changing experiences had forced Moby to look once again at the things that made him feel passionate as a naïve teenager. This road of contemplation took him back to punk rock. 'What Love' is punk rock's teenage angst reinvented for the techno generation.

It is from here that the album moved into territories that would later surface on *Play*. Tracks were more contemplative, moods thoughtfully downbeat. The atmospheres were almost meditational as Moby found solace in the warm and comforting blanket of melancholia.

'First Cool Hive' (an anagram of Love of Christ, and originally proposed as the album title) found another Joy Division-esque bass line caressed by a bongo-filled break, pulsing strings and a female voice humming a forlorn, distant melody. 'Into the Blue', featuring the stunning vocal from Mimi Goese, sounded like a cross between John Barry's soundtrack to *Midnight Cowboy* and the Julee Cruise songs from *Twin Peaks*. As a track, it depicted Moby's ability to create left field pop songs with a classic, timeless air. Throughout the track the recurring theme of buoyancy pervades, with vocals which seemed to accentuate the mood with their liquid sound. When Moby and Goese played the track live on *Later With Jools Holland* on British television, it proved to be one of the highlights of the show's history, so stunningly theatrical was the performance.

The next track, 'Anthem', further explored this sense of weightlessness. However where 'Into the Blue' centered on water, this track was more concerned with flight, the combination of pulsating bass and beats with sequenced synths in a minor key providing an incredible sense of rebirth.

The album's title track offered Moby's take on Eric Satie with its simple but effective piano melodies, while 'God Moving Over The Face Of The Waters' echoed Philip Glass's system music, New Order's more downtempo mood pieces and Roxy Music's 'In Every Dream Home A Heartache'. Once again, despite being almost overbearingly melancholic, the resulting ambience was one of great power and positivity.

The final track, 'When It's Cold I Like To Die', once again featuring Mimi Goese, took this mood juxtaposition to its furthest extreme. Lyrics begged the question, "Where were you when I was lonesome?", over an ambient score of simple minor chords. When Goese comes in with the words, "I don't want to swim the ocean, I don't want to fight the tide", you are left with the feeling that Moby had finally come to terms with his loss. Despite the depressing nature of the track's title and the song's downbeat feel, he seemed to have realized and accepted his limitations as a human being.

Moby had undergone a period of reassessment in his personal life, coming to the conclusion that free will of the individual was a fundamental right, as long as it didn't violate another's freedom.

There was, however, an argument that in this album Moby was forcing his melancholia onto his fans. Possibly even exorcising his ghosts before a public who would undoubtedly have been expecting an album of upbeat, positive techno - albeit, laced with that trademark pathos–laden, melancholia.

"It's not a malicious violation, like killing a cow where some empirical damage is done," he exclaimed. "To use a sexual analogy, if I force myself on a woman, it's a violation of her rights, but if we've mutually consented that we'll tie each other up, beat each other, experiment with sex toys, then that's fine because we've asked each other to do it. When you buy my album, I'm only imposing myself by sharing a part of myself. It's not like I've marched up into someone's bedroom and forced them to listen to it - they've actually asked me to join the party by buying the album."

With its combination of anthemic rave, speed metal, kitsch art-house soundtracks and neo-classical systems music, any party that would include *Everything Is Wrong* on its play list would have been a strangely eclectic affair. Of the ideology behind this wide-open approach to often-oppositional genres, Moby declared: "People do embrace many quality things without being told to by the marketing process. The thing is, people's lives are structured by purism. White supremacists, football fans, favorite television shows, music, clothing, whatever. This purist approach is anti-evolution because growth relies on hybridization. Sure people try to define dance music by an acceptable number of bpms - never faster, never slower, only sampled vocals, no live guitars - if anything, I feel there should be the 'pure' pragmatic approach to music of 'if it works, it works, and it doesn't matter where it comes from.' With life in general, you're free to do most things and, y'know, most legislation doesn't actually apply. You can walk down the street screaming, talking to people, singing out loud, and you won't get arrested. But we have these little internal policemen saying you can't do this or that."

In terms of his relationship with the listener, the biggest change that occurred with *Everything Is Wrong* was quite simply that he was not just trying to make people dance any more. Of course his ambient output had always demanded a different approach from his more dance floor-oriented tracks. However, what he was now doing was actively challenging people to break down their "internal policemen".

On the surface this meant that many of the aspects of Moby's music which had previously challenged on a subconscious level were now brought to the fore. In many ways, he was making his musical position almost too obvious. Moby's own vision of what an album should be like was challenging to the point of being antagonistic. Much in the way some of his earlier DJ sets had been.

"I don't write music to intentionally challenge people," he said at the time. "I'm more honest about it in the fact that I put music out in a more unconventional way, rather than aim to screw with listeners' minds – I only make music that I love and I hope that people can deal with that. Some people do use their specialized knowledge to ostracize people but I don't. I mean anyone can write a dance record, where's the challenge in that?"

"What I do challenge and what I hope to challenge are, I think, very different things," he continued. "In reality I may only wish to challenge people's musical tastes. However I guess I hope to encourage people to realize that it is possible to broaden the scope of their cultural influence. And, just as I'm interested in breaking down barriers culturally, I would also like to see the rigidly defined notions of masculinity and femininity changed. All types of music can be wonderful, all of these different cultures can be great and so too can all different sexual experiences. At the moment, I guess I'm trying to present a spirit of experimentation and sexual open-mindedness. I'm sure that God will understand this, but I embrace the idea of aware, sensual hedonism because people have been too wound up for far too long. And that spirit of awareness, open-mindedness, sexual experimentation, and so on is, I think, at the heart of my record."

In initial quantities of the UK pressing of *Everything Is Wrong* a bonus disc called *Underwater* was added. An ambient piece in the same style as the 'Alt. Quiet Mix', *Underwater* was essentially a five-part exploration of, once again, weightlessness. If 'When It's Cold I'd Like to Die' was supposed to leave the listener with the feeling of "quiet resignation" then these pieces of music delve into, what was for Moby, fast appearing to be a blanket of depression.

On the promotional film Mute produced to plug the album, Moby could be heard reading a list of things that were wrong with the world over the liquid and air moods of *Underwater*. The visuals were taken from Moby and Loeb's Super 8 film *New York*.

This list of things that were wrong was printed on the inside sleeve of the album along with two essays on things that concerned Moby. Although the second essay offered some heartfelt thoughts on what Moby perceived would be God's reaction to the near-fascist attitudes of the Christian right, it was with the first essay, in which he laid out the basic premise for the album's title, that we are given an insight into the dichotomies of everyday life for Moby: "By *Everything Is Wrong*, I mean EVERYTHING. I look around me – I'm typing on a plastic and metal and glass computer perched on a desk made from cut-down trees and toxic paint. I sit in a building made of wood and bricks that were taken from the earth on a street made of poisonous asphalt that was laid over an eco-system that thrived for thousands of years."

This insightful line of thought goes on and progresses to cover people's almost suicidal use of tobacco and drugs, the global dominance of Hollywood's pulp culture in the face of the breakdown of local communities, before urging us to look to our everyday lives for ways to change. He also says "the thing is my life is just a bunch of contradictions," with particular reference to his position as an ecologist who makes a living from making records, which as products are "basically toxic."

Unsurprisingly, Moby's sleeve notes were not taken as him trying to do his bit for mankind. In the British press especially, he was ridiculed for what was seen as him imposing his ideology onto his fans. He was thus painted even further into the corner marked "humourless, didactic preacher." His records, far from being seen in terms of their beauty and power, were apparently just soapboxes for Moby's sermons.

CHAPTER FIFTEEN

"If Moby has a problem, this footlessness, this lack of a singular style is it. One minute he's just a techno artist, the next an acid revisionist, then a peddler of piano house... just what exactly is he?" NME, 1996

If Moby had wanted to make a point about his increased lack of interest in the dance scene, then his activities in the remaining months of 1995 seemed to say otherwise. It was a period in which he rediscovered Voodoo Child, reworked one of the most contemplative tracks from *Everything Is Wrong* into a mind-boggling number of dance mixes and eventually released a mix album. In the end, however, it was to turn out to be a smokescreen of some magnitude, as little rocker Moby was about to rear his cartoon head.

In June 1995, Moby delved back into his Voodoo Child guise for what was an incredibly minimal, underground dance track. Called 'Higher' it was, once again, little more than a DJ tool, empty of all forms of individual personality. In many ways this type of track holds the same prerequisites of ambient. Here the sound, and how it will mix into a DJ set, is all-important. Subsequently the track will invariably be an extended, minimal cut where the sonic nuances gradually develop. The intention is to create mood over substance. In this case the mood is all about dancing.

Naturally this release proved to be little more than a diversion from Moby's day job. 'Higher' was almost universally ignored. However, when the next single arrived it was impossible not to take note. 'Into The Blue' had been given the remix treatment by DJs and producers as diverse as The Beatmasters, Junior Vasquez, DJ Seduction, Phil Kelsey and, most surprising of all, Jon Spencer of noise rockers The Jon Spencer Blues Explosion. The latter of these remixes came about after Moby had remixed 'Greyhound' for Spencer – the Blues Explosion frontman provided his remix in return.

Spencer's 'Into The Blues' mix stripped the track right down to a slow-burning rocker. Guitars strained at the leash, as though they were about to explode at any moment, while drunken slide guitars gently sway in the background. Although it was an interesting idea (and one that gave more than a hint as to where Moby's passion lay at the time) all sense of space found in the original was lost. The track may not have suited the Blues Explosion treatment but it was by far and away superior to any of the dance mixes. The main problem here being the fact that this was one Moby track that just did not need to be worked in the clubs.

The package of extensive dance versions did call into question the record label tactics at this point. Undoubtedly the album they had been delivered would have come as something of a surprise. Where Mute Records boss Daniel Miller would have been able to accommodate such maverick behavior, Elektra in the States would surely have preferred it if he had turned out an album full of 'Go' replicas. These remixes sounded like a label trying to market their artist on the dance scene, for which Moby had increasing criticism.

Even though the 'Into The Blue' single managed to reach #31 in the British charts, it made few ripples in the US. Ironically, the song was so strong that, had it been mailed to the media without the plethora of mixes to choose from, it probably would have picked up considerably more radio play both in the UK and on the other side of the Atlantic.

With *Everything Is Wrong* already the source for five singles (six if you include the US seven-inch promo of 'What Love'), it seemed excessive to release yet another cut from it. However, in September 1995, 'Bring Back My Happiness' was unleashed, once again in a multitude of mixes.

As a typically Moby single it certainly suited the new versions which ranged from 'Josh Wink's Acid Interpretation', which was, exactly as its title suggested, a 303 acid workout, to the 'Interactive

Mix' by Ramon Zenker of German trance pioneers Hardfloor.

At this point it seemed, despite rumors to the contrary, that the more eclectic side to the album had quenched Moby's thirst for guitars and ballads. His output had become increasingly dance floor-oriented, so when a promo for his follow-up album arrived at the end of the year, it appeared that his rocker days were over. That album was a remix version of *Everything Is Wrong*. A collection that never dropped the bpms, picked up the guitar nor strummed a ballad. Moby, it seemed, was back in the dance fold.

Everything Is Wrong - Mixed & Remixed was released on January 15, 1996. A two-record, non-stop mix collection which was attributed to "Evil Ninja Moby" (it was the first time that one of Moby's cartoon alter-egos appeared) "with two turntables and a mixer". Consisting of entirely new recordings of versions of some tracks, as well as many unreleased mixes, Moby decided to put the album together as a way of getting these otherwise lost tracks out into the shops.

"To make the CDs, I used two Technics 1200 turntables, a Numark mixer and a portable Sony DAT machine. The sound quality you get is actually pretty terrific; it's all recorded straight to DAT, using just a mini-plug! No XLRs, just two phonos going into a stereo socket on a Sony DAT Walkman!" he explained to *Mix* magazine.

"The problem with working on your own is that you have no concept of how much work you are doing. I can just knock out mix after mix, song after song, but most of it is never released. I just wanted to make something that people, in buying the record, weren't buying some arbitrary CD, but it was something which could serve a function or a purpose in life."

Ironically, after a year of criticizing the increasing ghetto-ization of the dance scene, Moby's mix set made direct reference to a number of different sub-genres (or ghettos). CD1 features hard techno, joyous anthems and quiet ambience, while CD2 covered New York hard house, groovy acid and melodic trance. "Yes I can see the irony in this. Having spent a year complaining about how ghetto-ized dance music has become, I'm now as guilty of it as anyone."

However it was an ill-considered criticism. The breadth of vision displayed on these mixes was just as broad as on the original album. The only difference was that *Mixed & Remixed* was all about getting into the minutiae of dance culture. Much in the same way that Voodoo Child was his DJ tools guise at this point, Evil Ninja Moby was a genre-surfing dance master. Furthermore, that Moby understood these different aspects of dance culture to the degree that he could master them all, meant that he had as great an understanding as ever before, of the needs of the dance floor.

One of the other interesting points about this album was that he was one of the first artists to present a remix set in this way. It is a concept that is extremely common now; however at that time the mix set was considered to be of less importance than the artist album. Moby, on the other hand, considered the mix set to be a new art form that demanded respect.

"I see it [the mix album] as a new musical form, the seamless mixing of music, but what I think has a lot more impact is the way it effects other musical forms in the way a DJ will approach making a record, or that records are made specifically for DJs to work with; and it's strange because I'm coming at it from both angles. I've been making music for twenty years and DJing for about eight years. But I can only speak subjectively about the way it's affected me as a DJ and a musician."

Of course, the album did get criticized in some areas of the press. In defunct UK indie magazine *Raw*, Sam Pattenden called it "twice as long but half as interesting" as *Everything is Wrong*. In an accompanying interview Moby was also asked "The remix album… wasn't it good enough the first time?"

Moby replied with a certain amount of irritation: "It's so different from the original album. There's no connection between the remixes and the original songs. There were thirty or forty songs lying around. It was a shame for no one to hear them so

I put them out."

It wasn't all bad though. *NME* summed up the album and its maker in glowing terms: "If Moby has a problem, this footlessness, this lack of a singular style is it. One minute he's just a techno artist, the next an acid revisionist, then a peddler of piano house... just what exactly is he? The thing is, it's his ability to specialize in *and* blend together every musical genre that makes him so damn vital. And here he pulls off the double whammy of demonstrating near-genius in yet another field, and validating every concept of remixing in the process. Don't you just hate a smart-arse?"

Melody Maker's Carl Loben said: "Moby is a man born to entertain and confuse, in equal measure - *Mixed and Remixed* is true testament to that. There's something seriously wrong if you can't find something here to love."

Born to entertain and confuse, perhaps, but at this stage it was more often than not the latter situation. Because just as the remix machine plugged away, another story was unfolding. Since the summer of 1995 Moby had been touring with a set which included a huge amount of straight-ahead punk rock songs. Among those dates was a slot on former Jane's Addiction vocalist Perry Farrell's Lollapalooza tour.

Stranger still was the fact that LA metal funk band Red Hot Chili Peppers had seen Moby and practically begged him to support them on a UK tour. Bassist Flea said: "We caught his show in Hollywood and were just blown away by the energy."

By the time the tour hit the UK, rumors were rife that the next Moby album would be a punk rock record. A fact which Moby was happy to confirm. "At the moment there's nothing electronic or dance about it," he said. "If I had to make a more electronic record like the last one, I don't think it would be very good, because my heart wouldn't be in it. This is causing a lot of trouble at the record company, because the last record and all the singles sold pretty well. There's a good chance that this next record will alienate everybody. Rock people won't, like it 'cos they'll think, 'Oh, he's coming from a dance background' and dance people will feel betrayed. So I'll only have three fans in the world. I might be calling you in a few years' time to borrow money."

His musical affiliations may have been changing - however, as one tour story suggested, it appeared that his ideologies were just as strong as ever. In fact he had now resorted to direct action, waging a personal war on the tobacco companies: Moby had taken to sabotaging cigarette machines in the venues and towns where they played.

"I'm wary of getting into this because I wonder how much trouble you can get into for admitting this kind of thing... in places like airports and hotels, I try to sabotage cigarette machines... in New York State, and most of the United States, cigarette machines are actually illegal, so I don't have to think about it at home. But whenever I find one I just try to unplug it, and just do something to try to monkey wrench the system a bit.

"A lot of rave culture in Germany is sponsored by tobacco companies. You get these Philip Morris raves, and Camel raves, which I just find so offensive. Catching kids when they're fourteen or fifteen years old, and somehow subsidizing things so they associate that with their youth culture - *yeucch!* It's disgusting. There was one we went to a few years ago which had this of Marlboro truck outside. We ended up letting all of the air out of its tyres.

"Really I have no problem with smoking so much as I have a problem with tobacco companies. Nicotine is extremely addictive, and the tobacco companies exploit it at such a level with no regard for people's health and well-being, and try and make smoking seem somehow cool and sexy and young when it isn't. If someone chooses to smoke, that's fine, that's their choice... I don't think it's possible to make an objective choice whether you smoke or not, because there's so much baggage attached to it." That Moby had such anti-tobacco convictions is no surprise considering the earlier run-ins he had with his British touring companions and their smoking habits.

At this point in time, Moby seemed to be in a state of turmoil.

Where his previous output had reveled in juxtaposition and eclecticism, suddenly he seemed to be careering from musical extreme to musical extreme. In fact, just as rumors grew about Moby's rock record he released a contemplative, beautiful, trance album... and hardly anyone noticed. For this subdued release, he once again reverted to his Voodoo Child guise, for an album to be entitled *The End Of Everything*. Indeed, at a time when his Moby output seemed to be surrounded by inconsistencies, Voodoo Child remained the only constant. It was his link to the underground. A stealthy outlet for the music he made which remained completely devoid of ego.

The album, *The End Of Everything*, was released in the UK on July 15, 1996, through Moby's own Trophy Records (a subsidiary of Mute). Initially it had been intended as an accompanying album to the proposed punk rock album. However, the record label decided that it would be better to give the album its own release time so that neither would compete against each other.

In the United States, however, Elektra decided not to sanction a release until the following year. When it finally came out on July 29, 1997, it featured different versions of the tracks 'Honest Love' and 'Dog Heaven' and also had slightly different art work.

"I think it's the best record I've ever made," explained Moby in 1997. "It's just the nicest, gentlest record. It's very emotional, melodic, very simple and naïve, and very functional. You can put it on from the beginning and listen all the way straight through to the end and it can either exist as musical wallpaper, or if you pay attention to it, it can be... y'know, very substantial. It's the only record I've ever made that I could actually go out and promote enthusiastically. It's the only record I've made that I can actually listen to all of the time. I honestly think that it's a record that could improve the quality of anyone's life."

So why didn't he release it as a Moby record? "Because I didn't want to have to worry about hit singles. I almost wanted to preserve it a little. I didn't want to expose it to the rigors of the world. It's kind of like a precious little thing to me."

The *NME* agreed with Moby's sentiments, calling the album "a seven-song suite of synthetic orchestrations, doomy mood music, and subdued rhythms that's weighty enough to fit an old movie about a knight playing chess with Death perfectly, it'll make sense to students of the esoteric and alienate anyone who wants a quick-hit techno buzz. A fine diversion."

The End Of Everything was an album in which Moby explored subtle trancey mood music. It referenced 80s synth pop artists such as Gary Numan as much as it echoed minimalist composers like Michael Nyman. Above all, however, it was an album of incredibly sensual, evocative soundscapes.

On the stunning 'Patient Love', he sounds like Kraftwerk, Laurie Anderson and New Order (again) all rolled into one. 'Great Lake', 'Honest Love' and 'Gentle Love' all echoed Bowie's *Low* as if updated by *New Gold Dream*-era Simple Minds. While 'Slow Motion Suicide' again evoked Bowie, but this time in his *Heroes* period ('Nuekoln' specifically) with its brooding synths and elastic echoes. Finally, opening cut 'Dog Heaven' and closing track 'Animal Sight' offered slow-drip Euro bleeps and pulsing synths to disturbingly portentous effect.

There is no doubt that this album offered Moby's most focused vision yet. That it was reminiscent of other artists was in no way a bad thing, as, in reality *The End of Everything* may have been a collection of messages from disparate minds, but it still sounded like it came from one voice. Indeed, so personal in nature was it that the feeling of eavesdropping on the most private of all conversations seemed all-pervading.

If this album slipped past the attention of most people, then the next album release was designed to capitalize on the hype surrounding Moby's move back to punk. On August 6, 1996, a mere twenty days before the first of Moby's punk records was due to be released, Instinct returned to the arena with a retrospective album. Called *Rare: The Collected B-Sides (1989 - 1993)*, it not only brought together some of Moby's finest hard-to-find early mixes, but also came with an extra album collecting together every version of 'Go'.

This double-CD set threw fuel into the techno purist fire as dance fans bemoaned the loss of *their* Moby to the evil God of rock. Indeed, so incensed were the dance fraternity that UK club magazine *Muzik* had already seen fit to include Moby in their regular *Hang the DJ* column. Next to a picture depicting Moby's head superimposed over a body with a noose around its neck, Moby was 'hung' for his musical crimes.

"(Moby) we were told was going to save techno and make it the new rock'n'roll. The first dance superstar apparently. A camera-friendly, stage-hogging crowd-pleaser, they reckoned... He gave good interviews but boy did his records start to stink... He is the Liberace of dance music, up there with Guru Josh and Scatman John in the laughing stakes."

Moby, it would seem, had very few friends left in the dance media.

CHAPTER SIXTEEN

"I started dancing pretty wildly to Iggy's 'Lust For Life'. Then I bumped into this guy on the dance floor and when he pushed me back, I thought - being the old hardcore kid I am - that he was up for a mosh."

Moby, 1997

On August 26, 1996 the long-awaited but much-ridiculed first single from the punk rock Moby arrived. Called 'That's When I Reach For My Revolver', it was in fact a cover version of an old track by Mission Of Burma. Even at this stage it seemed Moby was giving little away about his own material, the choice of a cover version also sending cynical shockwaves around the music media that his own stuff was just not good enough.

'That's When I Reach For My Revolver' was in itself surprisingly laid-back. Most of the verses featured tastefully plucked guitars while the chorus was lifted with the aid of distorted power chords. As a record, it hardly had the explosive quality of some of his techno material, indeed it was relatively sedate.

It is debatable whether Moby added anything intrinsically new or different to the track. Just like his aforementioned cover of 'New Dawn Fades', it seemed as though he was more interested in remaining faithful to a song he had loved. The only thing he added on either track that was distinctively Moby (apart from his voice) was a distorted, heavy metal guitar sound, which was used to full effect on the guitar solos of each record.

For the single, Moby was forced to drop the references to guns for radio edits of the UK release, coming as it did so soon after the Dunblane massacre in which a gunman killed a number of schoolchildren in a small Scottish town. "Neither the BBC nor MTV would play the song before 9pm because of Dunblane. I re-recorded the choruses to play the guns down a bit. I realize that the lyrics are provocative and I wouldn't want to hurt anyone unintentionally, so I was happy with the changes. It just wasn't a big deal."

The video for the single was perhaps Moby's most effective promo to date. With his new band playing center stage on a piece of concrete wasteland, kids were depicted all around in various states of boredom. It was an effective attack on the plight of urban youth, with little future other than drug addiction, unwanted pregnancies and, of course, crime. The latter of these would inevitably involve the use of handguns.

"The gun situation is insane in the States," he explained. "Anyone can just walk into a store and buy a gun. Kids of only sixteen can buy them. You can get these things that can kill people as easy as you can... buy a packet of gum!"

Moby himself was almost involved in a shooting around this time. "I was recently threatened by a guy outside a nightclub and it was a pretty heavy deal," he said, with a look of amused disbelief. "Some friends and I had all been drinking free vodka at this party. I started dancing pretty wildly to Iggy's 'Lust For Life', y'know. So then I bumped into this guy on the dance floor and when he pushed me back, I thought - being the old hardcore kid I am - that he was up for a mosh, so I slammed into him!

"Next thing I know, his friends have jumped on me, my friends have jumped on them and everyone has been thrown out by the bouncers. I was feeling pretty bad about it, so I went up to this guy and apologized, but he turned around and said: 'It's a good thing you apologized, because I was going to wait until you came out and shoot you in the head.'"

It wasn't the first time Moby's love of slam dancing had got him into trouble. A few years earlier, at the height of his techno days, he was in a club when he slammed into one guy a bit too hard. "I was twenty four. I was at a party in Connecticut and I was DJing and I put on an old punk record by Black Flag and started slam dancing with a couple of friends and I moved my head forward just as someone else moved their head forward," he explained. "And if you've ever been hit in the face, it doesn't slow you down it makes you go mad. So it gave me more adrenaline, so I didn't realize I'd been badly hurt. So I went back to put on the next record and someone came over to request something and their eyes just went wide open because I had blood all over the side of my face. But I'm kinda disappointed because the scar is going away, slowly over time." Happily for Moby perhaps, the scar under his left eye is still clearly visible almost a decade later.

Although the story about his near-shooting experience showed a new side to Moby, in that he started the night drinking free vodka, and thus had dropped his anti-alcohol stance, the fact still remained that his beliefs were based on an ideology of non-aggression towards others. So why exactly had Moby decided to record a song which seemed to support gun use?

Well, on the surface it was true that the chorus of "That's when I reach for my revolver/that's when I blow them all away..." seemed provocative. However the song itself is all about loss of innocence in the face of betrayal. A rites of passage song which faces the sense of despair and emptiness that plagues many people when they feel that society, community and family have let them down.

If the video talked about the wastelands of young urban America, then the single artwork depicted another kind of emptiness, that of hotel life. In it, Moby is shown dressed in a woolen dressing gown and slippers, leaning against a wall. His friend Paul Yates adopts a similarly hopeless position, leaning against the opposite wall in the background. At first the picture seems to be of a lunatic asylum, with Moby and Paul acting out the part of patients. A closer inspection, however, reveals the ornate decor of a hotel corridor. Moby's room is 425.

It's a desperate image, void of emotion and somehow spiritually bereft. Once again Moby is presented as an outsider although this time with an associate - no matter how far apart they are. It's as if he's attempting to key into the despair he felt as a teenager. Or perhaps, depicting the emptiness he felt following the breakdown of his relationship with his long-term lover.

If the single hardly trumpeted the arrival of this bold new

Moby sound, then the accompanying tracks merely added to the confusion that surrounded him at the time. 'Lovesick' was an average thrash metal track, played at high speed with Moby screaming vocals over the top *a la* 'What Love'. 'Displaced' was a gentle bluesy acoustic guitar tune while 'Sway' offered a down-tempo, ambient-style song with no guitars at all.

The second CD of the single package for 'That's When I Reach...' further depicted this confusion. In fact with the inclusion of a trance remix by Faithless' Rollo and Sister Bliss and a version of 'God Moving Over The Face Of The Waters' (as re-recorded for the film *Heat,*), it seemed that the record company had little faith in Moby's punk rock material. Of the other tracks on this CD 'Everyone Of My Problems' could have come from *Everything Is Wrong* with its thrusting beats, female screams and epic strings, while 'Dark' sounded like an out-take from the previous album thanks to the combination of junglist breaks and dislocated ambience.

If 'That's When I Reach For My Revolver' was supposed to herald a bold step into a different musical world for Moby, then little else about the singles seemed to back this up. If anything, the package hinted at a struggle between Moby and his record labels. Somehow, the freedom that he reveled in on the last album had been lost.

Only a month later all became clear.

CHAPTER SEVENTEEN

"I do have this naïve dream that at some point people will stop using animals for human purposes." Moby, 1996

On September 23, 1996, the album *Animal Rights* was released in the UK (the US would have to wait until the following February). If the preceding single had raised doubts about Moby's ability to rock, then this album laid them to rest. Furthermore the album clearly showed that Moby's songwriting skills could adequately translate to the rock format.

"I find an honesty in some of the rock music that is coming out today that I don't hear in dance music anymore," he said. "Stuff like Pantera I find to be creative and exciting... I just love the way that rock music reinvented itself in the face of techno to become this far more vital form of music."

Animal Rights was not however the straightforward punk rock album that had been rumored. Among the twelve tracks were instrumental ballads where acoustic guitars and violins explored similar themes to those Moby had already visited with synths and samplers. Furthermore, on initial quantities of the UK version of the album an extra CD called *Little Idiot* was included. It featured a further nine acoustic explorations.

The opening track to *Animal Rights* was one such song. 'Let it Go' featured a lilting violin melody over picked acoustic guitar in a style reminiscent of Crosby, Stills, Nash and Young. Yet, despite the unfamiliar instrumentation, the energy and ambience of the track were immediately recognizable as Moby.

The same could not however be said of what followed. Musically, *Animal Rights* was very much about first loves. Each track hinted at the bands that had inspired Moby to take up the guitar in the first place, even if the treatments were more inspired by the contemporary rock sound of the day.

'Come On Baby' sounded like Pantera covering Iggy And The

Stooges' 'TV Eye'. A full-on guitar assault competed with over-the-top solos and the finest impersonation of Iggy Pop's trademark scream to have ever been committed to tape. 'Heavy Flow' similarly featured heavy Black Sabbath-style riffing guitars complete with a middle eight breakdown that then erupted once again – as was standard in rock music of the time. The whole track was pushed by Moby's growled vocals.

'You' offered an update of Moby's early fascination for Flipper; 'Someone to Love' and 'Say It's Mine' were thrash versions of constant musical companions Joy Division. 'My Love Will Never Die' sounded, to all intents and purposes, like an homage to Bad Brains' *Rock to Light* period. 'Soft', on the other hand, echoed the relatively up-to-date sound of Metallica.

Just as *Everything Is Wrong* was designed to leave the listener on a low, *Animal Rights* attempts the exact opposite. It was an angry album with ever-present themes of lost love, betrayal and enduring faith (in the ex-lover rather than Christ, although in view of Moby's love of ambiguous lyricism it is probably fair to say that God was in his mind to some extent). However, the last two tracks seemed to offer an incredible ray of hope.

'Living' featured a slow groove over which a beautiful lead line was picked out. It was the kind of melody that Moby would normally play on piano, as minor chords grew through a series of flowing progressions. The final track, 'Love Song For My Mom', was an exquisite acoustic ballad evoking the opening track with its plucked guitar and violin arrangement. Once again a deeply positive song, despite its melancholic feel.

On the UK's limited bonus CD, Moby explored similarly melodic themes. This collection was called *Little Idiot* after a nickname given to Moby by his European manger Eric Härle. "It goes back to a time when I was getting offered all of these raves to play at and I really wanted to do them all. Eric just said to me, 'are you going to go ahead and do them all like a little idiot?' I just thought, 'Hey, I like that'. It kinda sums me up really. I am little, and I do idiotic things sometimes."

The nickname has subsequently stuck (it's also the name of Moby's publishing company) as has the cartoon image which adorned the inside cover for this UK double-CD version of *Animal Rights*. Essentially a caricature of Moby looking like a cross between Bart Simpson and an insect, it is an image which has subsequently endured many changes.

The first time this image appeared was on the previous *Mixed & Remixed* collection, on which Moby depicted a black and white "Evil Ninja Moby". Since then the character has taken any number of permutations including "Mobyhead" (a take-off of Motorhead), "Festival Moby" and even a little girl Moby.

"The cartoons came from a time when I was about eighteen and I was working in a record store. We used to sell all our records in these plain brown bags and we were supposed to draw little cartoons on each one of them. I was doing maybe, I dunno, fifty a day or so. Anyway, after a while I got pretty good at these little characters. And they've just stayed with me ever since."

Little Idiot depicted a far more recognizable Moby. It may have still featured heavy use of guitars but it was a contemplative version of the rock song. If Voodoo Child's *End Of Everything* was intended to be the quiet companion to *Animal Rights*, then this album must have been intended as the hushed underbelly of *End Of Everything*.

Where *Little Idiot* differs from Moby's ambient mood music was in the way that it displayed a strong and demanding sense of melody. Tracks were all short with defined, individual voices of their own. Unlike say, *Underwater*, which worked directly on the senses. The way these quiet, almost poppy, monologues interacted with the listener was, by their very nature, far more immediate then his mood pieces.

So, although not quite the full-on punk rock assault that had been rumored, *Animal Rights* still proved to be a commercial failure both in the UK and in the US. The obvious reason would be to suggest that his audience just couldn't take the guitar material. However, this would be too simplistic. The problem lay in the fact that Moby seemed unable to create the same level of power when he strapped on a guitar than when he hammered away at his synths.

"*Animal Rights* is a fairly reactionary, petulant record," he says of the album now. However, the main problem was that it wasn't reactionary or petulant enough. *Animal Rights* was almost too restrained; too thin. Song structures were largely self-conscious, and invariably predictable. For any long-time fan of Moby, such accusations against his music had previously been completely alien. Far from being an album of shocks as promised, *Animal Rights* was almost entirely unchallenging.

It was almost as though Moby approached this punk rock album like an uninvited guest as opposed to the usual stance of outsider with his own party to enjoy. Like an unwelcome gatecrasher, *Animal Rights* laughed at all of the right jokes, slam danced to all of the right tunes and drank far too much beer to fit in with the 'cool kids'. Much in the way that the young Richard Hall had experimented with alcohol and drugs in order to fit in with the in-crowd.

Surprisingly for what was his most explicit title yet, *Animal Rights* featured no lyrics that directly dealt with the subject matter. Indeed, the only time Moby had directly referred to his strong beliefs on animal rights issues came a year earlier on the B-side to 'Every Time You Touch Me'. Called 'The Blue Light Of The Underwater Song', the track started almost like a parody of the kind of relaxation tapes that include water sounds and calming voices talking in hypnotic tones.

Opening with the sound of waves and seagulls, Moby urged you to "close your eyes, relax. Feel the warmth of the sun and imagine yourself as a beautiful dolphin..." If ever there was justification for all of the cynics that had slated Moby as a New Age fanatic, then it was here in this track – until the reasoning for such saccharine words became clear. Moby delivered the pay-off line: "Suddenly you are caught in a drift net laid by commercial fishermen. And you start to panic." At this point the track erupted in a mass of chaotic acid squelches and techno beats.

Animal Rights, on the other hand, included no such references, although the CD booklet did feature extremely well-formulated and persuasive arguments on the subject in the form of his now traditional essays. "To be honest," explained Moby, "I only really called the album *Animal Rights* so the journalists would have something to focus on that was interesting to talk about. I was fairly sure that they would all ask me about why I was playing punk rock, but I wanted a way of also talking about something which was dear to me."

In the end, few journalists ever got the chance to ask any questions about *Animal Rights*, largely because no one was interested. Indeed, when the album was promoted in the UK, where he had previously received the biggest support, only one magazine was prepared to run a feature on him. *Animal Rights* seemed to spell the beginning of the end for Moby in the media spotlight. The press simply hated his new sound.

"When the dance press criticized me for *Animal Rights* it was just part of a great tradition of people getting pissed off at me for liking different types of music. I've been dealing with it most of my musical life," he says. "When I first stated playing guitar I was studying music theory with this guy who mainly played jazz-fusion. He also played guitar in a jazzy heavy metal band, which sort of had eighty-minute guitar solos, and he tried to tell me that, as a serious musician, I was only allowed to like jazz, classical, jazz-fusion and stuff like King Crimson. I liked the Clash and he was just mortified. So when I started a punk rock band, he came to watch us play and was so disappointed. He was like: 'All of those years that we worked together and you're playing Sex Pistols covers.'

"And then, I was playing in this punk rock band, doing hardcore shows and I was also into Kraftwerk and New Order, and Psychedelic Furs and so on. All of my friends were like, 'How can you like that stuff?' Then I started DJing, playing stuff like New Order, DAF, Test Department and also playing hip hop – and then playing early proto-house music. I'd like play a New Order record and then play a dancehall reggae record straight afterwards and people would get so offended. So I just got used to this. I just accepted that I love lots of different kinds of music and in doing that I'm bound to offend people. I'm not trying to offend people; I'm just trying to react naturally. I'm not trying to paint myself as a martyr, nor am I trying to paint myself as a visionary, it's just this kind of criticism is something that I got used to very quickly when I was young.

"So when people were shocked and offended by *Animal Rights*, on the one hand I was a little bit nonplussed at the severity of people's reaction. In some quarters of the dance press I was Trotsky, like I'd personally betrayed the movement. I kept expecting Lenin or Stalin's henchmen to come and visit me in Mexico City and shoot me. Is that where Trotsky died? Somewhere in Mexico anyway."

CHAPTER EIGHTEEN

"After five months of touring, I finally got back to New York and I was so happy to be back. I had a few months of going out and sleeping around. It was really fun. But I'm not a particularly successful flirt." Moby, 1997

With the disappointing reaction to *Animal Rights*, Moby decided to take the show on the road where the songs would make more sense. Stripped down to a basic guitar, bass and drums line up, he toured extensively over the following five months. It was a gruelling experience, but one which was necessary, both in commercial and personal terms. His live shows slowly won people over and the rock scene increasingly accepted the one-time techno artist.

At the time, while writing a review of his Electric Ballroom gig in London for *Melody Maker*, I pondered on his current position: "Moby's transition from hands-in-the-air raver to fingers-on-the-six-string thrasher should come as little surprise to his fans. He had, after all, a couple of years back, slipped out a single with a hard-rocking version of Joy Division's 'New Dawn Fades'; his *Everything is Wrong* album was littered with guitars and he rarely missed the chance to proclaim his dissatisfaction with dance music in interviews.

"So, are we to understand that the all-new Moby, the born-again rocker, has seen the error of his ways and rejected the rave scene? The answer of course, is a resounding NO! Like tonight's audience who are as happy in Goldie or Prodigy T-shirts as they are in Oasis of Cast garments, Moby understands that in the real world, it's attitude which connects bands, not simple generic similarity.

"Moby's musical attitude has always been centered around a thirst for energy. He was attracted to the rave by the spiritualism of the energy and when that dissipated he fused a plethora of styles, all energetic in their own way. Now he's rediscovered the skate punk of his youth, and the brutal adrenaline buzz that walks hand in hand with it. And, as such, there's little difference between Moby now and Moby then.

"As if to underline this fact, a number of the tracks played tonight are from the pre-guitar days. OK, so they're adapted to suit the new band, but the energy remains intact. 'Go', the rave scene's first worldwide hit, gets the power chord over haul; 'Into The Blue' is transformed into an Evan Dando-esque strum-along; even the happy hardcore classic 'Every Time You Touch Me' gets the treatment – revamped into a hardcore garage stomper that DC straight edgers would have been proud of.

"Moby is clearly turned on by it all. Bare-chested, with eyes bulging and neck stretched, he looks like a turtle on crystal meth as he runs through some rediscovered classics – Black Sabbath's 'Paranoid', 'Hendrix's 'Voodoo Chile' and, of course, Joy Division's 'New Dawn Fades' (echoed by Moby's own slow prog workout 'Face It') These are simply songs he's loved and this is what tonight is all about – Moby having fun, rediscovering a feeling he had when he was in his first punk rock band, drunk with the energy of it all.

"Which is why you know he'll be playing many of these songs in three years' time in a completely different style, still in search of that core life force of music, that all-important abstract element – energy."

This was a time when he toured with Soundgarden and reworked one of their tracks, 'Blow Up The Outside World', on his favored 'swaps' basis. He also struck up a friendship with Billy Corgan of The Smashing Pumpkins.

And if these two (virtual) endorsements weren't enough, he'd also been approached by two of rock's biggest legends for future collaborations or production work. One invitation came from fellow New Yorker Iggy Pop, who called Moby to suggest that they work together in the near future. The second came from Guns N' Roses frontman Axl Rose who wanted him to produce the band's follow-up to 1991's *Use Your Illusion* album. As if to underline Moby's increased standing, he was also asked to join a canon of artists (which has included Shirley Bassey, Louis Armstrong, Tom Jones and Duran Duran, among many others), in being asked to record a new version of the James Bond Theme.

"I got a message from Iggy on the answering machine the other day. And Iggy wants to get together and work on something," he confirmed at the time. "But it was like, I wish I had a tape-based answering machine, 'cause I had so many good messages from people. Like I still get calls from Axl Rose every now and then. And it's so disconcerting to come home and there be a message from Axl, you know: 'Hi Moby, it's Axl calling.' But the other day I hit play on my answering machine and it was like: 'Hi Moby, it's Iggy calling up, uh... give me a call, I think we should get together.'

"I guess the strangest message on my answering machine... I was in a hotel room in Los Angeles and I got a call from John Lydon. That really freaked me out, 'cause when I was much younger, I was a huge Sex Pistols fan, and the first three Public Image records I just loved. And he was you know, when I was fifteen or sixteen years old, he was my hero and role model. There was no one above John Lydon. Then suddenly it struck me to be a nice sort of post-modern experience to have my hero call me up and ask if I wanted to go and get a cup of coffee.

"Actually it was a very strange day, 'cause it was the day I was in Los Angeles and it was the day I got asked to produce the Guns N' Roses record, it was the day I got asked to do the James Bond theme, and then I got a call from John Lydon! I realized just how strange my career is, you know. Very strange."

In the end neither the G N' R or the Iggy offers came to fruition. But Moby did remix one of John Lydon's solo tracks ('Grave Ride') and also ended up accepting the James Bond offer. And these weren't the only production offers Moby was to receive during his so-called rock period. Talking in October 1997, on the eve of the release of the 'James Bond Re-Version', he told me: "The only thing I've ever produced for anyone else is a song for Ozzy Osborne for the *Beavis And Butthead* soundtrack. It was not... I mean it was an OK experience, but it wasn't great, uh, and so the only things I've been asked to produce are Hole. Courtney Love asked me to produce the next record and Rick Ocasek also asked me to help him on his new album and this band Clutch - they're this heavy metal band from West Virginia.

"The weirdest thing is that most of these people from the rock world are responding to the more like, instrumental dance stuff that I do. Rather than the rock stuff. Strangely enough I did get some response from the dance people for my rock record. I got a message from, I forget, one of the guys in Leftfield, when I first sort of put a rock thing out. It was the mix of 'All I Need Is To Be Loved', that sort of speed metal mix and I got a message from him saying how much he liked it. But no dance people called after *Animal Rights*!"

Subsequent to Moby's huge success with *Play* he has received a number of requests for his production magic. Among them came one from Madonna who wanted to collaborate with him. Moby turned her down: "I like to work alone and her version of 'American Pie' is absolutely awful!' he said. But rumors were rife that Moby had ventured into the studio for tentative early sessions with Axl Rose. The sessions allegedly lasted only a couple of days before the pair were rumored to have had a huge fall-out. It's something Moby has strenuously denied.

"I did go out to LA and kinda hung out with them for a few days and I listened to a lot of their new songs," he said at the time. "They were really good, the direction that they're moving in is really interesting. But I couldn't agree to produce the album because I just couldn't commit to moving to LA for that long. I know it's not the smartest move I've ever made financially, but I've got too many other things going on to relocate to California, although I would have really loved to have worked with them under different circumstances. [Axl] is misunderstood and more sensitive than most musicians. He's not the drug-addled misogynist that the press make him out to be."

Axl may not have been the man the media made him out to be, but increasingly neither was Moby. He had slowly gained a reputation for womanizing and drinking. Typically, in an attempt to catch Moby out, the media started to question his faith in the face of this 'normal' behavior. After years of castigating Moby for his ideology, he was now being criticized for his apparently anti-social behavior. For once it seemed, the media could take the moral high ground.

"In 1996 I was on tour for five months in Europe," Moby recalls. "I did a lot of festivals, went on tour with Soundgarden, did my own tour, and I don't like touring very much, and well I kind of did start drinking again. I actually think that it's a really worthwhile experience to be really drunk. You get a unique perspective of everything, a perspective that you can only get through drinking alcohol. I'm sure I have a much better understanding of myself, and my friends now."

And as for these rumors of the increasingly lecherous Moby? "After five months of touring, I finally got back to New York and I was so happy to be back. I had a few months of going out and sleeping around. It was really fun. But I'm not a particularly successful flirt. If I'm in a nightclub and I see someone I'm attracted to, I have a tried and true approach. It works every time. I sit there. I look at them a while, and I look at them for a little bit longer, then I usually leave. Occasionally I'll try and make conversation but fail. I'm fine if I'm introduced to someone but approaching someone out of the blue - I'm so bad at it. Part of that is because I've watched so many men do it badly and seen so many women respond negatively, and I don't want women to respond negatively to me, so if I see someone I find attractive, the chances of me talking to them are pretty much zero."

Despite his humility on the subject, Moby's increasingly flirtatious nature started to become more and more apparent in his dealings with the media. Indeed, midway through one interview, he asked the female journalist: "Wouldn't it make a great feature if the artist and journalist actually had some kind of romantic involvement? Have you got a boyfriend or a girlfriend? Are you exclusive? The one thing I'd hate is to make someone's partner jealous."

On discovering the journalist was a lesbian however, his talk became even more personal. "How's sex with your girlfriend?" he asked. "Do you use prosthetics? I'm ninety-eight per cent exclusively heterosexual. I can completely understand why women might be more attracted to other women. Men get better with age and experience. I had a really disappointing one-night stand in Greece recently; this woman wouldn't let me go down on her. Can you imagine not wanting someone to give you pleasure? Sometimes sex should be completely selfish - you should be able to give or receive it."

With each interview Moby seemed to become more and more preoccupied with matters of the flesh. Indeed, it was suggested that he took to his more relaxed attitudes in the same way that a born-again Christian takes to religion: obsessively. "I like oral sex, it's important to give and receive, I think," he would say, in varying versions to a number of journalists between 1997 and 1999. Could it be that he was making up for lost time?

"Oh yes, definitely I am. When I was young I spent my entire youth being ignored by the opposite sex... my first sexual experience was absolutely miserable. I met this very thin, pale, gothic girl at a party and we went back to my house and had bad sex as the sun was starting to come up. I was beginning to feel hungover, and this girl was so reserved and other-worldly, it wouldn't surprise me if someone told me she'd been dead for forty years! I almost have an inherent distrust of anyone whose first sexual experience was good; most of my close friends had equally bad or mediocre ones."

If Moby was intent on catching up, it seemed that he was giving this project more than 100 per cent of his energy. It was an aspect of Moby that called into question his attitudes about women, love and relationships. Was he just becoming someone who used women with a made-up set of ideologies to support his behavior?

"I know musicians that are always fucked-up in clubs and having indiscriminate sex with groupies," he defended himself. "I can't go to bed with someone unless I really admire and respect them. I don't want to disappoint anybody but I think I'm fairly normal in regards to my tastes and appetites. I'm actually a shameless flirt. I really enjoy it, although it doesn't necessarily lead anywhere.

"I was in a relationship that wasn't very good, and when it ended, I realized I had always viewed romance in a very black and white way, either somebody was my friend or they were my girlfriend. But living like that didn't make me happy. I live more open-mindedly now, and its wonderful to go out and flirt with people.

"I'm torn, because on the one hand I really like being single, and on the other, I kinda romanticize the idea of a specific monogamous commitment with someone. Infidelity is damaging and terrible and I don't have a hard time being faithful – that's the easy part – I just have a hard time finding someone I want to do that with."

So, had Moby ever actually been in love? "Definitely not in the conventional sense," he replied. "I'm perhaps a little too analytical? My ideas of love change all the time. One of the ways I know I love someone is if they do things I would find upsetting in others, but find quite endearing and lovely in them. I don't want to sound like Morrissey, but I don't know."

There was another side to Moby's openly flirtatious behavior. In many ways it had become his way of understanding the hundreds of new people he was continually meeting. Openly flirting, or talking indiscreetly about sex (as with the aforementioned female journalist) became a way of shocking people. Those who were offended by it, Moby had realized, were certainly not the kind of people he would want to spend his time with.

These shock tactics manifested themselves in other aspects of his social life. Not least in his attitudes to public nudity. Or more to the point, public urination. "I like people who aren't easily offended. I have this way of finding out if people - especially girls that I like - are easily offended," he explained to me just before the release of *Play*. "One of my best friends, Damian, has a girlfriend and we were out one night drinking and she went to the bar and there was this huge queue to the bathroom. And I didn't want to get up, so I pee'd into a beer bottle. And she came back and put fresh beer bottles down on the table and accidentally grabbed mine and was about to drink it when I grabbed it back and said no, 'cos I pee'd in it. They'd just started going out and her response could have been like, she could have been disgusted and furious. Instead she was just laughing and laughing, she thought it was the funniest thing. And I knew at that moment, 'you know, I like this woman'.

"That doesn't mean that all women have to pass a public urination test. I just like girlfriends to not be uptight about things. One ex-girlfriend, she got arrested twice. Once for nudity and once for public urination. How can you not love a women like that!?"

That Moby was an exhibitionist should have come as no surprise to anyone who had ever caught his live show where he would invariably pose shirtless. However during the support tour with the Chili Peppers, he took to performing naked, influenced by RHCP bassist Flea. During one interview (in 1999) Moby was keen to tell me about his exhibitionist tendencies.

"One time I was with a girlfriend of mine, the one who got arrested those times," he explained of his liking for the great outdoors, "and she lived on the second floor and it was a hot night, so we were out on the fire escape having sex. People started walking by and no one looked up. At one point we thought this was weird, so we started yelling at people and still no one looked up. I mean, if you were walking down the street and you saw two naked people having sex and yelling at you, you'd look up, right? No one did!"

Exhibitionist or not, one thing that he has admitted to openly is his love of social voyeurism. Not in any perverted sense, but just as a form of observation. "I'm a social voyeur. I love watching people and I love listening to people's conversations. One thing that really disappoints me, I've always lived with apartment buildings within easy view. In the place where I used to live I could see maybe thirty apartments from my window. But I've never seen people having sex at home! I'm so disappointed. Maybe its comic retribution because I've never really had sex in public view *in* my apartment, but whenever I'm voyeuristic and look into people's apartments, they're watching TV. I just think people should turn off their TV and have sex and do more interesting things so I'll be more entertained."

On the entertainment front, rumors also started to circulate in the press that he had developed something of a taste for strip clubs, and had instructed his tour manager of the time to organize a visit for him at every new port of call while on the road - these rumors are something he denies *strenuously*.

"Strip joints don't do anything for me sexually. I really don't go out of my way to go to strip joints either. But I have frequented them on occasion. I like to put myself in different situations so I can understand myself and other people, better."

One of these "different situations" he had experienced was with two dominatrix friends in a role-playing session. "I played the part of a jealous boyfriend who had to watch," he explained. Of course this had very little to do with shocking people. It had far more altruistic overtones, with Moby simply helping out some friends. That he was happy to be involved did however suggest that these tendencies were well developed. However, it is likely that this voyeurism was more an act of people-watching than for any kind of sexual gratification.

Moby's need to shock people did start to go way beyond

"peeing in bottles." There was one story that told of him attending a record company party, where he decided the bottle trick wasn't enough. Instead, he pee'd all over the sushi bar. Doubtless the fact that he didn't endear himself to any of the other guests would not have caused any lost sleep in Moby. He was more likely to have felt a sense of pride as no one would have been able to eat raw fish that night. Or possibly ever again.

Although Moby's increasingly public interest in sex had a lot to do with his open-minded approach to life, his more anti-social behavior suggested some kind of inner turmoil. Of course, much of it could be put down to his old punk attitudes – and his love of public nudity goes back to his school days when he admits he used to take his clothes off and run around the school corridors. However, in the background a tragic story was unfolding. And one which had an undoubted effect on Moby.

In February, 1997, Moby received some news which turned his world upside down. Following a routine health check his mother, Betsy, was diagnosed with lung cancer. She died seven months later in September. "She was a really special woman," Moby's friend Damian Loeb told *Spin* in 2000. "Just giving and kind and quirky and understanding basically, it was always the two of them. Then that was gone."

It would be easy to paint a picture of Moby turning into an idiot as opposed to the "Little Idiot" during this process of mourning. However, that would be miles from the truth. Yes, he had been doing a number of things in public that had turned him into a one-man gossip column. But these were things he had always done, albeit to a lesser extent.

Furthermore, the experience of suddenly losing his last living relative seemed to inspire Moby to rediscover the joy of music for music's sake. Rather than instantly dive headlong into making his next proper album, he teamed up with some friends and simply let loose.

Of these sonic adventures, one of the funniest was as a member of a lounge rock covers band. Dressed in black tuxedos, black button-down shirts, skinny white ties and over-sized glasses, the band who called themselves America's #1 Fun All-American Cover Band, took to the stage at New York's Coney Island High nightclub and presented an evening of "all fun, all covers, no original music guaranteed." The band was made up of Moby on bass, Keith 'Disque 9' Fancy on guitar and Mystery Guy on drums. The latter turned out to be Duke Mushroom, one the founder members of New York dance troupe Stomp. The band also featured Paul Yates on tambourine.

As promised, the set was drawn entirely from the 80s. Among the tracks played were Twisted Sister's 'We're Not Gonna Take It', Jim Croce's 'Time In A Bottle', Bob Seger's 'Night Moves', Kenny Rogers's 'The Gambler', Guns N' Roses' 'Sweet Child O' Mine', Nena's '99 Red Balloons', Neil Diamond's 'Sweet Caroline', Bonny Tyler's 'Total Eclipse Of The Heart' and Billy Idol's 'Dancing With Myself'.

Reporting on the show for webzine *Addicted To Noise*, Dakota Smith noted: "The usually reserved Moby howled the lyrics and paraded around the stage like fluff pop star Rick Springfield conducting a cheerleading rally. Like a mirror facing a mirror, the band was obviously a parody of itself; it was like listening to a cover band covering itself." Shelby Meade, Moby's publicist at the time, was reported as saying "Hot, sweaty, uncontrollable dancing. Horrible at moments, breathtaking at others."

"We're going to LA next week to start recording," enthused Mushroom after the show which closed with Bow Wow Wow's 'I Want Candy'. "It's just going to be fun recording party songs. To make a lot of money for our musician friends who did the songs." "It's always been fun to be terrible!" concluded Moby.

Playing 80s cover versions wasn't Moby's only outlet. He was also involved in a rock band called The Pork Guys. Once again Paul Yates was present alongside Tarquin Katis from indie rock band Philistines Jnr. "Punk rock as performance art," is how Moby looks back on the band, "fun and a lot better than it was supposed to be."

Moby appeared with The Pork Guys on a number of occasions throughout the summer of 1997 while a year later a seven-inch single emerged. Recorded at *The Anthrax* in Stamford CT, the previous summer, 'Nutmeg HC' featured four tracks pressed on transparent brown vinyl.

Moby was the drummer.

CHAPTER NINETEEN

"My favorite James Bond was probably Roger Moore (laughs). I'm just going on the one I'm familiar with because when I was growing up, he was, well, Live And Let Die. *He was James Bond when I was like eight to sixteen."*   Moby, 1997

There was, of course, a slightly more serious musical venture than The Pork Guys in 1997, Moby's reworking of the 007 anthem. 'The James Bond Theme (Moby's Re-Version)' combined the infamous melody from the original score with a fierce breakbeat, heavy-duty wah-wah funk guitar and massive horns, to create a powerhouse of a single.

Stylistically the single was very much in tune with what was going on in the UK dance scene once more. It was a big beat track which echoed many of the sounds of The Prodigy in its use of high-energy guitars and huge drums. If Moby had wanted to fanfare his rediscovery of the good groove then this was the perfect tool.

There was another side to this track however. Moby's critics suggested he was merely jumping on the bandwagon having watched dance music, especially The Prodigy, take off worldwide in the very year he had rediscovered punk rock. While Liam Howlett was busy reinventing punk for the 90s, Moby was just dredging up history. Now here he was back again riding the coat tails of the very people he previously rejected.

In retrospect this was an unfair criticism in that Moby had been extremely supportive of the eclectic melting pots that fired the big beat scene. Indeed, arguably his 'All I Need Is To Be Loved' predated many of the developments in this scene by a couple of years. The fact that the dance fraternity had taken up their guitars once again actually offered a sense of vindication. When he delivered *Everything Is Wrong*, the dance scene was trapped in a state of stagnant purism. With that album he argued the only way to move forward was by hybridization. Suddenly he was entirely justified in his argument.

"Yeah, the irony is not wasted on me," he told me as we sat in his hotel room on the first day of August 1997. "I'd feel vindicated if there was some contrition, on the part of the dance press or the dance community to say, you know, gosh, well, we slagged off Moby for trying different things and now we've sort of ended up in the same place he has. But, it's kind of like, a lot of pop culture tends to be myopic. So one year I get slagged off for playing guitars, and the next year everyone discovers guitars as if they're the ones that invented it. And I can't worry about it, you know, life is too short to get upset at the failings of other people (*laughs*). I'd rather just do what I do, and try to make myself happy through that."

Another aspect of this debate is that, quite simply, the James Bond Theme already rocks like a runaway juggernaut. The addition of breakbeats would have seemed obvious to any producer who had spent time making dance records. In many ways this was a track which was already produced before Moby put it together.

Beyond the simple mechanics of the track there was an irony in Moby's involvement with this project that didn't escape too many of his critics. In the UK, James Bond represents some of the country's less favorable qualities. He is a Cold War figure, standing for the British Empire. In him, Britain (or more accurately, Oxbridge Englishness) is depicted as more intelligent, craftier, better equipped and smoother than the rest of the world. Beyond any notions of racism and classism, James Bond also carries with him many sexist connotations. All things that Moby was supposed to be totally opposed to.

"To me James Bond was almost farcical and very tongue-in-cheek. You know, when I think of James Bond, the one thing that sticks out is the sense of humor of it. It's almost like a caricature, and sort of self-mocking, that's how it's always struck me."

Of course the self-mocking is in itself very much wrapped up

in the Englishness of the Bond film. That self-deprecating humor
being as British as the stiff upper lip. But at the same time there is
an elaborate grandeur in that the British are shown as always
having the upper hand over everybody else. According to one of
the subtexts of the Bond film, the British have the graduates, the
secret service and of course the imperialistic stance, which in
many ways undermines the humor.

"Um, well I'm not an imperialist, I'm not a white supremacist.
You know, I don't put much stock in the West over the East. I'm
not a misogynist. But the main reason I wanted to do it was that
I liked the piece of music. They asked me to which was kind of
an honor in itself. It's such a sort of archaic institution that I can't
and don't respond to it as any viable representation of ideology.
It's kinda like been around for such a long time and it is such
a caricature. I don't know, that didn't even cross my mind 'cause
I don't associate James Bond with any sort of political or
ideological overtones.

"It's funny, maybe if I was British I might see James Bond as
a more British institution, but I always just saw James Bond as an
institutional institution. No sorry, an international institution. But
I think this resurgence of interest in James Bond, I think it's more
of a playful interest in the style, you know, in that sort of slick
aesthetic. 'Cause I know in the last few years in the United States
at least, lounge culture has gotten big, you know, people wearing
suits and it's fun. I love putting on a suit and going out and have
a couple of Martinis and dancing to Nancy Sinatra. Yeah, I mean
it's playful, and it's kinda fun. And I think for a British person
James Bond represents much more of a British aesthetic. But for
the rest of the world it's entered that realm of the international
institution. Kinda like... the Beatles would be a good example.
A lot of the people in the rest of the world see the Beatles as an
international pop band, whereas if you're British it might be that
they're British first. Tom Jones is a good example (*laughs*). If you're
from Wales you know he's Welsh, and that's a source of pride but
anybody else in the rest of the world thinks he's a pop musician,

but who knows where he's from?"

So none of the subtextural themes in James Bond had, according to Moby, ever touched him. It is sure that, as an American, he would have a different view on the ideology of the film genre than someone from the UK. However, many of these themes are universally understood.

"I can't take it seriously, you know, I mean it's so goofy. It's fiction... the only time that fiction upsets me is when it reports or pretends to be non-fiction. Like the movie *Kids*, did you ever see the movie *Kids*? The violence, like the sexual violence, and the violence in that really bothers me because it was presented in a sort of *cinema verité*, almost like documentary style. That's upsetting to me, you know, maybe it's supposed to be upsetting. But obviously if you go to see an Arnold Schwarzenegger movie, and he kills 500 people, and it doesn't represent the destruction of human life, it represents a cartoon character."

A particularly pertinent aspect of the Bond genre are the sexist connotations. James Bond, it has been argued, represents Britishness at its most misogynistic and by carrying such ideology into the popular cultural marketplace, the 007 genre actually encourages such behavior.

At the time of Moby's reworking of the 007 theme, the debate about the effect that art can have on popular culture was rife in the UK. This was thanks mainly to 'Smack My Bitch Up' by The Prodigy, which lifted a Kool Keith sample and turned it into a breakbeat epic. Indeed, such was the concern over the track that the British Parliament even debated its apparent ideology.

"Yeah, I mean a lot of art can definitely influence people, and it can set dangerous questions," Moby considered. "You know, talking about The Prodigy, I can't listen to The Prodigy record 'cause of the 'Smack My Bitch Up' song. And I'm not a prude and I don't believe in censorship but that song really offends me. You know I have a few friends who have been involved in abusive domestic relationships. The week that Prodigy video came out I had to go visit a friend of mine in the hospital because her boyfriend had just pushed her down a flight of stairs. And it's really hard for me to take a light-hearted view of spousal abuse, or misogyny. So as much as I like The Prodigy, I can't support that record. I mean, I love the shock value, I love challenging people's aesthetics and morals, but that's really dangerous. 'Cause maybe you have like a bunch of fourteen-year-old kids in Ohio on the football team and they hear a song like 'Smack My Bitch Up' and for that moment it legitimizes misogyny and that's a really bad thing."

With the James Bond theme, Moby's record company saw the perfect chance to recoup some lost favor on his behalf. In order to remind people that Moby had been a serious electronic artist long before any flirtations with punk rock, and also to put him back where he belonged within the dance fraternity, they collected together a host of Moby tracks which had been used in films on a compilation called *I Like To Score*.

"I think, in all honesty, the album is designed more for America than for England. Like 'Go' was never properly released in America - some of these songs that are well-known over here in the UK might not be known at all in the States. And also America is a much more album-oriented market.

"There was the James Bond theme and I realized there were some songs that had never been released, like the Joy Division cover and a bunch of stuff lying around, so we figured, well, why not put it out? I mean, it's a sort of unplanned record. You know normally when I make an album, the songs are all written and recorded specifically for that record. Well, it's sort of a catalogue record, I guess, I mean you can treat it as a strange sort of *Greatest Hits*. Although it's not a greatest hits 'cause, apart from Go, there aren't any hits on it!"

I Like To Score was released on October 21, 1997 and was an interesting, if not essential Moby album. However, as an introduction to Moby's involvement in film soundtracks it was a very useful artefact. Moby had first had his music used on movie soundtracks as early as 1992 when his tracks 'Ah-ah' and 'Next Is

The E' were used on *Cool World*. Since then his music has graced numerous soundtracks. Furthermore, in tracks like 'Go' he had so obviously been influenced by movies.

When you consider that Moby was a keen film-maker (with his long-term companion Paul Yates) then it is fair to say it was perhaps inevitable that his music would become used in soundtracks. His style was already extremely visual and massively evocative. It is almost as though he has always dealt with music in visual terms.

Another distinguishing factor of *I Like to Score* is that it brought together all of Moby's different styles in a far broader sense than *Everything Is Wrong*. More to the point, as a collection it hangs together very naturally, underlining Moby's feelings that people can listen to more than one kind of music without feeling uncomfortable. On this set he put together rock, ambient, funk, rave, techno and all styles in between, and at no point does it seem strange.

'Strange' is exactly what people said about Moby when the promo shots for *I Like To Score* were sent out. In them Moby was depicted strapped in a studded leather harness and reins, being controlled by a busty blonde. The sexually explicit nature of these shots was not lost on a media once again asking the strangely right-wing moralistic questions, "Is it OK for a Christian to behave like this?" The humor in the photos, alas, was lost on many.

The James Bond theme may have heralded Moby's return to dance music; however, no one could have predicted what might come next. Throughout his interviews for *I Like to Score*, he talked openly about doing more film scores. He suggested that he might do an "unplugged" version of his songs. However the biggest clue came when he told me of his current listening habits.

"Over the last couple of years I have developed this really deep love for pre-World War Two old blues stuff like Leadbelly and Lightning Hopkins," he said. "I've got wonderful blues albums which I think are really visionary. I'm already finding huge inspiration from them."

So was his next album likely to be another punk rock record? "No, the way it's shaping up now, I still love punk rock and heavy metal but I've also rediscovered my love for dance music. If anything you have to go away from something for a while to see it clearly again. And I discovered even though there are some really despicable and hateful elements to dance culture (*laughs*) that we're all aware of, the positive aspects of dance culture vastly outweigh the negative. And the positive aspects for me are basically people going out dancing enthusiastically and people making really good dance records, and I had sort of lost sight of that.

"Last autumn and last winter I was going out dancing, going out to dance clubs and going out to parties hearing dance music and getting excited about it again and then looking back at my own musical output and realizing a lot of the dance stuff that I've done I really like.

"Then I had an epiphany when I went to see John Fogerty (laughs). Actually, this one night I went to see John Fogerty *and* The Prodigy, but not together! I went to see John Fogerty first and he was gracious and kind and playing songs that people loved, and talking to the audience and making people happy and it was wonderful. You know, like just a wonderful experience playing old Credence songs, playing his old songs and he makes such an effort to make people happy and I was like, 'Wow, what an important thing that is you know'. It may sound very clichéd and naïve, but if you can make music that makes people happy that's a wonderful thing. What a gift. And that kinda made an impression on me.

"Then I went to see The Prodigy. Once again, as much as I love them the first song they did was 'Smack My Bitch Up' and I had to leave. You know, like Maxim was like insulting the audience, saying you know, 'fuck you, get off my stage'. The contrast of John Fogerty being as kind to the audience and then having Maxim saying, 'fuck you, get off my stage before I kick your ass'.

"There's enough horrible nasty stuff in the world that people don't need to pretend to represent that world. Because I know the guys in The Prodigy, they're nice guys, you know, the world doesn't need any more people pretending to be tough, and I'm not saying that as a dis against The Prodigy I'm just saying the world doesn't need that. 'Cause they're wonderful guys if they just let themselves be themselves, that's terrific.

"But then we need the end of this long story *(laughs)*. So listening to the old dance music that I've made and going to see John Fogerty and going out dancing again made me realize I love dance music, especially the dance music that I make. It makes people happy. I had a conversation with one of my managers and he said, 'You know, the rock music you make is good and interesting but the dance music you make seems to make people more happy.'

"But rather than saying happy, I would rather say emotional, and so the next album will be melodic and emotional, probably, maybe more eclectic, along the lines of everything that I've done. Because I certainly couldn't imagine making an album of twelve dance tracks, and I couldn't imagine making an album of twelve punk rock songs again. So I imagine it's gonna be a nice, emotional, powerful, melodic, eclectic, record."

And so, in Moby's long-winded way, it was confirmed. The next album would be a dance album. Albeit a "nice, emotional, melodic, eclectic record" influenced by the closeness of John Fogerty and the innovation of old blues.

CHAPTER TWENTY

"The album definitely has a very specific melancholic quality, but it's not oppressive. When I finish listening to the record I don't want to jump out of the window." Moby describing *Play*

In July, 1998, I was approached by Mute Records to write Moby's biography for the forthcoming press campaign to promote his next album and associated singles. If his previous all-new album, *Animal Rights*, had left me with a number of criticisms of his musical direction, then one listen to this brand new material blew any doubts out of the water. No longer was he working the skate punk themes, instead he had amalgamated many of his ever-present themes of down-tempo beats, sombre minor-chord structures and epic, cathedral-esque strings, and added copious measures of hip hop flavoring and deep swamp blues. The result was the astounding eighteen track collection *Play*.

That Moby was headed into creatively inspired territory had already been made obvious only a week previously when promo copies of 'Honey' arrived. Possibly Moby's most obviously sexual song, 'Honey' took a sample of blues singer Bessie Jones singing the standard 'Sometimes' and laid it over luscious shuffling breaks, wah-wah guitar and heart-wrenching string flourishes. The glue that held the whole thing together was a repeated bluesy piano riff picking out a downlow bassline.

Almost inevitably the single was accompanied by a plethora of remixes ranging from the funky junglist beats of Aphrodite and Mickey Finn to the epic trance workout from Rollo and Sister Bliss. Such mixes were important to the UK market especially, as Moby's image remained tainted among the dance scene following his foray into rock music. Not even the big beat assault of the James Bond theme had managed to bring back those fans.

One listen to the pre-tape of *Play*, however, and it seemed certain that Moby would not only reassert himself as a one of electronic music's leading talents, but also win over an army of new fans. From the opening gambit of 'Honey' to the closing melancholic ambience of 'My Weakness', the album presented Moby at the height of his creativity, compounding all of his previous explorations into a cohesive and fully realized whole. Indeed, it was the first time he had fully achieved this on an album.

Despite only making up a minority of the album, it was the blues-influenced cuts which dominated *Play*. The obviously seductive qualities of 'Honey', the haunting passion of Vera Hall's 'Trouble So Hard' as sampled on 'Natural Blues' and the deep spirituality of 'Find My Baby' which featured a sample of Blue Boy's recording of 'John Lee's Rock'. All inspired and sampled from the field recordings of musical archivists Alan Lomax and his father John. These historians spent years scouring the small towns of America's deep south in order to amass a considerable recorded archive of the indigenous black music of the United States. It was through a subsequent compilation of these field recordings called *Sounds Of The South*, released in the mid-50s, that Moby discovered the music. He had been lent the compilation by a friend a few years previously and had long considered sampling aspects of those tracks.

Other blues-fuelled tracks included the gospel-tinged 'Why Does My Heart Feel So Bad?' with its recording of the Shining Light Gospel Choir, and 'Run On' which in fact sampled from a recording by Bill Landford and the Landfordaires called 'Run On For A Very Long Time'. Moby's initial inspiration, however, came from a version recorded by Elvis Presley in his earlier years.

Perhaps one of the reasons that these blues tracks seemed to dominate the album was due to the fact that on many of the others, Moby seemed to be intent on updating the blues for his own needs. Cuts like the gloriously contemplative 'Porcelain' or the aching lament of 'Why Does My Heart Feel So Bad?' tapped directly into the same optimistic sadness at the heart of the blues.

"The recordings made around those field recordings were

actually a very small part of the recording process," explained Moby. "Although they figure very prominently on the album, in the wider scheme of things they were only a minimal part of the entire recording."

Indeed, the entire recording amounted to some 200 tracks. Although Moby had a number of moments of self-doubt while creating *Play*, it cannot be said that he let such matters affect his work-rate. "Out of these 200," explained Moby, "about forty were punk rock songs, thirty were faster techno/house things and I also made about twenty straightforward pop songs, because I have in the back of my mind this anonymous pop project. I knew that I didn't want to make an album from any of these styles this time. After the last album, *Animal Rights*, which was very aggressive, I wanted this album to be more inviting. Still very personal and emotional but a little bit warmer and less self-indulgent."

Of the remaining tracks, some sixty were quieter instrumentals. From these Moby chose his favorites to appear on the album. These included the folksy picked guitar and hummed vocal of 'Everloving' which emerges from a sea of moody pianos and somber strings; the film soundtrack-style 'Inside' with its ghostly tone, distant echoing choral effects and simple piano melody. Another notable track in this section of the album was 'Guitar Flute & String' which featured the instruments of its title in a gorgeous yet dark piece, reminiscent of Canadian folk artist Leonard Cohen's first two albums.

"I'm in love with string-piano combinations," Moby revealed. "I go back to it a lot because I feel I can accomplish a lot. I also go back to flute or woodwind quite a lot. I just love the way they sound together." If these instrumental tracks had a certain somber air to them, then this was only added to by the tracks in which Moby himself added vocals. The lyrics were seemingly exhortations of a man in the depths of depression. On 'The Sky Is Broken', a song of lost love and isolation, Moby talked of the rain washing away his very presence, to the beat of a desolate drum break and piano motif, until the spirit of the track was lifted by one of Moby's trademark minor key string fills. 'If Things Were Perfect' (originally titled 'Good Love') brought together downtempo beats, slow-hand scratching, a gospel-style vocal begging the line "give me summer" and a bassline once again reminiscent of Joy Division. Over this, Moby again offered lyrics of loneliness. He also reintroduced one of his recurring themes: that of coldness. In fact it is a theme he also explored on the more uptempo cut 'Machete' in which he sang through a vocoder, "Yesterday I felt so cold I thought I was going to die" (echoing the closing track from *Everything Is Wrong* called 'When It's Cold I'd Like to Die').

"I wouldn't say I was obsessed with the cold," he argued. "I like the way that things shut down in the cold. Kinda like the way, in New York, when it's really cold, there's this silence almost. 'If Things Were Perfect' was inspired by this one night about three years ago. I went for a walk at about 3am. It was in January and it was just the coldest night of the year, bitterly, bitterly cold. And New York at night is sorta desolate.

Any suggestions that the lyrical content of *Play* was the work of Moby at his most personal was, according to Moby himself, completely untrue. His lyrics are, he argued, intended to be more ambiguous. "[The lyrics] are not personal in that they're not about anything specific. They're based on certain things but they're descriptive of more ambiguous idealized things. Every song to me has a theme. Roughly they're all about something but they're not specifically about something. I mean 'Porcelain' is sort of like a simple love song about romance gone awry. But the lyrics for that are so simple that there's little evolutionary psychology thrown in there.

"'Southside' – actually I feel dumb talking about what the songs are about because maybe they can be about different things to different people – but essentially 'Southside' is supposed to be about being in some post-apocalyptic gang. It's a post-apocalyptic gang song where the world has destruction and violence as a natural part of life."

Despite the inclusion of the big beat-inspired 'Bodyrock' with its sample of Spoony G and the Treacherous 3's 'Love Rap', and the indie pop-rock energy of 'Southside', the overall theme on *Play* is an almost overpowering sense of melancholy. Yet the album never delves into the self-indulgent territory usually associated with more somber music. In many ways, what Moby tapped into on *Play* was the universal need for depressing art forms. Music (or any other creative form) allows people a space to purge themselves, or creates a space for catharsis or release. As a result, creative contemplation can be as addictive as church confession.

"The album definitely has a very specific melancholic quality," he agreed, "but it's not oppressive. When I finish listening to the record I don't want to jump out of the window, I don't feel depressed. But my favorite records are melancholic, or somber at least. It's that age-old conundrum of why does feeling bad make us feel so good? Why is *Titanic* such a popular movie and why did that Celine Dion song sell ten trillion copies when it's actually a real depressing song? It's a real tear-jerker. Why do people feel good when they're crying? I know I do.

"Before I started work on this album, I was thinking about the records that I loved and what purpose they served in my life. It's kind of like a three or four-fold purpose. On the one hand you want to play a record that has some kind of emotional communication, while you also want a record that can create an atmosphere that is almost separate, but connected to what it's communicating. And my favorite records are warm, whether it's like early Roxy Music, or Nick Drake, Massive Attack's 'Protection', or Prince's 'Purple Rain, or 'Closer' by Joy Division, all records that are quite inviting, sonically, atmospherically, they're inviting. I wanted to make something which was warmer and more inviting."

Despite being Moby's finest work to date, there still seemed to be an air of resignation about the album. At this pre-promotion, tape copy-only stage, no one seemed to believe that *Play* was going to be huge. Moby himself expected it to be largely ignored, selling modest amounts to his fans. Indeed, Elektra, his record company in the US, showed a classic case of cold feet when presented with the album. They decided not to option another album from him and he was effectively dropped from his domestic label.

CHAPTER TWENTY ONE

"I've read an interview with DJ Shadow where he's said that he wants to master ever single thing about the sampler and be like the sample king. I'm not at all like him." Moby, 1997

Ironically the first single from *Play*, 'Honey' told its own story about the making of the album. Throughout the process of recording the new album, Moby was stricken with periods of intense self-doubt. It was a situation which drove him to chase a number of different alternatives.

At first he attempted to record tracks in expensive studios. He had a clear idea of the sound he wanted for the record and felt he would not be able to achieve it in his home studio. However, using outside studios was not entirely fruitful.

"Every record I've ever made I've done everything myself. Mainly because whenever I work with other people in other studios, I get kind of nervous. This is because I've been working by myself since 1983 when I had a little Mattell drum machine and a Task M four-track which set up my basic methodology of working, and when I go into an outside studio, I have that added pressure of having to do something good because I've just spent $2,000 a day on it. At home I can spend a week and get garbage and not feel bad about it. While I was recording these tracks I always felt this immense pressure to produce something exceptional. I kinda felt that these external pressures were blocking the creative process."

Often these sessions in expensive studios were with the simple aim of mixing the tracks he had already recorded at home. Yet even here the process was fraught with problems, forcing Moby into a creative depression from which he found it increasingly difficult to escape. So he enlisted the help of other producers to mix the tracks for him. Again the majority of the resulting mixes were simply not what he hoped for. 'Honey', however, was one of the success stories.

For this track he called upon Beastie Boys producer Mario Caldato Jnr. Perhaps due to the fact that Mario was already fully experienced in working magic with the Beastie's eclectic melting pot, he was able to bring together all of the disparate elements of Moby's original recordings into a cohesive vision. Furthermore, his apparently innate sense of rhythm helped to add a funky underbelly to 'Honey', subsequently underlining the track's intrinsically sexual imagery.

Of the other tracks on the album, only 'Natural Blues' and 'Southside' came from these external mixing sessions. In the former's case, Moby brought in the UK's Sheffield-based production team All Seeing I. For this mix they called themselves I Monster although, as The All Seeing I, they had been responsible for the haunting house tune 'Beat Goes On'. A huge hit in the UK, it featured a sample of a young Tina Turner, and was in itself very similar in style to the blues sample-based tracks on *Play*. 'Southside' on the other hand was a Moby mix, but was executed in an outside studio equipped with a Solid State Logic mixing desk. The final version would have been impossible to mix in Moby's studio.

"These days there's so much to know about engineering in the studio," said Moby in 1999. "With 'Southside', I went into this studio with SSL. I'd always found them quite daunting but I succeeded and thought, 'Wow, I'm like a real engineer now'. It'll be interesting in like twenty to thirty years, to autopsy the brains of sound engineers from the late 20th century!"

Of the other producers approached during these times of self-doubt, perhaps the most notable was Prodigy main-man Liam Howlett. Moby explained: "When you're working by yourself you can lose objectivity so quickly and molehills become mountains. Like I'll be working on a song and if I can't get the kick drum to sound right I'll think I'm a failure. I'll walk around Manhattan like mourning my fate. It doesn't matter that I've made lots of records in the past. All that matters is that I can't get one kick drum right. And all I can think is that my career's over and I'm going to have to become a fries chef at McDonalds.

"Anyway on one of these nights that I was just walking around Manhattan, I just thought I'd listen to a mix that I'd done. Then I thought it would be kinda fun to play The Prodigy's *Fat Of The Land* straight after. And I was just totally depressed about it. I felt like a total failure. *Fat Of The Land* is such a remarkable sounding record and it sounded about a million times better than what I'd done. So I asked Liam if he'd be interested in mixing some, or all, of the album but he was too busy. It was a fortunate thing in the end because I am really happy with the way the album turned out." Ironically, all of Liam's Prodigy material was recorded and produced in a home-based studio, employing similar basic techniques to those used by Moby, and using similarly basic equipment.

"I've been playing music for twenty five years now, so I don't think about the process that much," Moby explained as we walked into his studio. "It's got to the point where it's neither an intellectual nor a visceral process. It's just something immediate and almost automatic."

In 1999, Moby's home studio was swamped by two things: fly posters advertising all of his albums and singles, and his Soundcraft desk. Along one wall sat a rack of keyboards while his samplers and effects stood in a single tower. Next to the desk sat two Apple Macs. However it was the older model he reached for to demonstrate the tools of his trade.

"Isn't it pathetic," he laughed, "I have this brand new Macintosh *G3* and I'm still using an old *IICi*. My friends think I'm a retard. I bought the brand new *Cubase VST* for the *G3* and I don't like it. This old version from about 1993 on my *IICi* has like these four different built-in shuffle parameters and it just feels livelier."

As you might expect, Moby's studio seemed to have an energy all of its own. A small but comfortable space, perfectly set up for hours of solitary recording sessions. It was also the only place in his apartment that was not ordered to the point of obsession. Each corner seemed to house another piece of kit, each nook apparently hiding an equipment graveyard.

"In 1987 when I was messing around with my *TR606* and my Casio *CZ101*, all I wanted was more equipment," he said of his studio set-up. "I'd read magazines and look in the stores and drool over things. I'd be like, 'If only I could afford a *Midiverb*, everything would be fine'. I used to know my equipment inside out. But now that I've got loads of gear, I'm not so into pulling stuff apart. I'll even stick with the factory presets on the synths."

With his Apple Mac up and running *Cubase* software, he pointed to his collection of samplers; all of which were used in tandem in order to create as much sampling time as possible for *Play*. "I have this Akai museum in here," he said, pointing to the array of Akai samplers. "I bought the *S950* in 1990. In 1993 I bought an *S1000* and then two years ago I bought the *S3200*. For this album I decided that I wanted to create as much sample space as possible so I bought the *S3000*. So I have pretty much every Akai sampler they made between 1989 and 1998. Now they have all these big huge crazy ones with the removable face-plates but I don't have any of those.

"One of the reasons I bought the extra sampler was for the memory. For the album *Everything Is Wrong*, every song had a completely different set-up. Different sample discs, different everything. With this record I wanted to create this huge palette of sounds to choose from, so I could just load it up and start playing rather than spend twenty minutes loading a song." To the uninitiated, of course, one sampler is much the same as another. However, for Moby, each different Akai has its own strengths. As such, each one was employed on *Play* to its best advantage.

"To me the *1000*, *3000* and the *3200* are pretty much the same machine. There's a world of difference between them and the *S950* but those three are pretty much the same. The differences are subtle. I mean the *3200* is a waste of time for me. It does all these things that I'll never do. The *950* is a wonderful machine. It's really special for looping samples. For some reason it's just more intuitive," he said.

Samplers are also intrinsic to the way Moby created the rhythm for his music. Where many artists would use the machine to lift entire breaks from other recordings then simply loop them, Moby has generally sampled individual drum sounds from his record collection.

"I tend to use the sampler as a drum machine by sampling drum sounds from my favorite hip hop, jazz, rock or house records," he says. "There are some loops on the record, but generally you get so much more flexibility from sampling the sounds and building your own breaks."

Also he generally sticks to, or certainly re-uses those favorite drum sounds already sampled. Indeed, unlike many of the producers to have emerged from the rave scene, he is relatively disinterested in the twists and turns in sampling studio trickery. For him the song remains paramount, the sampler merely an instrument through which he is able to bring his ideas to life. As a result, in terms of production technique, Moby's material is surprisingly straightforward.

"I've read an interview with DJ Shadow where he's said that he wants to master ever single thing about the sampler and be like the sample king. I'm not at all like him. My approach is pretty rudimentary. I sample things, then I use the sample. The only thing I do tend to do is play with the filters. The 3200 has two filter banks which I really like. You can send things like an LFO to the filters. On the track 'My Weakness' from the latest album, I have this African choral vocal which has just been filtered to death. Now it bears no relation to the original. And there's a song called 'Down Slow', and it's got this drum loop which has been really manipulated through the filter banks. But that's about as far as I go into the trickery."

The foundation of all electronic music production is in the choice of sequencing software. For so many artists, this is an area of huge debate, indeed it is possible to chart the growth and development of dance music through the technological improvement of sequencers. For Moby however, usability is the most important thing. Less the eager tech-head, he's far happier sticking to what he knows. In his case, that's *Cubase*.

"When I bought my first Macintosh the guy who sold it to me recommended *Cubase*. So I went with that. Basically I've never used anything else since," he explained in a matter of fact manner. "Until 1991 I used an Alesis *MMT8*, a potato chip sequencer that I love. It's a wonderful piece of equipment but so limited. I loved the way it was parts-based rather than being linear like *Cubase*. It's really easy to make monotonous music on modern sequencers like *Cubase* as opposed to thinking about linear blocks and segments. Sometimes, for me, it's the limitations of a piece of equipment that make the composition so special. The piano will always sound just like a piano but that limitation makes a piano wonderful. The only piece of equipment that comes close to being limitless is the sampler. The only real limitations are what we as humans bring to it."

With all the studio running, he then turned to his keyboards and played a few of his key string motifs from past recordings. From 'Go' to 'Hymn', he demonstrated both the simplicity and the power of the string sounds he has looked to time and again. "I have a sort of like stereotypical string sound on the SY22. I use the same two patches for everything. For bass sounds I use the *Juno 106* and occasionally the *Waldorf Pulse Plus*. The *Juno* is nice because it's so flexible."

Indeed, just as he often uses similar drum sounds, then the favored use of a particular string sound is one of the ways in which he has created a sonic unity in his recordings. Listening back to his whole output a definite link exists between each album and single.

Despite Moby's apparently well-defined working methods, he has made a few mistakes when buying equipment. Much in the same way he used to believe that a new Alesis *Midiverb* would improve his music overnight, so he has continued to buy kit in a search for improvement. Obviously this is a natural trait of any studio-based musician, yet in Moby's case it offers an insight into the mind of the man who would walk the streets of Manhattan at night, fretting about his songs. Central to the way he makes music is a basic insecurity. An insecurity which has driven him to invest in a number of redundant pieces of equipment.

"I do have a graveyard which I haven't looked at in a long time because it's so depressing," he said. "The Roland *GP100* guitar pre-amp/processor entered the graveyard really quickly because it's got unusable sounds. It was cool in the show room, but when I got it home it sounded too Japanese. Not that I'm anti-Japanese. Another mistake was this *Drawmer EQ*. I got the idea that I needed a valve EQ so it bought this. It's really expensive, and it's good but I never use it. There's loads more like this. And I'm sure there's more to come."

CHAPTER TWENTY TWO

"Bar a few isolated outbreaks of talent, it's all rubbish."

                    Melody Maker reviewing *Play*

It seemed to come from nowhere. An invisible force sliding through the back door. A ghost in the cultural machine, seen but unseen, working its potent magic with a slow-burning ferocity. Some saw it appear. Some welcomed it with open hearts. But they made up a pathetic minority against the huge, lumbering strength of the critical majority. Believers were just cast aside as mindless fools, idiots with no real ability to read and understand anything deeper than a soap commercial.

Despite the blind indifference from the cultural gatekeepers the force grew of its own volition. Gradually building up momentum and shifting into the greater subconscious of society. It became a shadow on the ether, moving through the airwaves like a stealthy messenger. It melted over television adverts, flowed through the fades of the movie world and slowly spread its spectral fingers across the airwaves. And then, a year after it had first emerged, the force finally seemed to have dominated the planet. It poured through every radio station, every TV corporation soundtracking the hustle of life. No movie seemed untouched. It seemed omnipresent.

That unseen force, the sinuous presence, which seemingly caught the entire world in state of cultural narcolepsy, was an album called *Play*.

While 'Honey' reignited the UK's interest in Moby, its release was overshadowed by the lack of a US label. The situation was not a desperate one however, as a number of imprints were interested in him. In the end, V2 signed Moby for the US and Canada. However, it wasn't until May 4, 1999, almost a year after 'Honey' was first promo'd in the UK, that the first tracks from *Play* were released in the US. That single was the combination of 'Honey' and 'Run On', the latter of which had been issued in the UK on April 26, 1999.

But 'Honey/Run On' received only a low-profile release as V2 were not yet fully geared up to push their new signing. Also, they were developing a campaign which aimed to use the single 'Bodyrock' to fully reintroduce Moby. If it seemed that the US and European labels were working at odds with one other, then these thoughts were compounded by the full release of *Play*. In a market where a unified worldwide release date is paramount to an album's success, *Play* alarmingly received a staggered schedule. The album was released on May 17, 1999, throughout Europe and only hit the streets in the US some two weeks later on June 1.

The title of the album was inspired by some graffiti sprayed along a wall of a playground nearby to Moby's apartment. Just a simple four-letter word, sprayed in an unusually straight, non-stylized manner along the edge of a basketball court, it's a word that evokes the idea if downtime, of letting loose. It is also a word with connotations of freedom and space, as much as it suggests performance or even sexual invitation. It is a word which is both naïve and knowing, innocent and wild. Play seemed to conjure up many images - many of which were as contradictory as Moby himself. Moby would later suggest that the title was also chosen in tribute to post-punk band Magazine who released a live album called *Play* in 1980.

The cover artwork to the album featured Moby in typically hyperactive mood, jumping on a bed. The photo shoot by Corinne Day took place in one of the rooms at New York's legendary Chelsea Hotel (where, among other things, Sid Vicious allegedly killed Nancy Spungen, Arthur C. Clarke devised *2001: A Space Odyssey* and Janis Joplin gave head "on an unmade bed" to Leonard Cohen). The cover photos were the result of a happy accident as the bed-jumping concept only came about through Moby's natural exuberance. Seeing the bed, he could not resist the urge to test the springs to the full. Where most musicians might only do this through sexual endeavor, Moby simply preferred the method that most children would enjoy. Indeed, so rigorous was this test, that he actually broke the bed!

The photos do, however, provide a deeper insight into the character of Moby than any of his previous albums' art work. When all the ideology is stripped away and the rumors removed, Moby is at his happiest when he is simply at play. Indeed, when he showed me the graffiti that inspired the album title, he was immediately drawn to the climbing frame in the park where he immediately made the acquaintance of a dog and a couple of young kids.

"I may be inhibited when I meet a girl at a party," he said while hanging upside down on a monkey bar. "I'm just not good at flirting - although I enjoy it very much. But with dogs and children I can just be myself." In this moment Moby, the real person, emerged from Moby the myth. This was the Little Idiot; the man who loves to watch *The Simpsons* with friends and knows all of the scenes from the programme to the point of obsession.

"My love of *The Simpsons* is justified and excessive. My friend Damian [Loeb] and I can't watch it with other people because we're so annoying - we know all the words so we spoil all of the punchlines. It's a wonderful program because it's so overtly political; an area of profound public discourse."

Upon its release, *Play* seemed to be almost universally ignored by the wider media. Most music magazines only provided downpage reviews, rather than the usual lead, while a number simply ignored it. Of these reviews, however, almost all were positive. In the US, *Rolling Stone* said "the ebb and flow of eighteen concise, contrasting cuts writes a story about Moby's beautifully conflicted interior world while giving the outside planet beats and tunes on which to groove. Read it with your heart and hips." *Newsweek* were equally impressed, describing the album as "one of the seasons most appealing CDs. Only musicians and techies will know how it works - and God only knows *why* it works. But you don't need to be a club kid or know the rock-crit lingo for it to work on you." *Spin* enthused: "To hear an electronic music album looking backwards as intently as it dreams forward is a real time jolt. *Play* is as real an image as rave or alternative culture has ever imagined." While *Village Voice* echoed these sentiments: "A perfect blend of sacred and secular, once touched in the head, now touched by an angel, the holy idiot Moby has finally come up with the masterpiece he's threatened to make since the beginning. *Play* should not only rehabilitate his reputation among electronic music fans; it should also ensure that when Moby finally meets his maker, God will give him the job he's always wanted – resident DJ in heaven's celestial disco."

In the UK, the response was perhaps a little more reserved. However, those who did support the album did so with huge enthusiasm. London listings magazine *Time Out* said: "Quite simply one of the best albums of the year so far. *Play*, with its weave of influences and originality, will delight fans and convince the most hardened skeptic that this New Yorker means business." Elsewhere the self-styled street fashion bible *The Face* delighted that "his wholesale achievement is to have tweaked more from *Play*'s folksy atmospheres than mawkish campfire bonhomie. That, and giving the otherwise woolly headed spiritualism of 1999 a sharp modernist, soulfully retro tweak." Even the usually cynical weekly music title *NME* were won over by the album, saying: "Moby's much-vaunted eclecticism works brilliantly, ploughing a unique furrow in pop music, he demands your enjoyment as much as your respect." There were bad reviews however. In a moment of blind obstinacy the now-defunct UK weekly *Melody Maker* went against the grain of general consensus and declared "Bar a few isolated outbreaks of talent, it's all rubbish."

"Some people have said that this is a wildly eclectic record," Moby exclaimed, when questioned about some of the most common criticisms of *Play* that he'd heard. "My intention was to make an album that was a lot more cohesive. That held together and that could be used as background music, and as foreground music. And would work either way. I mean, *Animal Rights*, no one is going to put that on in the background when they're making dinner."

Of course the suggestion that *Play* was intended to be dinner party music was like a red rag to a bull for those critics who imagined that these kinds of music were simply coffee table sounds. To criticize something as 'coffee table' has been one of the most damning things you could level at a dance artist. Despite the fact that the coffee table is the natural home for albums as diverse as Marvin Gaye's *What's Going On,* Stevie Wonder's *Songs In The Key Of Life,* Orbital's *Insides,* etc. Indeed the list of classic 'coffee table' albums is endless.

In the case of *Play*, however, the biggest criticism came less from the fact that the album was a dinner party soundtrack, but that the album was all on one level and sounded too similar throughout. But this was a ridiculous criticism suggesting that the reviewer had failed to actually listen to the album beyond the most cursory level. Surprisingly, many of the early critics of *Play* (among the UK media) kept their feelings to conversations (and editorial meetings) choosing not to put their thoughts into print. Not surprisingly many of the same people could be found praising the album when it became an international hit!

"Its funny how people will employ something sounding the same as a criticism, yet at the same time people have shown how much they like nice things that happen a lot," Moby argued. "Like eating breakfast. Nobody gets bored eating breakfast. Or sex. No one gets bored with sex, even though it's pretty much all the same, it can be mundane, it can be inventive but basically it's always the same. You don't complain that you're bored of taking a shower even though it happens every day! If something's nice then you'll do it over and over again with a minimum of variety.

"One of the wonderful things about western music is that it's so inherently limited," he continued. "I mean basically its just twelve notes. And the billions of pieces of music made using these twelve notes is remarkable. The human capacity for invention within such a limited framework is unbelievable. I'm told that seventy per cent of #1 songs have the same chord changes and I'm not in the least bit surprised. There's only so many chords you can use."

This last comment slices open the very thing that is wrong with the electronic music conundrum, that it has a duty to be innovative. All too often artists are criticized for not experimenting with sound just because they are creating music through sampling technology. In the same breath, these critics applaud guitar bands who are happy to adhere to the basic structure of rock'n'roll.

In Moby's case however, his music is born from the incalculable aspects of electronic music. Yet the finished results place the song itself in the spotlight, rather than the tricks and tools used to get the final results. In order to achieve the simplicity of many of the tracks on *Play*, the creative process involved a number of complex equations.

"I wonder how many times in the past forty years someone's been driving home from work and heard a wonderful piece of music and just started crying in their car?" pondered Moby. "Hundreds of millions of times. It's a mundane thing but it's still deeply profound. I mean, I've been thinking a lot about musical innovation recently and it seems to me that, for the most part, musical innovation happens completely accidentally. That's one of my problems with people who approach music from too academic or too analytical a viewpoint, because true innovation just happens. No one plans it. Rock'n'roll, jazz and the blues, hip hop and house music and psychedelic rock and drum'n'bass. These things just happened. It wasn't like a bunch of people sitting down at Berkeley College of Music and saying 'Let's invent a new innovative style of music.' Usually its just kids doing something that is fun and sexy. Rock'n'roll is just white-trash kids trying to sound black. Hip hop was just people trying to make a party more fun.

"That's one of the joys of electronic music, there's so many ways that things can go wrong. There's so many variables in creating electronic music that there's room for chaos. Or chaos can happen really easily. On 'Find My Baby' for example, there's so many weird elements on that song. The main vocal is from 1926. There's a secondary vocal from the late 80s, like a disco song. Then there's me playing acoustic guitar and bass. Then there's a drum loop from an old funk record from about 1968 and a weird analogue synth sound, and Mellotron and string sounds and a 909. So, it's almost like a post-modern symphony. I didn't think of it that way when I was making the record. I just thought 'why don't I do this'. I was open to trying different things. Like with that song I was playing with the vocal sampler and put some drums underneath of it and then I thought why don't I put some acoustic guitar on it. Which is kind of like a revolutionary approach to electronic music."

Another criticism leveled at *Play* was that Moby had appropriated black music much in the same way as the white industry did with the creation of rock'n'roll. This argument was also tied in with the usual negative comments about sampling and the creativity of the producer doing the sampling. Indeed, when songs like 'Run On' featured samples of original songs so heavily, at what point do they cease being remixes and start becoming original recordings?

Moby was quick to point out that as far as he was concerned all of the people he had sampled had been paid where possible. Also springing to his defense was the Alan Lomax Foundation who picked holes in the argument by praising the way that Moby had used the samples in a brand new context, with such sensitivity to the source material. So in both economic and artistic terms it wasn't as simple as saying he had cynically appropriated the blues aspects of the records.

As for the argument about sampling culture? This had followed Moby since 'Go', a tune many people had criticized as a rip-off of the *Twin Peaks* theme. Despite the work that Moby had put into the track, it was still the instantly recognizable aspect that people homed in on.

Despite the largely positive reviews for *Play*, few magazines were interested in running features on Moby to coincide with the album's release. Furthermore the radio reaction seemed decidedly underwhelming. What followed, however, was a case of the public discovering the album for themselves. *Play* slowly gathered momentum and started to sell through simple word of mouth.

Play, it would seem, contained a positive melancholia which tapped into the mood of the people. This was especially the case throughout the post-millennial comedown of 2000 when many came to realize that nothing had changed but the date. Not even the much-publicized 'millennium bug' had appeared to make our lives more interesting.

There was, however, another argument to support the album's increased success. The campaigns Moby's record companies employed were almost unique. They utilized every subterranean trick in the book to open the public's eyes to the record, without ever reducing to the level of hype. It was tactic known as stealth marketing.

"From the start we knew we had something unique, but something that could appeal to a wide demographic range," explained the V2 president Richard Sanders to *Billboard* in February 2000. "It was just a matter of exploring the various avenues necessary to expose the music properly."

In the US this involved a carefully planned campaign which opened fully with the release of 'Bodyrock'. The label's first step was to re-establish Moby as a club-friendly artist. Much in the same way that Mute Records had promo'd 'Honey' with a string of remixes, V2 mailed out reworkings of 'Bodyrock'. Most notable was Olav Basoski's 'Da Hot Funk Da Freak Funk Remix' which introduced a deep trance flavor that was perfect for the dance floor of trendy New York club event Body & SOUL. This was an important point as, at this time, Body & SOUL was wielding a huge influence on the world dance scene. Olav Basoski had developed a style which perfectly captured the essence of the club. In return, his remixes provided worldwide hits for artists such as Moloko (whose 'Sing It Back' was remixed without their knowledge by Basoski and subsequently bootlegged. Such was the demand for the mix that the band's label signed it and Moloko deservedly enjoyed their biggest hit).

Coinciding with the US club DJ promotion, 'Bodyrock' was also targeted at the modern rock radio DJs to positive effect. The track went Top Ten in *Billboard*'s Modern Rock Tracks chart. That this was essentially a hip hop-influenced track with an almost big beat feel seemed of little consequence and, as a result of the single's radio success in this unlikely territory, the album itself gained increased radio exposure.

The next piece of the 'Bodyrock' jigsaw offered what was perhaps the clearest indication of the route that *Play* would take into the public subconscious. The track was given huge TV exposure, being used throughout the fall commercial campaign for ABC's *Dharma & Greg* sitcom. Similarly the track was used as the opening theme to NBC's *Veronica's Closet* while Moby himself also performed on a handful of talk shows.

Over the course of the next few months Moby's songs would start to crop up in a multitude of TV shows. Furthermore they were increasingly used on movie soundtracks including *Any Given Sunday*, *The Next Big Thing*, *Play It To The Bone*, *The Beach*, *Body Shots* and *Big Daddy* among many others. Increasingly, the public knew Moby's music, even if, on the whole, they hadn't quite worked out who had created it.

It was this combination of licensing exposure and performance that would find Moby becoming an increasingly mainstream name. Indeed, if the US marketing campaign offered a test case for stealth tactics, then the UK situation was similarly persuasive.

As *Play* slowly moved up the charts, so his music became a common presence on TV. Although it isn't unusual to hear some of the most obscure underground dance tracks soundtracking trailers for TV shows in the UK, the rapidity with which Moby's songs seemed to suddenly be everywhere was shocking. It was not uncommon to hear 'Honey' played over the 'Goals of the Month' on the weekly soccer show *Match of the Day* for example. 'Bodyrock' was deemed perfect to soundtrack the replays on satellite TV soccer show *Sky Football*. Similarly, soaps like *Brookside* and *Hollyoaks* would regularly play host to a number of cuts from *Play* while Moby's music also trailered shows like *The Simpsons, Buffy The Vampire Slayer, The Sopranos* and even Spice Girl Victoria Beckham's TV presenting debut, *Victoria's Secrets*.

The presence of *Play* was also felt in between TV shows. His songs were increasingly licensed to soundtrack commercials throughout the world. A fact which brought with it an enormous amount of criticism. The plethora of corporations which would go on to use tracks from *Play* to advertise their product included Galaxy, Learndirect, Grolsch Lager, Thorntons Chocolate, Maxwell House, Bosch and France Telecom among many others. If such commercial actions were attacked by many observers who believed that Moby was being hypocritical, then nothing compared to the reaction that his highest-profile advert-licensing ventures would bring, namely the use of his music on car ads, only a few years after his outburst about 'Go' being used in a similar campaign. Even more poignant was the fact that he used to refuse to use cars for anything but emergencies. The cars that were sold to the tune of Moby's track included the Nissan Almeira, the Renault Kangoo, the Renault Scenic and the VW Polo.

Among the many public attacks on Moby was this one from UK rock artist David Gray. When asked by *Select* magazine in October 2000 why he didn't allow his music to be used for adverts, he exclaimed: "That's what's fucking wrong with the world! There's purity – the things in your soul that are most dear to you revealed in a musical way. And to put it on some arsehole beer advert, you're lending your kudos to some globe-destroying fucking company. Fuck the argument as well that people get to hear your music. Yeah, but at what fucking cost? It becomes some inane fucking wallpaper, just like everything else in the fucking world. For example, take Moby. The biggest twat of all in my opinion, because he still talks the talk as if he's got some integrity, 'I'll get on any fucking advert known to man and then I'll talk about the environment.' You fucking idiot. Shut up!"

Moby himself was unrepentant about the licensing deals. "I'm not sure about what my record company are going to license, however I am happy to support them. Mute are a small independent label and if they can make some money then I'm happy for that to happen. After all, they've been supportive of me."

As for the apparent about-turn on the car ads, Moby simply replied: "Obviously I would rather my songs weren't used on these adverts, but the ads are going to be made anyway. And if I can use the proceeds to help my friends then it's more worthwhile."

The obvious thing about this last comment is the fact that he no longer aimed to use the proceeds to support anti-automobile lobbyists (as with the reissue of 'Go'). It was a hypocrisy which baffled many of his long-time fans who increasingly called him a 'sell-out'. Moby did, however, maintain his anti-tobacco stance, refusing permission for any of his songs to be used for cigarette ads.

By March, 2000, every track from *Play* had been licensed out. It may have been a first for any artist, but it came with a huge cost. Among his fiercest critics was one of his oldest friends Paul Yates. What followed was one of the most public breakdowns of a friendship ever seen outside of the celebrity gossip columns of *Hello* magazine.

CHAPTER TWENTY THREE

"There's a part of me that really enjoys being rootless. I have periods of being obsessive about the weirdest things. Just now that's what obsesses me." Moby

In the Fall of 2000, Yates took the unusual step of offering Moby's soul for sale online. He claimed that Moby had already sold it to the corporate devil, so in reality it wasn't really worth much anyway. He suggested potential bidders get in touch with "previous owners" such as Rover Limited and Dodge cars, and went on to further suggest they might even get the soul purified and then sell it back to the star, making sure they "charge him plenty". Along with the soul, the winning bidder would receive several photographs of Moby, some copies of his writing and a video tape of him.

Bidding took place and Moby's soul was duly dispatched to Mark Lincoln Seiler, who runs the *Mobilicious* fan site. "The money went to the American Lung Association (which I respect, being an American with bad lungs)," explained Mark. "Anyway, bidding started at five cents to make a point. I was the highest bidder, as most other people who would have bid on it know me and knew to just lay off. I ended up paying $45 with shipping, also getting some great old photos and videotapes with some great stuff on it, and a few other things. The soul thingy had to be held for a photo shoot 'cause there ended up being so much press about the whole situation (NYC papers, *Time*, *Spin*, *Select*, etc) but he sent a photocopy in the meantime."

The breakdown of this friendship was extremely poignant. Yates was Moby's only remaining friend from his Connecticut days. Over the course of twenty years, Moby and Yates had worked together on musical ventures like Shopwell and The Pork Guys. More recently the two of them had recorded a spoof Germanic disco track under the guise of Schaumgummi (released as a seven-inch single in the summer of 2000 and accompanied by 'The Ballad Of Paul Yates', a track by Philistines Jnr). Yates had directed the original black and white video for 'Hymn', appeared on the sleeve for 'That's When I Reach For My Revolver' and played keyboards on stage for Moby. Furthermore, Moby had written the score for, and acted in, Yates's short film *Space Water Onion*.

In the end, the source of the argument seemed not to lie in Moby's commercial ventures (although, given Yates' fiercely independent, underground stance it would have clearly angered him) but in a fall-out over a film that Moby had funded and acted in for Yates. Moby even provided the score which he performed with one-time *Penthouse Pet* and singer with New York rock band The Stingers, Dyanna Lauren.

Called *Porno,* the movie was set in a sex shop on New Year's Eve and Moby played a handful of small parts in it. Moby himself was not involved in anything pornographic, despite his oft-proclaimed belief that he can't trust any man who says he doesn't like pornography. Although those who viewed the film considered it to be "very funny", Moby was widely reported in the press to have attempted to place an injunction on the movie ever being released. Yates was said to be angered by this and his public fall-out with his old friend began. On September 28, 2000, Moby posted the following response on the Moby wesbite, *www.mobymusic.com*:

"i don't know if you're aware of this or not, but i have an acquaintance named Paul Yates. he and i had been very good friends for a long time, but about four months ago i had to stop being his friend because he had grown very hostile towards me. now it seems that he is preoccupied with saying and writing really nasty things about me... it makes me sad that he's now so consumed with hostility towards me. if any of you are friends of paul's, please let him know that even though i can't be his friend i wish him well and i just wish that he would let go of this anger that he has towards me and get on with his life." (Despite Moby's efforts to stop *Porno,* information on the movie, including a synopsis, cast list and short clip could be found on line.

Throughout 2000 there were various turning points for *Play.* Many of these coincided with single releases which included 'Porcelain' (June 12) and 'Why Does My Heart Feel So Bad?' (October 16). However, the single that saw Moby finally gaining full recognition for *Play* came in early March, 2000, in the shape of 'Natural Blues'. For the video, arty photographer David LaChapelle (whom Moby declared "an absolute visionary genius") was brought on board to direct. Such was LaChapelle's respect for Moby that he agreed to work for free. In the resulting promo, Moby is depicted as an old man (as discussed, something he had considered doing as far back as 'Feeling So Real') lying in bed in a convalescent hospital pondering his life, when he is taken by an angel to his final resting place. In his last moments he remembers the various stages of his life.

Although two child actors were brought in to play Moby as a nine-year-old and a sixteen-year-old, Moby played both himself at thirty five, and as the old man. The angel on the other hand was played by Christina Ricci, to whom Moby was subsequently romantically linked. In fact, she had been Moby's ex-girlfriend's room-mate, although he did admit to me nine months prior to this video shoot that she was the actress he'd most like to have sex with. "There's something about her that's so sexy," he said.

Four weeks after 'Natural Blues' had been released, *Play* hit the #1 position in the UK. The tide had truly turned.

Although much has been made of the success of *Play* being due to the licensing exposure, one of the biggest factors was Moby's live show. Indeed, Moby toured the album for approximately eighteen months. It seemed he had become addicted to the rootlessness of being on the road.

"There's a part of me that really enjoys being rootless," he explained in 1999. "I have periods of being obsessive about the weirdest things. Just now that's what obsesses me. There was one time I got obsessed about furniture. I started buying all these books about furniture, I'd go to furniture stores all of the time. I was completely obsessed… buying my sofa started it. Before that I had no furniture, so I started going out and looking at furniture and I became fascinated. Then I became obsessed with architecture. Probably because of building this place [his apartment]. I started going out to libraries and bookstores and just read and bought books about architecture obsessively. And then a week would go by and I'm not interested anymore.

"My strangest obsession was probably Herman Miller. It's a furniture company from the mid-20th century. I have a couple of books on Herman Miller, those chairs [points to the corner of the room] are all Herman Miller. It became my mantra two or three years ago because he just had phenomenal furniture designers working for him; remarkable mid-20th-century furniture designers. Now it's very trendy so I'm ashamed about it. This was a few years ago before *wallpaper (interior design magazine) came on the scene and ruined it for everybody.

"Just now though, I have this romantic idea of just selling my apartment and kind of having no home. That way I'd just have some money in the bank and travel around and not live in one place. Sort of just how you then perceive yourself and perceive the world. Because, you know, if you're on an airplane and you look at the flight map I think people's eyes naturally gravitate towards the place where they live, followed by places they've known. I think it must be interesting to look at the globe and not do that." Being on the road was of course the next best thing to selling up and choosing homelessness. Through the tour to promote *Play* it was possible to view the ongoing success of the album and its immediate effect on Moby's circumstances.

During the early stages of the tour in late 1999 he was only augmented by drummer Scott Frassetto, bassist Greta Brinkmann and turntablist DJ Spinbad. Moby himself would dart between percussion, synths, guitar and vocals like a man possessed. Indeed, when on November 4, 1999 he performed in Milan for the *Show Case* program on Italian TV, the band was still in this relatively depleted state. In the broadcast, however, the band numbers were swelled by the inclusion of his tour manager Dick Meredith, who could clearly be seen standing behind the keyboards miming for 'Porcelain'.

Gradually over the course of the next twelve months, the band grew to include full-time keyboard players, a percussionist, three backing singers (including Dianne Charlamangne, best known for her vocals on Goldie's 'Inner City Life'), and eventually a three-piece string section. It was with this full band that Moby appeared on UK TV show *Later With Jools Holland,* where he presented a full hour of live renditions of old favorites. The additional musicians had clearly opened up new vistas for Moby as he explored 'Hymn' via grand piano and strings and 'Every Time You Touch Me' in a stripped-down, unplugged version among other gems. Clearly Moby was developing his oft-expressed desire to do an *Unplugged*-style album.

Moby had always excelled in the live arena. Whether throwing himself at his keyboard and pounding the living daylights out of drum pads to a tune played by a DAT player, or thrashing around naked, genitals hidden by his guitar, like a rock god, his performances never strayed too far away from being incendiary. However, in performance there had always been a clear stylistic division between raver Moby and rocker Moby. True, he would strap on a guitar during his dance sets, however the beats would remain techno-driven. His rock sets may have featured his old dance classics, but they were always delivered in a style that suited his skate punk musical persona. Indeed, when he was at his most willfully eclectic during the *Everything Is Wrong* shows, he would divide the set neatly between the dance numbers and the rock songs.

But with this latest outing, he seemed to have developed a new confidence in the music. As a result, the live shows found him pulling out a diverse selection of tracks. From the dance epics like

'Next Is The E' to the rock melodrama of tunes like 'New Dawn Fades'; he even interspersed some of his more ambient moments such as 'The Rain Falls And The Sky Shudders'. Suddenly, giving his fans the songs they wanted to hear, in a way in which they already loved them, seemed paramount.

Another, equally important area in which Moby appeared to have gained new confidence was in his actual stage-craft. His ability to hold the audience in the palm of his hands was almost masterful. From the 600-capacity venues of the early dates on the tour to the 40,000-strong audiences at the many festivals he appeared at throughout the summer of 2000, he captivated his fans with a warmth and personality which was unusual for a dance-related artist.

It is possible that he had developed this more relaxed style of performance following his aforementioned experience watching Credence Clearwater Revival's John Fogerty. This gig seemed to have an influence on his approach to his music and also his performance on stage. The way in which this development was most noticeable was in the ease with which he would banter in between songs. Introducing them with personal anecdotes, plugging in his electric guitar with declarations of how the instrument inevitably brings out the rock ego in him, before delivering a fully-fledged heavy metal guitar solo. Indeed, as he sat on the edge of the stage at Wembley Arena on November 18, 2000, joking with the audience, you could have been forgiven for thinking that he was playing to a crowd of fifteen, not an audience of 15,000. That he spent the moments before this walking the stage, picking up bits of rubbish, tossing them into the photographers' pit, while explaining his obsessional behavior, only made the warmth of his performance seem closer.

With shows selling out everywhere he played, Moby succeeded with this tour in both satisfying the fans of old and the more recent converts. Not that many of Moby's long-standing following appreciated the arrival of the new breed of Moby fan. As with most bands or artists who suddenly find popular success a few years after they first emerged, a division increasingly grew between his two sets of fans. Indeed, Moby's online mailing lists buzzed with accusations of people being 'bandwagon jumpers' just because they had only recently discovered him. Throughout December 2000 the question on *Mobility* was simply "what was your first Moby experience?" The answers showed the list of subscribers going to increasingly obtuse lengths to underline their long-standing position as a Moby fan. To admit that you had only heard of him through a car advert on TV seemed tantamount to admitting that you were the kind of fan that would move on to the next big thing as soon as it arrived.

Throughout the debate one thing did, however, remain constant. The depth of feeling that Moby's fans have for him. One of the main reasons for this was simply because he seemed to reciprocate the same feelings for them. Indeed, many of his fans wrote of their experiences meeting with him backstage, and just how gracious he seemed.

One such posting was this one from "Mike A7" who saw Moby on tour with Bush in the US: "We went to his show in Saginaw, Michigan on April 3, 2000. We watched Moby tear it up as usual opening the show – after his performance we said the hell with Bush, let's try and meet Moby. We went out to where his tour bus was and waited twenty to thirty minutes. By this time it was getting dark, but suddenly I saw a small bald figure approaching the tour bus.

I shouted 'Moby!' and he replied, 'Let me drop this off in the bus, I'll be out in two seconds', as he was carrying some stuff in his hands. He came back out with a marker in hand, prepared to sign something (he autographed my Voodoo Child 'End Of Everything' CD), but talked to us for at least five minutes... He was everything I had heard as far as kindness and humility... Moby was nothing but humble, kind and gracious in my meeting him. He was a great guy in person as he was on stage. Thanks Moby for making this fan feel welcome that night when one part felt like those silly gushing fanatics who follow rock stars around :)

With Moby's growing popularity also came increased celebrity status. Perhaps the clearest example of this came on the evening before the Grammy Awards in early 2000. Moby played a private party for the Hollywood celeb A-list at The House Of The Blues venue. Immediately before the set, Elton John ventured backstage to tell Moby how much he loved the album. He then joined Moby on stage for a rendition of 'Why Does My Heart Feel So Bad?' (a track which Elton has subsequently recorded). Not only was this the start of a friendship with Elton John – which would see the pair teaming up once again on UK music and chat show *TFI Friday* to perform both 'Why Does My Heart...' and the Lynyrd Skynyrd classic 'Sweet Home Alabama' – it also signified the Little Idiot's entry into the world of celebrity.

For the rest of the year it seemed that there wasn't an award ceremony in the world in which he wasn't nominated, winning, presenting or just hanging out. Suddenly Moby was decidedly high profile. He was increasingly linked to supermodels in the tabloid press ("I don't even have any supermodel friends! Who am I supposed to be dating? I mean, what would I have in common with a seventeen-year-old anorexic from Texas?"); he was romantically linked with nineteen-year-old Star Wars actress Natalie Portman ("there was never anything more serious than a bit of flirtatious behavior"); he was reported to be (quite literally) hanging out with *Trainspotting* star Ewan McGregor ("very drunk, delightful and sweet – he hugged everybody"); he was flown in especially to DJ at Donatella Versace's aftershow party where he dropped a combination of "Donna Summer, Aerosmith, tacky Euro disco, and old hip hop. Basically I was a wedding DJ!" Such was his appeal that he even modeled jeans for Calvin Klein. Indeed, a huge billboard depicting Moby dressed in 'Dirty Denim' and standing in an approximation of the Christ's crucifixion pose, stood on the corner of Moby's street for a number of weeks. "In reality, you know, I don't think that I'm an attractive person. I don't expect people to be looking at that ad and commenting on my six-pack! It would be terrible if I was ever with a girl and she could only get aroused by looking at the advert though!" he joked to *Spin*.

The requests for Moby's production skills also started to roll in. Madonna asked him to help out on tracks which would eventually appear on *Music*, However Moby declined, suggesting that he would be happy to collaborate with her when he was ready to work on his next album. Also looking for Moby's services was Irish pop star Ronan Keating of Boyzone fame. Despite Moby's pronounced love of pop music, he offered no comment on this particular request.

As *Play* continued to sell, the inevitable spin-off albums soon followed. Elektra Records in the US put together a compilation called *Moby Songs 1993-1996*. Far from being an unworthy addition to the Moby catalogue, however, this album – which was released in the US only on July 18, 2000 – was a carefully selected collection which depicted the road Moby had traveled to reach *Play*.

To any long term Moby observer, the roots of *Play* could be found as far back as *Ambient*. In terms of song structure, mood and atmosphere however, it was with cuts like 'Into the Blue' that the style of *Play* was first explored.

Moby Songs 1993-1996 included many of the mellower moments from *Everything Is Wrong, I Like To Score, Animal Rights* and the 'Move EP' alongside better-known material such as 'Go'. And while there was nothing new or previously unreleased, the album was beautifully packaged and sensitively programmed. As an introduction to the pre-*Play* Moby, this compilation was essential.

On October 23, 2000, Mute Records in the UK released a limited-edition version of *Play* which featured an extra album called *Play: The B-Sides*. Inevitably this box-set version of the album was criticized as being a cash-in, as the fans who already had the album had to buy it again in order to get the extra disc. It could be argued, however, that most of his fans would have already owned the tracks on the singles. Moby's reasons for wanting to release *Play: The B-Sides* was far more honest. The music was important to him and may have become lost as extra tracks on singles. As an album (albeit an extremely limited release) these tracks were given a more coherent platform.

"The fate of most B-sides is to be released on a single and then disappear into obscurity and MP3 files," wrote Moby on the album sleeve notes, "some of these songs might not be instantly accessible but I (immodestly) think that they're all quite special."

Featuring the same cover photo as *Play*, only with the blue background changed to deep orange, and inside illustrations of the Moby caricature, the album package was of a far greater quality than most bonus-CDs. The songs, on the other hand, were often a little saccharine and occasionally lacking the depth of his best work.

Play: The B-Sides opened with 'Flower', another of Moby's Lomax-archive sampling blues tracks. Featuring a sample of 'Green Sally Up', with the vocals of Jessie Pratcher, Mattie Gardner and Mary Gardner, it was a track which wouldn't have sounded out of place on the original *Play*. 'Sunday' was more reminiscent of his work on *Everything Is Wrong* with its shuffling hi-hats, driving piano riff and somber synth flourishes, while 'Memory Gospel' was a dark string-led piece with a repeated gospel-inflected voice picking out a simple, yet melancholic tune.

'Whispering Wind' featured Moby singing a heavily vocodered melody to a spacious keyboard refrain and simple hip hop beat. The song developed with what was fast becoming a Moby cliché; the introduction of a meandering piano over minor-chord string fills. A beautiful track nonetheless, but one which came with an almost overwhelming sense of *deja vu*.

'Summer' offered a piano and string combination once again. However, this time the track was tempered with the ambience of French movie soundtracks such as *Betty Blue*, thus offering a new spin on the Moby sound. 'Spirit' once again evoked the spirit of

Everything Is Wrong, this time echoing the Philip Glass ambience of 'God Moving Over The Face Of The Waters' before surging into a sequenced crescendo similar to 'Anthem'. 'Flying Foxes' on the other hand was a stunning track which brought together all of Moby's favored musical themes with a depth worthy of the best moments of any one of his albums.

'Sunspot' found Moby once again exploring systems music on the piano. But 'Flying Over The Dateline' was the sound of old-school drum programming which could have been lifted straight from the grooves of an old 80s tech-funk track, with abstract string stabs and a Japanese-sounding discordant ambience. Eventually the track broke down with an epic trance-style string motif, before the drum machine spluttered back in. 'Running', the only previously unreleased version on the album, featured stripped-down trance beats, muted 303s and strings repeating the same motif while gradually becoming more and more heavily filtered. Finally 'The Sun Never Stops Setting' was a poignant and touching pastoral piece which begged to be used a movie theme.

Perhaps not Moby's finest moment in terms of a complete albums, *Play: The B-Sides* did offer an insight into the problems Moby must have had compiling the eighteen tracks on *Play* from the 200 songs recorded.

Towards the end of 2000, Moby completed two new versions of tracks from *Play* which confounded many of his fans. First of all came 'Honey' featuring R&B vocalist Kelis, which was put out on October 16 as a B-side to 'Why Does My Heart Feel So Bad' in the UK. The second of these reversions was 'Southside', featuring added vocals from Gwen Stefani of No Doubt. It was released in the US only in late November. Of the two new versions, Kelis' 'Honey' was perhaps the most successful with the vocalist, who delivered one of the year's finest R&B /hip hop albums in *Kaleidoscope*, providing a sultry pop hook over reworked two-step beats. 'Southside', on the other hand, was reduced to the level of an average indie pop rock song. Perhaps, unsurprisingly, it went on to break the Top Fifty in the US.

Throughout this time Moby also expressed a desire to work with Spiller vocalist Sophie Ellis-Bextor, whose 'Groovejet' single was one of the year's dance anthems in the UK. The use of such obviously poppy vocalists may have seemed a little strange; however, Moby had long held a deep love of pop music. Indeed, as mentioned earlier, he had previously revealed to me that many of the songs recorded during the *Play* sessions were for an anonymous pop project he had in mind.

"One of the reasons I like pop music is because it can appeal to many people in a very personal way. There's arbitrary criteria applied to listening to music. It's only a subjective thing. Do I like it or do I not like it? And I think that's a much more enjoyable way to deal with culture. Rather than having preconceived criteria of like, I'm not allowed to like American films, or I'm not allowed to like independent films, or I'm not allowed to like dance music. If you like it, you like it! I mean, there are so few things in the world which make people happy (*laughs*) why, why, why limit the scope of things which can potentially bring you pleasure?" he argued.

"I think some pop music can be sublime, you know," he continued. "Some pop music can be way more transcendent than so-called serious music. I remember even when I was a punk rocker at the time, of being seventeen years old and hearing 'Total Eclipse Of The Heart' by Bonnie Tyler and actually getting kinda choked up by it. And you know, that's the thing, that subjective response to music.

"I try very hard to approach things without prejudice, and sometimes it's really hard. Like Oasis is a good example. There's a part of me that really wants to despise them (*laughs*). But you know, they write catchy little songs, and I finally had to admit to myself that I liked them. Green Day is another good example. When I first heard Green Day I thought, 'what's the point in making a punk rock record fifteen years after punk rock happened?' Then I finally got over my prejudices and realized it's enthusiastic and their songs are great."

By the end of 2000, *Play* had been declared the highest-selling album of the year in the UK, turning five times platinum in early December. The same story was being told all over the world.

CHAPTER TWENTY FOUR

"I'm not a very good star. I'm small. And I'm bald."   Moby, 2000

Saturday, November 18, 2000, Fabric, London's coolest club. Moby sits in the cordoned-off VIP area, surrounded by crew and friends. The atmosphere is one of pure celebration. Champagne flows and the in-jokes of the touring family spark throughout the jovial banter.

Only three hours earlier Moby had played a triumphant set to a sold-out 15,000 capacity Wembley Arena. Not only did the set represent the culmination of month after month of the nomadic life on the road, but it was also the biggest headline show Moby had ever played. The gig itself was a spectacular event which drew on every aspect of Moby's career; diving into past glories as if each song had just been written.

In between his energetic sprints from percussion to keyboards, microphone to guitar, Moby joked with the crowd like he knew each and every one of them personally. Each track was introduced with a suitable anecdote, each nuance of his expansive sound brought to the crowd with an immense feeling of warmth. Augmented by a blistering light-show (especially effective on the now-traditional strobe assault of 'Thousand') and even a full-size costume of the Little Idiot Moby character, worn by a friend on stage much to everyone's delight, the Wembley show proved once and for all that Moby's mastery of the live performance was now fully formed.

At the aftershow party upstairs in the Arena Restaurant, he moved from place to place, talking to different people like a professional social butterfly. Champagne bottle in hand, swigging directly from the neck, he continuously talked in wonderment at how great his crew were. Naturally everyone involved with the spectacle was in the mood to celebrate and following a brief tour bus ride, during which tracks by legendary rockers AC/DC were played at full volume on the in-bus soundsystem, we arrived at Fabric.

Slowly the clubbers recognized the small, bald man sitting in the corner, deep in conversation. Wearing his usual ensemble of gray sweater, black jeans and old sneakers, he looks like the most unlikely pop star ever, his wire-rimmed spectacles only adding to this image. Yet a star he most certainly is.

Slowly girls gravitate towards him and start dancing in a please-notice-me style. Arms are raised, hips sway and every now and then glances are thrown in Moby's direction. Gradually the VIP area fills up with more and more girls going through the same routine. The only men are the ones who came with him and John Digweed (the DJ for the Wembley show who is described by Moby and crew as the nicest DJ they had worked with on the entire tour).

As Moby grabs another champagne bottle, he looks up and flashes a smile at one of the girls. Not a lecherous smile, more like the kind of greeting you would offer an old friend who you haven't seen for a while. It's a moment that the tabloid press would love to have witnessed. Especially given the fact that over recent months the spotlight on Moby's personal life has moved away from the old Christian vegan cliché and was now centered squarely on Moby the hedonist.

In every article recently published, we have been told that he now occasionally takes drugs - or specifically magic mushrooms. Each journalist has reported with glee that he likes a drink as much as the next man. And even more have questioned him about his sex life as if each one was the first to have the courage to do so. Moby, it would seem had, in the course of ten years, gone from lonesome outsider to one of the lads.

Here in the sweaty ambience of a club in London's trendy East End, all of the above seems to be being played out to the letter. He's drunk, exuberant and surrounded by groupies. All that's missing is a plate of blue meanie mushrooms. It all seems a far cry from the image of Moby the political pundit who had vociferously campaigned against George W Bush throughout the farcical 2000 US Presidential elections.

Except this is only a perception of what is actually happening, distorted by magazine articles, industry rumor and more than a bit of media manipulation on Moby's part. Looked at from another perspective, Moby and his friends are enjoying a celebratory bottle of champagne like anyone else would after such a milestone-passing gig. Sure he's being stalked by girls, but this doesn't automatically mean they're groupies, and in turn, it isn't a done deal that he will be sleeping with one of them tonight. Even if he has declared his fondness for one-night stands.

In reality, any reading of tonight's events, or any other event in Moby's public life has been affected by his own intelligent handling of the media. Researching through ten years' worth of interviews for this book, it is astounding to see how often he repeats the same lines to different journalists – at times almost verbatim. Not that this is a cynical skill that he has acquired, more the defense mechanism of the overtly shy, or an honest reaction to the predictability of the questions he is asked. Indeed, at times it seems he rehearses quotes in order to take the conversation away from his faith, animal rights etc.

The articulate way in which he then delivers these conversation topics seduces the journalist into thinking that he/she is getting beneath Moby's skin like never before. Thus we are offered glimpses into his personal life, openly shown the inconsistencies in his ideologies and invited to shuffle around the detritus of his surface-level subconscious like amateur psychologists.

Read between the lines, however, and you are left with a feeling that the truly private Moby is nothing like the one we meet in interviews. At his core there seems to be a loner called Richard Hall who adopts personae in order to deal with the social world. Beneath the visible surface there seems to be a man uncomfortable with close relationships and insecure about many aspects of his own personality.

There is little doubt that Moby has a selfish side to him. Indeed he seems quite headstrong when it comes to getting what he wants. Ironically it is this aspect of his nature which has enabled him to create his no-lose morality. A Christian who does not believe in the formal structures of the church but in his own interpretation of Jesus Christ, thus side-stepping many of the usual issues which go hand in hand with Christianity. An ecologist who can support his creative involvement in car adverts by saying that he was actually being altruistic. The man who says that everything is alright sexually (and otherwise) as long as it involves consenting adults, yet openly indulges in one-night stands in the belief that no one ever gets hurt in these situations.

And it is in this way that Moby is much like the rest of us. Not as the media-friendly, womanizing, drinking lad but, just like everyone else on the planet, he is inconsistent, hypocritical, selfish and wrong; real in other words. That he tries to make sense of it all is no strange thing. That he has attempted to do so in public, however, is.

What makes Moby such a special person though is the fact that he can admit to these flaws in his personality. Just as he accepts flaws in every human being. And it is this spirit which flows through his music, rather than that of the supposed didactic moralist who walks an increasingly sexist and boorish path. As I walk out of Fabric into the wintry glare of the early-morning sun, I am immediately faced with a huge poster. It features a bald headed thirty-something man leaping for joy, arms outstretched, shirt undone and knees pulled up to his skinny chest. With eyes tightly shut and grin across his face he seems to be lost in a world of pure, undiluted ecstasy. It's a naïve image which begs us to forget our adult inhibitions and jump with him.

A wondrous moment perfectly captured which begs each and everyone of us to come on in and *play*.

DISCOGRAPHY
Although Moby's record labels have put out a huge number of promo items in support of his singles, only official releases are shown. All releases are US or UK, unless releases in other territories are substantially.

List is in chronological order.

For a definitive discography, including all cover versions of Moby's songs, movie discography and bootlegs I suggest you check out www.mobymusic.com/collectors/ or
 www.geocities.com/animal_sight/

SINGLES

MOBILITY (Instinct 12" US Only) 1990
Mobility/Mobility (Aquamix)/Go/Time Signature

GO (Instinct US 12") 1991
Go (Woodtick Mix)/Go (Low Spirit Mix)/Go (Analog Mix)/Go (Night Time Mix)

GO (Outer Rhythm UK 12") 1991
Go (Woodtick Mix)/Go (Low Spirit Mix)/Go (Voodoo Child Remix)

GO DEMIXES (Outer Rhythm UK 12") 1991
Go (Analog Mix)/Go (Nightime Mix)/Go (Soundtrack Mix)

GO MIXES [Outer Rhythm UK 12") 1991
Go (Rainforest Mix)/Go (Video Mix)/Go (Analog Mix)

GO REMIXES [Instinct US 12") 1991
Go (Radio Edit)/Go (Rainforest Mix)/Go (Subliminal Mix)/Go (Woodtick Mix)

GO REMIXES [Instinct US 12") 1991
Go (Woodtick Mix)/Go (Radio Edit)/Go (Rainforest Mix)/Go (Subliminal Mix)

GO REMIXES (Instinct US CD) 1991
Go (Radio Edit)/Go (Rainforest Mix)/Go (Subliminal Mix)/Go (Woodtick Mix)/Go (Soundtrack Mix)/Go (Original Mix)

DROP A BEAT (Instinct US 12") 1992
Drop A Beat/Electricity/Drop A Beat (Deep Mix)

DROP A BEAT (Instinct US CD) 1992
Drop A Beat/Drop A Beat (Deep Mix)/Electricity/UHF 2

THE ULTIMATE GO [Outer Rhythm/Roughmix Germany 2x12") 1992
Go (Delerium Mix) [Jam & Spoon]/Go (In Dub Mix) [Jam & Spoon]/Go (Mover Mix) [The Mover]/Go (Arpathoski Mix)/Go (Amphetamix)/Go (Barracuda Mix)

THE ULTIMATE GO (33:45) [Outer Rhythm/Roughmix Germany CD) 1992
Go (Delerium Mix) [Jam & Spoon]/Go (Arpathoski Mix)/Go (Video Mix)/Go (Amphetamix)/Go (In Dub Mix) [Jam & Spoon]/Go (Barracuda Mix)

NEXT IS THE E (Instinct US CD) 1992
Next Is The E (Edit)/Next Is The E (Victory Mix)/Next Is The E (Synthe Mix)/Next Is The E (I Feel It)/Thousand/Next Is The E (Cool World Mix)

NEXT IS THE E (Rough Trade Germany 12") 1993
Next Is The E (Synthe Mix)/Next Is The E (T.H.K. Tekk Mix)/Next Is The E (I Feel It)/Thousand

NEXT IS THE E (Rough Trade Germany CD) 1993
Next Is The E (Edit)/Next Is The E (T.H.K. Tekk Mix)/Next Is The E (Victory Mix)/Next Is The E
(Synthe Mix)/Next Is The E (I Feel It)/Thousand/Next Is The E (Cool World Mix)

I FEEL IT [NEXT IS THE E-REMIX] (Rough Trade/ Roughmix Germany 12") 1993
I Feel It (Contentious Mix)/I Feel It (Invisible Brothers Mix)/Go (Barracuda Mix)

I FEEL IT [NEXT IS THE E-REMIX] (Rough Trade Germany CD) 1993
I Feel It (Invisible Brothers Mix)/I Feel It (Contentious Mix)/Go (The Mover Mix)

I FEEL IT (Equator UK CD) 1993
I Feel It (Radio Edit)/Thousand/I Feel It (Contentious Mix)/I Feel It (Synthe Mix)

I FEEL IT [Equator UK 12"] 1993
I Feel It (I Feel It Mix)/I Feel it (Synthe Mix)/Thousand/I Feel it (Victory Mix)

I FEEL IT [Equator UK 12"] 1993
I Feel It (Contentious mix)/I Feel It (Synthe mix)/Thousand/I Feel It (THK Tekk mix)

MOVE [Elektra US 12"] 1993
Move (You Make Me Feel So Good)/Morning Dove/All That I Need Is To Be Loved/Unloved Symphony

MOVE (Elektra US CD) 1993
Move (You Make Me Feel So Good)/All That I Need Is To Be Loved (MV)/Morning Dove/Move (Disco
Threat)/Unloved Symphony/The Rain Falls And The Sky Shudders

MOVE - THE E.P. (Mute UK12") 1993
Move (You Make Me Feel So Good)/Morning Dove/All That I Need Is To Be Loved [Hard Trance
Version]/Unloved Symphony

MOVE (Mute UK limited edition 12") 1993
Move (You Make Feel So Good)/Move (MK Blades Mix)/Move (Sub Version)/Move (Xtra Mix)

MOVE (Mute UK CD) 1993
Move (You Make Me Feel So Good)/All That I Need Is To Be Loved (MV)/Unloved Symphony/The Rain
Falls And The Sky Shudders

MOVE - THE MIXES (Mute Intercord Germany CD) 1993 "The German(y) Mixes"
Move (DJ Kid Paul Mix)/Move (Electro Mix) "The Remixes"/Move (Sub Version)/Move (You Make Me
Feel So Good) [radio edit]

MOVE(Mute CD UK) 1993
Move (You Make Me Feel So Good) [radio edit]/Move (Disco Threat Mix)

ALL THAT I NEED IS TO BE LOVED (Elektra US 12") 1994
All That I Need Is To Be Loved (Vocal Dance)/All That I Need Is To Be Loved (Speed Trance)/All That I
Need Is To Be Loved (Moby Dub)/All That I Need Is To Be Loved (Flashin' Dub)

ALL THAT I NEED IS TO BE LOVED (Elektra/SOL(Singles Only Label) US 7") 1994
All That I Need Is To Be Loved (House Of Suffering Mix)/New Dawn Fades

HYMN (Mute UK CD12") 1994
Hymn (This Is My Dream Extended Mix)/Hymn (Laurent's Wake Up) [Laurent Garnier]/Hymn (Upriver)/Hymn (Dirty Hypo)

HYMN (Mute 12" UK) 1994
Hymn (Menacing)/Hymn (European Mix)/Hymn (Lucky Orgasm)/Hymn (I Believe)

HYMN {Part1} (Mute UK CD) 1994
Hymn (This Is My Dream)/All That I Need Is To Be Loved (H.O.S. Mix)/Hymn (European Edit)/Hymn (Laurent's Wake Up) [Laurent Garnier]

HYMN {Part 2} (Mute UK CD) 1994
Hymn.alt.quiet.version (33:45)

THE ORIGINAL GO (Mute UK 12") 1994
Go (Woodtick Mix)/Go (Arpathoski Mix)/Go (Delirium Mix)/Go (Amphetamix)

THE ORIGINAL GO (Mute UK CD)1994
Go (Woodtick Mix)/Go (Delirium Mix) [Jam & Spoon]/Go (Arpathoski Mix)/Go (Amphetamix)/Go (In Dub Mix) [Jam & Spoon]

FEELING SO REAL (Mute UK 12") 1994
Feeling So Real (Westbam Mix)/Feeling So Real (Original Mix)/Feeling So Real (Ray Keith Jungle Mix)/Feeling So Real (Old Skool Mix)/Feeling So Real (Unashamed Ecstatic Piano Mix)

FEELING SO REAL [Mute UK limited edition 10") 1994
Feeling So Real (Ray Keith Mix)/Feeling So Real (Original Mix)

FEELING SO REAL {Part One1} (Mute UK CD) 1994
Feeling So Real (Original Mix)/Feeling So Real (Unashamed Ecstatic Piano Mix)/Feeling So Real (Old Skool Mix)/New Dawn Fades

FEELING SO REAL REMIXES {Part 2} (Mute UK CD) 1994
Feeling So Real (Westbam Mix)/Feeling So Real (Ray Keith Jungle Mix)/Feeling So Real (Moby's Dub Mix)/Everytime You Touch Me parts for sampling in remix competition

FEELING SO REAL REMIXES (Elektra US CD/ Warner/Elektra Australia CD) 1994
Feeling So Real (Radio Edit)/Feeling So Real (Ecstatic)/Feeling So Real (Old Skool)/Feeling So Real (Westbam Remix) [Westbam and Klaus Jankuhn]/Feeling So Real (Moby's Dub)/New Dawn Fades/Feeling So Real (Main Mix)/Feeling So Real (Ray Keith Mix)/Everytime You Touch Me (Remix Parts)

FEELING SO REAL - Part one (Mute/Intercord Germany CD) 1994
Feeling So Real (7" Edit)/Feeling So Real (Unashamed Ecstatic Piano Mix)/New Dawn Fades/Everytime You Touch Me parts for sampling in remix competition

FEELING SO REAL REMIXES - Part two [Mute/Intercord GE CD) 1994
Feeling So Real (Westbam Mix)/Feeling So Real (Original Mix)/Feeling So Real (Old Skool Mix)/Feeling So Real (Moby's Dub Mix)/Feeling So Real (Ray Keith Jungle Mix)

EVERYTIME YOU TOUCH ME [Elektra US 12") 1995
Everytime You Touch Me (Na Feel Mix)/Everytime You Touch Me (Freestyle Mix)/Everytime You Touch Me (NYC Jungle Mix)/Everytime You Touch Me (12" Beatmasters Mix)/Everytime You Touch Me (John Blackford Mix)

EVERYTIME YOU TOUCH ME (Elektra US CD) 1995
Everytime You Touch Me (Jude Sebastian Remix) [UK contest winner]/Everytime You Touch Me (NYC
Jungle Mix)/Everytime You Touch Me (John Blackford Remix) [US contest winner]/Everytime You Touch
Me (Na Feel Mix)/The Blue Light Of The Underwater Sun/Everytime You Touch Me (Beatmasters' 7"
Mix)

EVERYTIME YOU TOUCH ME - Part one [Mute UK CD) 1995
Everytime You Touch Me (Beatmasters 7" Mix)/The Blue Light Of The Underwater Sun/Everytime You
Touch Me (Jude Sebastian Mix)/Everytime You Touch Me (Freestyle Mix)

EVERYTIME YOU TOUCH ME REMIXES - Part two { Mute UK CD} 1995
Everytime You Touch Me (Uplifting Mix)/Everytime You Touch Me (NYC Jungle Mix)/Everytime You
Touch Me (Na Feel Mix)/Everytime You Touch Me (Pure Joy Mix)/Everytime You Touch Me (Progressive
Edit Mix)/Everytime You Touch Me (Beatmasters Dub)

EVERYTIME YOU TOUCH ME [Mute UK 12") 1995
Everytime You Touch Me (Uplifting Mix)/Everytime You Touch Me (Jude Sebastian Mix)/Everytime You
Touch Me (NYC Jungle Mix)/Everytime You Touch Me (Na Feel Mix)/Everytime You Touch Me (Freestyle
Mix)

INTO THE BLUE [Mute UK 12"] 1995
Into The Blue (The Buzz Boys Main Room Mayhem Mix) [Phil Kelsey]/Into The Blue (Underground Mix)
[Steve Mason and P.E.T.E.]/Into The Blue (Hard Mix) [Steve Mason and P.E.T.E.]/Into The Blue (Voodoo
Child Mix)

INTO THE BLUE - Part one (Mute UK CD) 1995
Into The Blue (Beatmasters Mix)/Into The Blue (Sound Factory Mix) [Junior Vasquez]/Into The Blue
(Follow Me Mix) [Junior Vasquez]/Into The Blue (Summer Night Mix)/Into The Blue (Into The Blues
Mix) [Jon Spencer]

INTO THE BLUE REMIXES Part two (Mute UK CD) 1995
Into The Blue (Voodoo Child Mix)/Into The Blue (Spiritual Mix)/Into The Blue (Simple Mix)/Into The
Blue (Uplifting 4 Beat Mix) [DJ Seduction]/Into The Blue (Summer Wind Mix)/Into The Blue (The Buzz
Boys Main Room Mayhem Mix) [Phil Kelsey]

BRING BACK MY HAPPINESS [Elektra US 12")1995
Bring Back My Happiness (Extended Mix)/Bring Back My Happiness (Para Los Discos Mix)/Bring Back
My Happiness (Wink's Acid Interpretation) [Josh Wink]/Bring Back My Happiness (Underground Version)

BRING BACK MY HAPPINESS (Elektra US CD)1995
Bring Back My Happiness (Extended Mix)/In My Life/Bring Back My Happiness (Para Los Discos
Mix)/Bring Back My Happiness (Underground Mix)/Bring Back My Happiness (Josh Wink Mix) [Josh
Wink]/Into The Blue (Jr. Vasquez Follow Me mix]/Alone

BRING BACK MY HAPPINESS (Mute UK 12") 1995
Bring Back My Happiness (Extended Mix)/Bring Back My Happiness (Interactive Mix) [Ramon
Zenker]/Bring Back My Happiness (Voodoo Child Mix)/Bring Back My Happiness (Wink's Acid
Interpretation) [Josh Wink]/Bring Back My Happiness (Para Los Discos)

BRING BACK MY HAPPINESS (Mute UK CD) 1995
Bring Back My Happiness (Extended Mix)/Bring Back My Happiness (Interactive Mix) [Ramon
Zenker]/Bring Back My Happiness (Voodoo Child Mix)/Bring Back My Happiness (Wink's Acid
Interpretation) [Josh Wink]/Bring Back My Happiness (Para Los Discos)

THAT'S WHEN I REACH FOR MY REVOLVER (Mute UK 12")1996
That's When I Reach For My Revolver (The Rollo & Sister Bliss Vocal Mix)/That's When I Reach For My Revolver (The Rollo & Sister Bliss Instrumental Mix)

THAT'S WHEN I REACH FOR MY REVOLVER - Part one (Mute UK CD) 1996
That's When I Reach For My Revolver (Single Version)/Lovesick/Displaced/Sway

THAT'S WHEN I REACH FOR MY REVOLVER REMIX - Parrt two (Mute UK CD) 1996
That's When I Reach For My Revolver (The Rollo & Sister Bliss Vocal Mix)/Every One Of My Problems/God Moving Over The Face Of The Waters (Heat Mix)/Dark

COME ON BABY - Mute UK 12" (1996)
Come On Baby (Crystal Method Mix)/Come On Baby (Eskimos & Egypt 12" Mix)/Come On Baby (Eskimos & Egypt 7" Mix)

THAT'S WHEN I REACH FOR MY REVOLVER (Sub Pop Records US 7") 1997
That's When I Reach For My Revolver (Album Version)/Whip It (Death Metal Version)

THAT'S WHEN I REACH FOR MY REVOLVER (Elektra US 12")1997
That's When I Reach For My Revolver (Moby's Mix)/That's When I Reach For My Revolver (Psychotic VE-GUN Mix Edit Vocal Dub)[Philip Steir]/That's When I Reach For My Revolver (Moby's Mix 1 - Edit)/That's When I Reach For My Revolver (The Rollo & Sister Bliss Vocal Mix)

JAMES BOND THEME (MOBY'S RE-VERSION) (Mute UK 12) 1997
James Bond Theme (Moby's re-version) (LSG Mix)/James Bond Theme (Moby's re-version) (Moby's Extended Mix)/James Bond Theme (Moby's re-version) (Danny Tenaglia's Twilo Mix)

JAMES BOND THEME (MOBY'S RE-VERSION) (Mute UK CD) 1997
James Bond Theme (Moby's re-version)/James Bond Theme (Moby's re-version) (Grooverider's Jeep Remix)/James Bond Theme (Moby's re-version) (Da Bomb Remix)/James Bond Theme (Moby's re-version) (CJ Bolland Remix)/James Bond Theme (Moby's re-version) (Dub Pistols Remix)/James Bond Theme (Moby's re-version) (Dubble-Oh Heaven Remix)

HONEY (Mute UK 12") 1998
Honey (Rollo & Sister Bliss Remix)/Honey (Sharam Jey's Sweet Honey Mix)/Honey (Low Side Mix)

HONEY (Mute UK CD) 1998
Honey/Micronesia/Memory Gospel

HONEY REMIXES (Mute UK CD) 1998
Honey (Rollo & Sister Bliss Blunt Edit)/Honey (Moby's 118 Mix (Radio Edit))/Honey (Westbam & Hardy Hard Mix)/Honey (Aphrodite & Mickey Finn Remix)

HONEY REMIXES (Mute UK 2x12")1998
Honey (Risk Mix)/Honey (Dark Mix)/Honey (Westbam & Hardy Hard Mix)/Honey (118 Mix)/Honey (Aphrodite & Mickey Finn Remix)/Honey (RJ's Mix)/Honey (Original Mix)/Honey (Bammer's Mix)

RUN ON (Mute UK 12")1999
Run On (Moby Young & Funky Mix)/Run On (Dave Clarke Remix)/Run On (Extended)

RUN ON (Mute UK CD) 1999
Run On/Spirit/Running

RUN ON EXTENDED (Mute UK CD) 1999
Run On (extended)/Sunday/Down Slow (full length version)

RUN ON (Mute/ Intercord Germany 12") 1999
Run On (Sharam Remix)/Run On (Plastic Angel Original Mix)/Run On (Dani König Remix)/Run On (Plastic Angel New Mix)

HONEY/RUN ON (V2 US CD) 1999
Honey (Album Mix)/Honey (Moby's 118 Mix)/Honey (Sharam Jey's Sweet Honey Mix)/Honey (Aphrodite & Mickey Finn Mix)/Run On (extended)/Run On (Moby's Young & Funky Mix)/Run On (Sharam Jey's Always On The Run Remix)/Memory Gospel

BODYROCK (Mute UK 12")1999
Bodyrock (Olav Basoski's Da Hot Funk Da Freak Funk Remix)/Bodyrock (B & H Bodyrob Mix)/Bodyrock (Dani König Remix)

BODYROCK (Mute UK CD)1999
Bodyrock/Sunspot/Arp

BODYROCK (Mute UK CD)1999
Bodyrock (Olav Basoski's Da Hot Funk Da Freak Funk Remix)/Bodyrock (Hybrid's Bodyshock Remix)/Bodyrock (Rae & Christian Remix)

BODYROCK (V2 US 12") 1999
Bodyrock (Olav Basoski's Da Hot Funk Da Freak Funk Remix)/Bodyrock (Rae & Christian Remix)/Bodyrock (Dani König Remix)/Bodyrock (Dean Honer Mix)

BODYROCK (V2 US CD) 1999
Bodyrock (Dean Honer Mix)/Bodyrock (Olav Basoski's Da Hot Funk Da Freak Funk Remix)/Bodyrock (Rae & Christian Remix)/Bodyrock (B & H's Bodyrob Mix)/Bodyrock (Dani König Remix)/Bodyrock (Album Version)/Sunday/Sunspot

WHY DOES MY HEART FEEL SO BAD? (Mute UK CD) 1999
Why Does My Heart Feel So Bad?/Flying Foxes/Princess
Also includes the PC and Mac animated video for "Why Does My Heart Feel So Bad?"

WHY DOES MY HEART FEEL SO BAD? REMIXES (Mute UK CD) 1999
Why Does My Heart Feel So Bad? (ATB Remix)/Why Does My Heart Feel So Bad? (Ferry Corsten Remix)/Why Does My Heart Feel So Bad? (Subsonic Legacy Remix)

WHY DOES MY HEART FEEL SO BAD? (Mute UK 12") 1999
Why Does My Heart Feel So Bad? (ATB Remix)/Why Does My Heart Feel So Bad? (Ferry Corsten Remix)/Why Does My Heart Feel So Bad? (Sharp Roadster Remix)

WHY DOES MY HEART FEEL SO BAD? (Mute UK 12")1999
Why Does My Heart Feel So Bad? (Original Version)/Why Does My Heart Feel So Bad? (Subsonic Legacy Remix)

NATURAL BLUES (Mute UK CD) 2000
Natural Blues (Single Version)/The Whispering Wind/Sick in The System

NATURAL BLUES REMIXES (Mute UK CD) 2000
Natural Blues (Perfecto Remix)/Natural Blues (Mike D Edit)/Natural Blues (Peace Division Edit)

NATURAL BLUES (Mute UK 12") 2000
Natural Blues/Natural Blues (Mike D remix)/Natural Blues (Peace Divison Dub)

NATURAL BLUES (V2 US CD) 2000
Natural Blues (Radio Edit)/Natural Blues (Perfecto Remix)/Natural Blues (Album Version)/Natural Blues (Mike D Remix - Edit)/The Whispering Wind

NATURAL BLUES (Mute UK 12") 2000
Natural Blues (Katcha Mix)/Natural Blues (Peace Divison Dub)

PORCELAIN (Mute UK CD) 2000
Porcelain (Single Version)/Flying Over The Dateline/Summer

PORCELAIN REMIX (Mute UK CD) 2000
Porcelain (Clubbed To Death Variation By Rob Dougan)/Porcelain (Futureshock Instrumental)/Porcelain (Torsten Stenzel's Edited Remix)

PORCELAIN MIXES Part one (Mute UK 12") 2000
Porcelain (Torsten Stenzel's Remix)/Porcelain (Force Mass Motion Remix)

PORCELAIN MIXES Part two (Mute UK 12") 2000
Porcelain (Futureshock Instrumental)/Porcelain (Futureshock Beats)/Porcelain (Clubbed To Death Variation By Rob Dougan)

SOUTHSIDE. (V2 US CD) 2000
Southside (featuring Gwen Stefani)/Southside (album version)

SOUTHSIDE (V2 US CD) 2000
Southside (featuring Gwen Stefani single version)/Southside (featuring Gwen Stefani Hybrid Dishing Pump Remix)/Southside (Pete Heller Park Lane Vocal)/Ain't Never Learned/Southside (album version)/Southside (Hybrid Dishing Pump Instrumental)/The Sun Never Stops Setting

SOUTHSIDE (V2 US 12") 2000
Southside (featuring Gwen Stefani Hybrid Dishing Pump remix)/Southside (featuring Gwen Stefani single version)/Southside (Pete Heller Park Lane Vocal)

HONEY FEAT. KELIS promo 1 (Mute UK 12" 2000)
Honey feat. Kelis (Fafu's 12" Mix)/Honey (Sharam Jey's Sweet Honey Mix)/Honey (Moby's 118 Mix)

WHY DOES MY HEART FEEL SO BAD? / HONEY FEAT. KELIS (Mute UK CD) 2000
Why Does My Heart Feel So Bad?/Honey Fteat. Kelis (Remix Edit)/Flower

REMIX WHY DOES MY HEART FEEL SO BAD? / HONEY FEAT. KELIS (Mute UK CD) 2000
Honey feat. Kelis (Fafu's 12" Mix)/Why Does My Heart Feel So Bad? (Red Jerry Strings And Break Mix)/The Sun Never Stops Setting

ALBUMS

INSTINCT DANCE (Instinct US Only) 1991
Party Time (Edit) - Barracuda/Drug Fits The Face (Edit) - Barracuda/Besame - Barracuda/Go - Moby/Mobility - Moby/Rock The House (Edit) - Brainstorm/Move The Colors (Edit) - Brainstorm/Drop A Beat - Brainstorm/Voodoo Child Remix - (Edit) Voodoo Child/Have You Seen My Baby? - Voodoo Child/Permanent Green - Voodoo Child

MOBY (Instinct US Version) 1992
Drop A Beat/Everything/Yeah/Electricity/Next Is The E/Mercy/Go/Help Me To Believe/Have You Seen My Baby/Ah Ah/Slight Return/Stream

THE STORY SO FAR (Equator) (UK Version of Moby) 1993
Ah Ah/I Feel It (I Feel It Mix)/Everything/Mercy/Help Me To Believe/Go (Woodtick Mix)/Yeah/Drop A Beat (The New Version)/Thousand/Slight Return/Go (Subliminal Mix Unedited Version)/Stream

EARLY UNDERGROUND (Instinct US) 1993 (Equator UK)
Besame/Rock The House (Edit)/Move The Colors (Edit)/UHF3/Party Time (Edit)/Protect Write/Go (Original)/Permanent Green/Voodoo Child (Edit)/Drug Fits The Face/Time Signature/Peace Head/Barracuda/Mobility/M-Four

AMBIENT (Instinct US/ Equator UK US) 1993
My Beautiful Blue Sky/Heaven/Tongues/J Breas/Myopia/House Of Blue Leaves/Bad Days/Piano & String/Sound/Dog/80/Lean On Me

EVERYTHING IS WRONG (Elektra US/ Mute UK) 1995
Initial quantities of the UK and German versions included a bonus CD called 'Underwater'.
Hymn/Feeling So Real/All That I Need Is To Be Loved [H.O.S. mix]/Let's Go Free/Everytime You Touch Me/Bring Back My Happiness/What Love/First Cool Hive/Into The Blue/Anthem/Everything Is Wrong/God Moving Over The Face Of The Waters/When It's Cold I'd Like To Die

UNDERWATER
Underwater (part 1)/Underwater (part 2)/Underwater (part 3)/Underwater (part 4)/Underwater (part 5)

EVERYTHING IS WRONG - MIXED AND REMIXED (Mute UK) 1996
Disc 1: Hard Techno, Joyous Anthems & Quiet Ambience
First Cool Hive (Minimal Version)/Feeling So Real (Unashamed Ecstatic Piano Mix)/All That I Need Is To Be Loved (Hard Trance Version)/Bring Back My Happiness (Extended Mix)/Move (Disco Threat Mix)/Everytime You Touch Me (Pure Joy Mix)/Feeling So Real (Westbam Mix - Westbam)/Into The Blue (Uplifting 4 Beat Mix - DJ Seduction)/Everytime You Touch Me (NYC Jungle Mix)/Into The Blue (Spiritual Mix)/Anthem (Cinematic Version)/Everything Is Wrong (Quiet Mix)

Disc 2: New York Hard House, Groovy Acid & Melodic Trance
Let's Go Free (Reversal Mix)/Hymn (I Believe)/Into The Blue (Voodoo Child Mix)/Everytime You Touch Me (Freestyle Version)/Bring Back My Happiness (Josh Wink Mix - Josh Wink)/Hymn (Lucky Orgasm Mix)/Everytime You Touch Me (Na Feel Mix)/Feeling So Real (Old Skool Mix)/Hymn (Menacing Mix)/Bring Back My Happiness (Para Los Discos)/Into The Blue (Simple Mix)/Move (Electro Mix)/All That I Need Is To Be Loved (Melodic Mix)/When It's Cold I'd Like To Die (Instrumental)

RARE: THE COLLECTED B-SIDES (1989-1993) + GO: THE COLLECTED MIXES (Instinct US) 1996 (Pinnacle UK) 1999
Disc 1:
Voodoo Child (Poor In NY Mix)/Next Is The E.(Club Mix)/Drug Fits The Face (Drug Free Mix)/Have You Seen My Baby (Baby Mix)/UHF 2/Time's Up (Dust Mix)/Drop A Beat (Deep Mix)/Mobility (Aquamix)/I Feel It (Synthe Mix)/Thousand

Disc 2:
Go (Woodtick Mix)/Go (Analog Mix)/Go (Subliminal Mix)/Go (Night Time Mix)/Go (Original Mix)/Go (Low Spirit Mix)/Go (Rainforest Mix)/Go (Delirium Mix)/Go (Voodoo Child Mix)/Go (Barracuda Mix)/Go (Arpathoski Mix)/Go (Soundtrack Mix)/Go (Amphetamix)

ANIMAL RIGHTS (Mute UK/ Mute Intercord Germany. UK and German version only) 1996
Initial quantities of the UK version included bonus disc called 'LITTLE IDIOT'.
Let It Go/Come On Baby/Someone To Love/Heavy Flow/You/My Love Will Never Die/Soft/Say It's All Mine/That's When I Reach For My Revolver/Face It/Living/Love Song For My Mom

LITTLE IDIOT (Mute)
Degenerate/Dead City/Walnut/Old/A Season In Hell/Love Song For My Mom/The Blue Terror Of
Lawns/Dead Sun/Reject

ANIMAL RIGHTS (Elektra US Version) 1997
Dead Sun/Someone To Love/Heavy Flow/You/Now I Let It Go/Come On Baby/Soft/Anima/Say It's All
Mine/That's When I Reach For My Revolver/Alone/Face It/Old/Living/Love Song For My Mom/A Season
In Hell

ANIMAL RIGHTS (Mute Japanese Version) (1997)
Dead Sun/Someone To Love/Heavy Flow/You/Now I Let It Go/Come On Baby/Soft/Anima/Say It's All
Mine/That's When I Reach For My Revolver/Alone/Face It/Old/Living/Love Song For My Mom/A Season
In Hell/New Dawn Fades

I LIKE TO SCORE (Elektra US/ Mute UK) 1997
Novio/James Bond Theme (Moby's Re-Version)/Go/Ah-Ah/I Like To Score/Oil 1/New Dawn Fades/God
Moving Over The Face Of The Waters [Heat Mix]/First Cool Hive/Nash/Love Theme/Grace

PLAY (V2 US/ Mute UK) 1999
Honey/Find My Baby/Porcelain/Why Does My Heart Feel So Bad?/South Side/Rushing/Bodyrock/Natural
Blues/Machete/7/Run On/Down Slow/If Things Were Perfect/Everloving/Inside/Guitar Flute & String/The
Sky Is Broken/My Weakness

PLAY LIMITED EDITION 1999 (Mute France 2xCD) 2000
Disc 1: PLAY, the same tracks as the UK and US release
Disc 2: PLAY CD-EXTRA
Audio part: Memory Gospel/Spirit
CD-Rom part: Video of "Why Does My Heart Feel So Bad?" - Mpeg format/Text interview with
Moby/Artwork from the *Play* singles.

PLAY LIMITED FESTIVAL EDITION (Mute/PIAS Belgium/ Netherlands only) 2000
Released to coincide with six festival dates in Belgium and the Netherlands during the Summer 2000
Disc 1: PLAY, the same tracks as the UK and US release
Disc 2: BONUS CD
The Whispering Wind/Honey (Rollo & Sister Bliss Blunt Edit)/Spirit/Why Does My Heart Feel So Bad?
(Ferry Corsten Remix)/Sunspot/Natural Blues (Mike D Remix) [Edit]

PLAY PLUS (Mute/Guts Taiwanese Limited) 2000
Disc 1: PLAY, the same tracks as the UK and US release.
Disc 2: LITTLE IDIOT MOBY (same track listing as bonus CD with UK/ Germany release of Animal
Rights)

PLAY THE B-SIDES (Mute UK Only) 2000
Limited edition bonus CD box-set with Play.
Disc 1: PLAY, the same tracks as the UK and US release.
Disc 2: PLAY THE B-SIDES
Flower/Sunday/Memory Gospel/Whispering Wind/Summer/Spirit/Flying Foxes/Sunspot/Flying Over The
Dateline/Running/The Sun Never Stops Setting

MOBY SONGS 1993-1998 (Elektra US Only) 2000
First Cool Hive/Go [ILTS version]/Into The Blue/Now I Let It Go/Move (You Make Me Feel So Good)/I
Like To Score/Anthem/Hymn/Feeling So Real/God Moving Over The Face Of The Waters/Alone/Novio/
The Rain Falls And The Sky Shudders/When It's Cold I'd Like To Die/Living/Grace

DJ MIX ALBUMS

MIXMAG LIVE VOLUME 2 (DMC US/ UK) 1996
Moby DJ mix set. CD also features set by Sven Vath
C3 Bells - Moby/Hypnotize Me - House 2 House/Your Touch - 2001-01-11/Dee Drive - Fiction/Barbarella
- Barbarella/Housewerk - Airtight/The Music is Movin' - Fargetta/Go - Moby/Next is the E (Intro Mix) -
Moby

MOBY RELEASES UNDER OTHER NAMES

SINGLES
THE BROTHERHOOD
Time's Up (Instinct US 12" only) 1990
Time's Up (Deep Mix)/Time's Up (Dope Mix)/Time's Up (Bonus Beats)/Time's Up (Radio Edit)/Time's
Up (Dust Mix)/Time's Up (Acapella)

VOODOO CHILD
Voodoo Child (Instinct US 12") 1991
Voodoo Child (Contracted)/Permanent Green/Voodoo Child (Expanded)/M-Four

BRAINSTORM
Rock The House (Instinct US 12"/ Low Spirit UK 12) 1991
Rock The House/Move The Colors/Help Me To Believe

MINDSTORM
Mindstorm (Instinct US CD, /Low Spirit UK CD) 1991
'Brainstorm' was changed to 'Mindstorm' due to R&S act with the name Brainstorm.
Rock The House/Help Me To Believe/Move The Colors

VOODOO CHILD
Voodoo Child Remixes (Instinct US 12") 1991
Voodoo Child (Brainstorm Mix)/Voodoo Child (Original Mix)/Voodoo Child (Poor In N.Y. Mix)/No
Buttons to Push

BARRACUDA
Drug Fits the Face (Instinct US 12") 1991
Drug Fits The Face/Drug Fits The Face (Drug Free)/Party Time/Barracuda

BARRACUDA
Drug Fits the Face (C.T. Records, UK 12") 1991
Drug Fits The Face/Drug Fits The Face (Drug Free)/Mad Love

UHF
UHF (XL UK 12") 1991
U.H.F./Peace Head/Everything/Protect Write

UHF
UHF (XL UK CD) 1991
U.H.F. (Edit)/Peacehead/Everything/Protect Write/U.H.F.

VOODOO CHILD
Demons / Horses (41:26) (Novamute UK CD/ 12") 1994
Demons/Horses

VOODOO CHILD
Higher (Trophy/ Mute UK 12") 1995
Higher/Desperate

VOODOO CHILD
Higher (Trophy/ Mute UK 12") 1995
Higher/Desperate/Sim 1

VOODOO CHILD
Dog Heaven (Trophy UK 12") 1996
ADog Heaven (Lopez Mix)/Dog Heaven (Extended Mix)

VOODOO CHILD
Dog Heaven (Trophy UK 12") 1996/Dog Heaven (Extended Mix)/Dog Heaven (Long Mix)

ALBUMS
VOODOO CHILD
THE END OF EVERYTHING (Trophy Mute UK/ Trophy Intercord Germany) 1996
Dog Heaven/Patient Love/Great Lake/Gentle Love/Honest Love/Slow Motion Suicide/Reject

VOODOO CHILD
THE END OF EVERYTHING [US only version] Voodoo Child (Elektra) 1997
Patient Love/Great Lake/Gentle Love/Honest Love (long version)/Slow Motion Suicide/Dog Heaven (alternative version)/Reject

RARITIES AND PROMOS
There are far too many rarities or promos to list here, so I have picked out some of the more interesting items.

SINGLES RELATED
WHAT LOVE (Elektra US CD promo) 1995
What Love/All That I Need Is To Be Loved [House Of Suffering Mix]

WHAT LOVE (Mute UK 7" promo) 1995
What Love

FEELING SO REAL (RAY KEITH REMIX) (Soapbar UK 10")1994
Feeling So Real (Ray Keith Remix)/Everytime You Touch Me (NYC Jungle Mix)

EVERYTIME YOU TOUCH ME (Mute UK limited edition 12")1995
These are the remaining remix competition winners.
Everytime You Touch Me (Totalis Remix) [Totalis]/Everytime You Touch Me (Quartermass Remix)[Quartermass]/Everytime You Touch Me (Dementia Remix) [Ron Verboom]/Everytime You Touch Me (Tabernacle Remix) [Tabernacle]

ANIMAL RIGHTS: LIVE AT THE SPLASH CLUB (Mute UK CD)1996
All tracks were recorded live at the Splash Club (London UK) on July 11, 1996. Single given away free at European dates.
Someone To Love/You/Say It's All Mine/Face It

COME ON BABY (Mute UK 2CD)1996
Limited edition of 10000 copies worldwide, including 5000 in the UK.

Disc one:
Come On Baby/Love Hole/Whip It (Death Metal Version)/Go (Live at the Splash Club)/All That I Need Is
To Be Loved (Live at the Splash Club)/Hymn (Live at the Splash Club)
Disc two:
Come On Baby (Eskimos and Egypt 7" Mix)/Come On Baby (Crystal Method Mix)/Come On Baby
(Eskimos and Egypt 12" Mix)

JAMES BOND THEME (MOBY'S RE-VERSION) (Elektra US CD promo) 1997
James Bond Theme (Moby's re-version)/Audio Bio

JAMES BOND THEME (MOBY'S RE-VERSION) (Mute UK 2x12") 1997
Limited edition of 4000 copies.
James Bond Theme (Moby's re-version) (Grooverider's Jeep Remix)/James Bond Theme (Moby's re-version)
(Danny Tenaglia's Acetate Dub)/James Bond Theme (Moby's re-version) (Dub Pistols Remix)/James Bond
Theme (Moby's re-version) (CJ Bolland Remix)/James Bond Theme (Moby's re-version) (Da Bomb
Remix)/James Bond Theme (Moby's re-version) (Moby Bonus Beats)

ALBUM RELATED
EVERYTHING IS WRONG INTERVIEW (Mute UK CD promo) 1995, Radio EPK

DISK (Elektra US E-CD) 1995
"Enhanced CD" which includes both regular CD audio, and multimedia content for PCs and Macs.
Includes interview clips, music, and parts of 'Everytime You Touch Me' for remixing.
Audio CD tracks: Everytime You Touch Me (album version)/Feeling So Real (Ecstatic Mix)/Shining (previously unreleased)
CD-ROM tracks: Into The Blue (album version)/Move (EP version)/First Cool Hive (album version)
Plus the following music videos: Hymn [This Is My Dream]/Everytime You Touch Me [Beatmasters 7"
Mix]

ANIMAL RIGHTS INTERVIEW (Mute UK CD promo) 1996, Radio EPK

PLAY INTERVIEW (Mute UK CD promo) 1999, Radio EPK

PLAY SAMPLER (V2 US promo cassette) 1999
Bodyrock (Album Mix)/Honey (Moby's 118 Mix)/Porcelain

PLAY PROMO SAMPLER (Mute UK CD promo) 1999
Why Does My Heart Feel So Bad?/Honey/Porcelain/Bodyrock

SELECTIONS FROM PLAY (V2 US CD promo) 1999
Porcelain/Why Does My Heart Feel So Bad?/Honey/Natural Blues/Bodyrock (Album Version)

MOBY PROMO FROM *THE OBSERVER* NEWSPAPER (The Observer UK CD), [15 Oct 2000]
Tracks chosen by Moby himself.
First Cool Hive/Porcelain/Go/Everloving/Anthem/Now I Let It Go/God Moving Over The Face Of The
Waters/Memory Gospel
+ CD-ROM portion with exclusive Moby interview

MOBY CALVIN KLEIN PROMO (V2 US CD) 2000
Free with Rolling Stone magazine.
Natural Blues/Porcelain/Memory Gospel (Non-Album Track)/Whispering Wind (Non-Album Track)

PLAY SAMPLER (Mute UK CD) 2000
Porcelain/Natural Blues/Find My Baby/Why Does My Heart Feel So Bad?/Run On/Everloving

RELATED
PHONICOID - BOOK OF DREAMS (underground/psychosound US CD) 1999
Moby gave Phonicoid permission to release this mix. The cd can be purchased online at
www.phonicoid.com:
Ah-Ah (Phonicoid Remix)

MOBY'S OTHER BANDS

THE VATICAN COMMANDOS
Hit Squad For God (Pregnant Nun Records US 7") 1983
Why Must I Follow/It's So Scary/Housewives On Valium/Hit Squad For God/Your Way/Wonder Bread

AWOL
AWOL (Purity Records US) 1984
Heart Flag/Happy Now/Holy Mountain/One More Dance/More Than Ever

SHOPWELL
Peanuts (HF US 12") 1985
No song titles

THE PORK GUYS
The Pork Guys (Nutmeg HC) (Self Starter US 7") 1998
Four Lights/Hannah/Face The Facts (You're Not Black)/Fuck X-Mas! Fuck You!

SCHAUMGUMMI
(US split-7") 2000
SCHAUMGUMMI - Schaumgummi/PHILISTINES JNR - Ballad of Paul Yates

TROPHY RECORDS RELEASES
NOTE: Trophy is Moby's own label. All Trophy releases are distributed by Mute in the UK and
Europe.This section includes all Trophy releases not previously listed.

VOODOO CHILD
Higher/Desperate (Trophy/Mute 12") 1995
Higher/Desperate

VOODOO CHILD
Higher/Desperate (Trophy/Mute CD) 1995
Higher/Desperate

LOPEZ
Why Can't It Stop? (Trophy/Mute, 12") Oct1995
Why Can't It Stop?/The Dirty Underground

LOPEZ
Why Can't It Stop? (Trophy/Mute, CD) Oct1995
NOTE: The sleeve has the same layout as VC's 'Higher', but with black letters on bright yellow, instead of
blue on silver. Credits: "Written and produced by M.Lopez".
Why Can't It Stop?/The Dirty Underground/Everybody Can Do It

LOPEZ
Emptiness (Trophy, 12"/CD) 1996
Emptiness/FuckedUp

DJ CAKE
Sugar Baby (Trophy, 12"/CD) 1996
Sugar Baby/I F ound A Way

SOUNDTRACK APPEARANCES

Moby has contributed to the soundtracks for the following movies: *Cool World, Hackers 2, Heat, The Jacka*l, *The Saint, Scream, Senseles, Spawn, Tomorrow Never Dies, Hit Squad For God, The Beach, Space Water Onion, Any Given Sunday, The Next Best Thing, Play It To The Bone, Bodyshots, Big Daddy, Porno - The Movie.*

REFERENCES

All quotes from interviews by Martin James 1992 - 2000 except as follows (listed in chronological order):

'Moby: Techno + Punk + Hippie = Ethical Rave Mobility', *Alternative Press*, 1991, by Dan Dinello
'Techno's Big Fish', *DJ Times*, 1991, by Marisa Fox
'Moby', *Melody Maker*, 14th June 1991, by Cosmic Cowboy
'A Vegetarian Surrealist Christian Raver', *Discotext*, Summer 1991, writer unknown
'GO!', *Disc Jockey*, August 1991, by Kid Hattan
'Rave On', *Band in a Van*, February 1992, by Tony Savona
'Moby Sails New Techno Waters', *Billboard*, November 20th 1992, by Larry Flick
'Raving in E Minor', *LA Weekly*, December 3rd 1992, by Sue Cummings
'Moby', *Syndicate*, July/ August 1993, by David Palmer
'Moby! Vegan, Christian techno nutter', *Mixmag*, 1993, by David Davies
'Moby FLAMEWAR', *USENET alt..rave*, October/ November 1993
Ecstasy and the Dance Culture by Nicholas Saunders, self-published, 1995
"EIW - Mixed and Remixed Review sidebar", *Raw*, January 1996, by Sian Pattenden
'News article', *Muzik*, 1996, writer unknown
'Moby Dicks Around with Fag Machines', *Melody Maker*, 13th January 1996, by Carole Clerk
'Hang the DJ', *Muzik*, March 1996, writer unknown
'Moby in the Mix', *The Mix*, April 1996, writer unknown
'Just Who the Fuck is Moby?', *Metal Hammer*, November 1996, by Chris Ingham
'America's #1 Fun All-American Covers Band', *Addicted To Noise*, 1997, by Dakota Smith
Energy Flash by Simon Reynolds, Picador, 1998
'V2 Builds Strong Base For Moby', *Billboard*, 26th February 2000, by Larry Flick
'Sex, Lives and Gaffa Tape', *Flipside* (UK), March 2000, by Sarah-Jane
'Rev enge of the Little Idiot', *Spin*, June 2000, by Charles Aaron
'The Think Tank with David Gray', *Select*, October 2000, writer unknown
'Definitely Moby', *The Observer Magazine*, 15th October 2000, by Andrew Smith